*Especially for*

..............................................................

*From*

..............................................................

*Date*

..............................................................

# THE BIBLE
# PROMISE BOOK®
## *for*
### *Morning and Evening*

## BARBOUR BOOKS
An Imprint of Barbour Publishing, Inc.

© 2015 by Barbour Publishing, Inc.

Compiled by Linda Hang.

Print ISBN 978-1-61626-410-9

eBook Editions:
Adobe Digital Edition (.epub) 978-1-63409-144-2
Kindle and MobiPocket Edition (.prc) 978-1-63409-145-9

Devotional thoughts and prayers are from *365 Daily Devotions from the Psalms, Wisdom from the Bible, Whispers of Wisdom for Busy Women, Daily Encouragement for Single Women,* and *365 Daily Devotions for Couples* published by Barbour Publishing, Inc.

Published by Barbour Books, an imprint of Barbour Publishing, Inc., P.O. Box 719, Uhrichsville, Ohio 44683, www.barbourbooks.com

*Our mission is to publish and distribute inspirational products offering exceptional value and biblical encouragement to the masses.*

Member of the
Evangelical Christian
Publishers Association

Printed in China.

The Bible is full of promises.
And when God makes a promise,
you can trust it.

---

*Evening, and morning. . .
will I pray, and cry aloud:
and he shall hear my voice.*

PSALM 55:17 KJV

---

This brand-new edition of Barbour's bestselling *The Bible Promise Book*® features themed Bible promises arranged into morning and evening readings for every day of the year. With Bible promises on topics like God's Word, Wisdom, Faith, Prayer, Encouragement, Love, Joy, and more, each scripture will speak directly to your heart, drawing you ever closer to your heavenly Father.

# DAY 1 - *Spiritual Refreshment*

## *Morning*

*For this is what the high and exalted One says—he who lives forever,*
*whose name is holy: "I live in a high and holy place, but also with*
*the one who is contrite and lowly in spirit, to revive the spirit of*
*the lowly and to revive the heart of the contrite."*
ISAIAH 57:15 NIV

*"In six days the LORD made heaven and earth,*
*and on the seventh day he rested and was refreshed."*
EXODUS 31:17 ESV

The giver of life is also the renewer of hope, and He is ready and waiting to fill you with new life, new hope—to transform your heart and lift you out of the pit. All you have to do is ask.

*Breath of life, breathe into me Your sweet joy and peace.*
*Help me see the coming years as an opportunity to*
*discard the old and embrace the new. Amen.*

## *Evening*

*Repent, then, and turn to God, so that your sins may be wiped out,*
*that times of refreshing may come from the Lord, and that he may*
*send the Messiah, who has been appointed for you—even Jesus.*
ACTS 3:19-20 NIV

*You who seek God, let your hearts revive.*
PSALM 69:32 ESV

You cannot minister to others when you are spiritually bankrupt. The Lord shapes you through quiet, contemplative prayer and Bible study—not a frenetic lifestyle. A frenetic lifestyle distorts, whereas, a balanced, spiritually nourished lifestyle shapes one into the image of God.

*O God, assist me in keeping life balanced so that my walk*
*with You might be first and foremost. Amen.*

# DAY 2 – *Faith*

*For it is by grace you have been saved, through faith—and this is not from*
*yourselves, it is the gift of God—not by works, so that no one can boast.*
EPHESIANS 2:8-9 NIV

*For whatsoever is born of God overcometh the world:*
*and this is the victory that overcometh the world, even our faith.*
1 JOHN 5:4 KJV

Reason and logic are important traits, but there is something more. Many
situations call for feeling, not just thinking. Faith is like that. It is vital that we
learn to think with our hearts, as well as with our heads.

*Too often, Father, I try to think my way through my problems*
*rather than feeling my way. Open my heart so that I might know*
*Your love in the deepest way possible. Amen.*

*And [Jesus] said to her, "Daughter, your faith has made you well.*
*Go in peace, and be healed of your affliction."*
MARK 5:34 NKJV

*Trust in the LORD with all your heart; do not depend on your own understanding.*
*Seek his will in all you do, and he will show you which path to take.*
PROVERBS 3:5-6 NLT

The Bible tells us to trust in the Lord with all our hearts and not lean on
our understanding. Though we are given minds to read, think, and reason,
ultimately our faith comes from abandoning hope in ourselves and risking
all on Jesus.

*Lord, I am often blind to my own weakness and my need of You.*
*Help me trust You. Amen.*

# DAY 3 - *Strength*

*The LORD is my strength, the reason for my song, because he has saved me.*
*I praise and honor the LORD—he is my God and the God of my ancestors.*
EXODUS 15:2 CEV

*My voice shalt thou hear in the morning, O LORD;*
*in the morning will I direct my prayer unto thee, and will look up.*
PSALM 5:3 KJV

We need to begin our busy days strong. Not with just a good cup of coffee but some time spent with our source of strength. Taking five minutes or an hour—or more if we're really disciplined—in prayer and Bible reading can make the difference in our day.

*Thank You, Lord, for another day. Be my source of strength.*
*In Jesus' blessed name, amen.*

*Blessed is the man whose strength is in thee; in whose heart are the ways of them.*
PSALM 84:5 KJV

*I am glad to be weak or insulted or mistreated or to have troubles*
*and sufferings, if it is for Christ. Because when I am weak, I am strong.*
2 CORINTHIANS 12:10 CEV

The apostle Paul stopped struggling against his thorn in the flesh when he realized it was God's gift to make him rely on God's strength. God wants us to do the same with our weaknesses. Where do we feel weak today? When we turn that area over to Him, God will demonstrate His strength.

*Christ Jesus, You are all-powerful. Step into our weaknesses, take over,*
*and demonstrate Your power and care on our behalf. Amen.*

# DAY 4 - *Wisdom*

## *Morning*

*Oh, the depth of the riches both of the wisdom and knowledge of God!*
*How unsearchable are His judgments and His ways past finding out!*
ROMANS 11:33 NKJV

*The fear of the LORD is the beginning of wisdom:*
*and the knowledge of the holy is understanding.*
PROVERBS 9:10 KJV

Often wisdom comes without great fanfare. It comes to those who wait with open heart and mind. It comes simply and quietly. It comes in the stillness, when God and His Word can get through.

*Open my heart, almighty God. Give me knowledge beyond ordinary knowledge.*
*Teach me more about Your love, Your Word, Jesus the Christ. Amen.*

## *Evening*

*How blessed is the man who finds wisdom and the man who gains understanding.*
*For her profit is better than the profit of silver and her gain better than fine gold.*
PROVERBS 3:13-14 NASB

*If you need wisdom, ask our generous God,*
*and he will give it to you. He will not rebuke you for asking.*
JAMES 1:5 NLT

There are no shortcuts to wisdom. The knowledge of the heart comes to us from patience, experience, and prayerful reflection. God wishes this wisdom for all His children, but it comes only over time.

*Lord, help me wait patiently for Your wisdom,*
*that I may become more like You with each new day. Amen.*

# DAY 5 - *Encouragement*

## *Morning*

*For I have sent him to you for this very purpose, that you may know*
*about our circumstances and that he may encourage your hearts.*
COLOSSIANS 4:8 NASB

*For whatever was written in earlier times was written for our instruction, so that*
*through perseverance and the encouragement of the Scriptures we might have hope.*
ROMANS 15:4 NASB

Faith and commitment to God are as challenging today as they were in
Bible times. Temptation surrounds us, and even when we obey the Word
of God and stand firm, we sometimes grow weak and afraid. But do not
fear. Take heart and be strong. You are deeply loved by God!

*Dear Lord, thank You for Your love and mercy.*
*Please give me Your peace and strength today. Amen.*

## *Evening*

*I am overcome with sorrow. Encourage me, as you have promised to do.*
PSALM 119:28 CEV

*A cheerful disposition is good for your health; gloom and doom leave you bone-tired.*
PROVERBS 17:22 MSG

Sometimes we have to fake it till we feel it. Experiment with this strategy.
Put a smile on your face when you feel discouraged over a setback or
frustrated about your circumstances. A cheerful heart is good medicine!

*Father, thank You for this day You have given me.*
*Create in me a happy heart that I may feel encouraged. Amen.*

# DAY 6 - *Eternity*

"Very truly I tell you, whoever hears my word and believes him who sent me has
eternal life and will not be judged but has crossed over from death to life."
JOHN 5:24 NIV

"Only I can tell you the future before it even happens.
Everything I plan will come to pass, for I do whatever I wish."
ISAIAH 46:10 NLT

Eternity is now! It starts with the realization that your salvation has granted
you a never-ending story—a life without end. Sure, you'll leave this earth at
some point, but you'll carry on as a child of God with Him forever and ever.

*God, help me live each day with an eternal focus. Amen.*

*Evening*

God will reward each of us for what we have done. He will give eternal life to
everyone who has patiently done what is good in the hope of receiving glory, honor,
and life that lasts forever. But he will show how angry and furious he can
be with every selfish person who rejects the truth and wants to do evil.
ROMANS 2:6–8 CEV

These things I have written to you who believe in the name of the
Son of God, that you may know that you have eternal life, and that
you may continue to believe in the name of the Son of God.
1 JOHN 5:13 NKJV

As a Christian, there is one thing that you can know for certain. Although
your earthly body will wear out one day, you will live forever in heaven with
God. Pray earnestly for unbelievers that they, too, may choose life!

*God, I claim the promise from Your Word that I will live forever with You.
As I lift their names to You, I ask that You touch the hearts of my
lost friends and family members. Amen.*

# DAY 7 – *Prayer*

## *Morning*

*Evening, and morning, and at noon, will I pray,*
*and cry aloud: and he shall hear my voice.*
PSALM 55:17 KJV

*He will respond to the prayer of the destitute; he will not despise their plea.*
PSALM 102:17 NIV

Prayer should be a precious thing since it is communication with our Lord. But how often do we skimp on prayer, pushing it out of our busy lives? Prayerless Christians become weak, helpless believers. But with prayer we can move mountains.

*Lord, sometimes prayer is a last resort as I try to live life*
*on my own power. Renew my prayer life today. Amen.*

## *Evening*

*Do not be anxious about anything, but in every situation, by prayer*
*and petition, with thanksgiving, present your requests to God.*
PHILIPPIANS 4:6 NIV

*Call unto me, and I will answer thee, and show thee*
*great and mighty things, which thou knowest not.*
JEREMIAH 33:3 KJV

When our prayers seem to hit the ceiling and bounce back, it's time to remind ourselves of God's greatness. Let's trust that God is still listening to our prayers. He will never fail us. All He asks is that our reliance on Him remains firm. At the right hour, we'll feel His love again.

*Even when I don't feel Your presence, Lord, You have not deserted me.*
*Keep me trusting and following You, O Lord. Amen.*

# DAY 8 - *Spiritual Growth*

## Morning

*Christian brothers, I could not speak to you as to full-grown Christians.*
*I spoke to you as men who have not obeyed the things you have been taught.*
*I spoke to you as if you were baby Christians.*
1 CORINTHIANS 3:1 NLV

*"The seed which fell among the thorns, these are the ones who have heard,*
*and as they go on their way they are choked with worries and riches*
*and pleasures of this life, and bring no fruit to maturity."*
LUKE 8:14 NASB

Christ never for one minute thought that we should be as perfect as God is. He knew that we are imperfect and sinful. He also knew how much God loves us and wants us to grow and be happy. With His help we can find joy and maturity.

*O Lord, help me know You, and through knowing You,*
*help me be like You. Amen.*

## Evening

*We are allowed to do anything, but not everything is good for us to do. We are*
*allowed to do anything, but not all things help us grow strong as Christians.*
1 CORINTHIANS 10:23 NLV

*As a prisoner for the Lord, then, I urge you to live a life worthy of the calling you*
*have received. Be completely humble and gentle; be patient, bearing with one another*
*in love. Make every effort to keep the unity of the Spirit through the bond of peace.*
EPHESIANS 4:1–3 NIV

If we will be dedicated to reading the Bible regularly, and do it prayerfully, God will help us understand it, and through understanding we will be able to live more perfectly, the way God intends.

*Lord, make me a faithful, loving follower, and be with me to guide me this day,*
*and every day to come. Amen.*

# DAY 9 – *Words*

—————————————————

Whoever of you loves life and desires to see many good days,
keep your tongue from evil and your lips from telling lies.
PSALM 34:12–13 NIV

What you heard from me, keep as the pattern of sound teaching,
with faith and love in Christ Jesus.
2 TIMOTHY 1:13 NIV

A person's words have great power to subtly shift the direction of any
conversation, whether encouraging or discouraging. God uses words to
guide and encourage His people. With His help, we can do the same.

*Father, thank You for the words You've given to show us Your love.*
*Help my conversations always reflect You. Amen.*

*Evening* —————————————————

But in a meeting of the church, it is better if I say five words that others can
understand and be helped by than 10,000 words in special sounds.
1 CORINTHIANS 14:19 NLV

Let no corrupt communication proceed out of your mouth, but that which is good to
the use of edifying, that it may minister grace unto the hearers.
EPHESIANS 4:29 KJV

Our Father desires that our words be soothing and inspiring, never bitter or
distasteful. In fact, His message of love cannot flow from a bitter mouth. We
can ask the Holy Spirit to filter our words so we can bring His message of
love to those around us.

*Heavenly Father, please forgive my harsh and bitter words of the past. Help me guard*
*my tongue, bringing Your comfort and joy to those whose lives I touch. Amen.*

# DAY 10 - *Loving Others*

*This is how we know what love is: Jesus Christ laid down his life for us.*
*And we ought to lay down our lives for our brothers and sisters.*
1 JOHN 3:16 NIV

*My dear, dear friends, if God loved us like this, we certainly ought to love each other.*
*No one has seen God, ever. But if we love one another, God dwells deeply within us,*
*and his love becomes complete in us—perfect love!*
1 JOHN 4:11–12 MSG

One of a Christian's greatest challenges may be to love others. People, after all, are so inconsistent. They cause us pain, even when they don't mean to. Let's face it—loving others can be a real sacrifice. But it's a sacrifice we can't avoid if we want to follow Jesus.

*Lord, Your call to love others is so clear. When I struggle, bring Your great love to my*
*mind so that I can love others as You would love them. Amen.*

*And this is his command: to believe in the name of his Son, Jesus Christ,*
*and to love one another as he commanded us.*
1 JOHN 3:23 NIV

*The one who loves his brother abides in the Light and there is no*
*cause for stumbling in him.*
1 JOHN 2:10 NASB

As Christians, we should reach out in love, not only to those who care for us and build us up, but also to those who devise our unhappiness. They are the ones who need it most.

*Father, when it is hard to love, I know I should love all the more.*
*Be by my side; show Your love through me. Amen.*

# DAY 11 – *Friendship*

## *Morning*

*And Jonathan made David reaffirm his vow of friendship again,
for Jonathan loved David as he loved himself.*
1 SAMUEL 20:17 NLT

*Never abandon a friend—either yours or your father's. When disaster strikes,
you won't have to ask your brother for assistance. It's better to go to
a neighbor than to a brother who lives far away.*
PROVERBS 27:10 NLT

Friendships don't always go smoothly. But even times of disagreement may benefit friends. Perhaps when friendships aren't candy coated, we can be more honest with each other. Let's listen to the courageous love of friends and avoid those who only want to please.

*Lord, I don't need a bunch of yes-friends. Give me relationships with those who care
enough to confront me. I need Your truth in all my friendships. Amen.*

## *Evening*

*The king's heart is a stream of water in the hand of the LORD;
he turns it wherever he will.*
PROVERBS 21:1 ESV

*Perfume and incense bring joy to the heart, and the pleasantness
of a friend springs from their heartfelt advice.*
PROVERBS 27:9 NIV

God uses our relationships to make us better people, better Christians. An honest friend full of forgiveness and grace can open our eyes to our faults so we can start making positive changes with God's help.

*Thank You, Jesus, for the example You have set for a true friend.
Help me be a better friend as I follow You. Amen.*

# DAY 12 - *Creation*

*In the beginning God created the heaven and the earth. And the earth was without form, and void; and darkness was upon the face of the deep. And the Spirit of God moved upon the face of the waters. And God said, Let there be light: and there was light.*
GENESIS 1:1–3 KJV

*One thing I ask from the LORD, this only do I seek: that I may dwell in the house of the LORD all the days of my life, to gaze on the beauty of the LORD and to seek him in his temple.*
PSALM 27:4 NIV

Do we seek God's beauty in our environment? Creation points to God's power and awesomeness! Ordinary things draw us into God's presence, where we can praise Him, enjoying His beauty and greatness all the days of our lives.

*Magnificent Creator, Your greatness and beauty surround me. May my eyes gaze at You, seeking You, that I may dwell in Your presence continually. Amen.*

*God saw all that he had made, and it was very good. And there was evening, and there was morning—the sixth day.*
GENESIS 1:31 NIV

*God's glory is on tour in the skies, God-craft on exhibit across the horizon.*
PSALM 19:1 MSG

Viewing creation puts everything into perspective. Our problems seem minuscule in comparison to the heavens above, the majesty of the mountains, and the grandeur of the trees. Knowing that God has favored us with His grace, mercy, and love, and has given us the responsibility to care for creation fills us with songs of praise.

*Lord, the beauty of this earth is awesome. Thank You for caring so much about me and for creating the magnificence that surrounds me. Amen.*

# DAY 13 - *Hope*

## *Morning*

*No one who hopes in you will ever be put to shame, but shame will come
on those who are treacherous without cause.*
PSALM 25:3 NIV

*I pray that God, the source of hope, will fill you completely with joy and peace
because you trust in him. Then you will overflow with confident
hope through the power of the Holy Spirit.*
ROMANS 15:13 NLT

God desires to fill us to the brim with joy and peace. But to receive it, we need
to have faith in the God who is trustworthy and who says anything is possible
through Him. When you begin to feel discouraged, exhausted, and at the end
of your rope, stop; go before the throne of grace and recall God's faithfulness.

*God of hope, I recount Your faithfulness to me. Please fill me with Your joy and
peace, because I believe You are able to accomplish all things. Amen.*

## *Evening*

*And not only so, but we glory in tribulations also: knowing that tribulation worketh
patience; and patience, experience; and experience, hope: and hope maketh not
ashamed; because the love of God is shed abroad in our hearts
by the Holy Ghost which is given unto us.*
ROMANS 5:3–5 KJV

*Hope deferred makes the heart sick, but when the desire comes, it is a tree of life.*
PROVERBS 13:12 NKJV

Jesus is your hope! He stands a short distance away, bidding you to take
a walk on water—a step of faith toward Him. Disregarding the distractions
can be hard, but the rough waters can become silent as you turn your eyes,
your thoughts, and your emotions to Him.

*Lord, help me not to concentrate on the distractions, but to keep my focus on which
step to take next in order to reach You—my hope! Amen.*

# DAY 14 - *Wealth*

——————————————————————

*As for every man to whom God has given riches and wealth, and given him power to*
*eat of it, to receive his heritage and rejoice in his labor—this is the gift of God.*
ECCLESIASTES 5:19 NKJV

*Do not wear yourself out to get rich; do not trust your own cleverness. Cast but*
*a glance at riches, and they are gone, for they will surely sprout wings*
*and fly off to the sky like an eagle.*
PROVERBS 23:4–5 NIV

Having money and possessions isn't wrong. Even having high-priced
possessions isn't wrong. But there is something missing when our desire for
wealth outweighs our desire for God. We may hold on too tightly to things that
don't have eternal value and not cling closely enough to the One who does.

*Lord, help me give back to You what You have given to me. Amen.*

*Evening* ——————————————————————

*Jesus answered, "If you want to be perfect, go, sell your possessions and give to the*
*poor, and you will have treasure in heaven. Then come, follow me. . . . It is*
*easier for a camel to go through the eye of a needle than for someone who*
*is rich to enter the kingdom of God."*
MATTHEW 19:21–24 NIV

*"For where your treasure is, there your heart will be also."*
LUKE 12:34 NIV

Are you gathering earthly treasures or eternal ones? Those on earth won't
last. When your best treasure is your relationship with Christ and His eternal
reward, you don't have to worry about where your heart is. It is safe with
Jesus. Worldly goods fade, but not those in Jesus' treasure vaults.

*Lord, help me send treasures ahead of me into eternity instead of grabbing*
*all the earthly items I can get. Amen.*

# DAY 15 – *Faith*

*Consequently, faith comes from hearing the message, and the message is heard through the word about Christ.*
ROMANS 10:17 NIV

*And PETER answered him and said, Lord, if it be thou, bid me come unto thee on the water. And he said, Come. And when PETER was come down out of the ship, he walked on the water, to go to Jesus.*
MATTHEW 14:28–29 KJV

To the skeptic, logic must pervade every situation. But to the person of faith, logic gives way to faith. Even when our prayers remain unanswered, we continue to pray. Even when God is silent, we continue to believe. And though we grope for answers, we continue to trust. In all situations, God asks us to hold fast to our faith.

*Dear Lord, please forgive me for allowing my problems to undermine my faith. I trust You, knowing that my faith in You is never futile. Amen.*

*Love the LORD, all his faithful people! The LORD preserves those who are true to him, but the proud he pays back in full.*
PSALM 31:23 NIV

*And I say unto you, Ask, and it shall be given you; seek, and ye shall find; knock, and it shall be opened unto you.*
LUKE 11:9 KJV

As growing Christians, we want to improve our faith. The Bible encourages us to do good works, but mature faith relies more on living as God wants us to live than on filling our calendars with spiritual disciplines. Are we just doing good things or doing the things God wants us to do?

*Lord, help me fill my days with Your will, not all the works that come my way. Amen.*

# DAY 16 - *Helping Others*

## *Morning*

*We who are strong [in our convictions and of robust faith] ought to bear with the failings and the frailties and the tender scruples of the weak; [we ought to help carry the doubts and qualms of others] and not to please ourselves.*
ROMANS 15:1 AMP

*Yet it was good of you to share in my troubles. Moreover, as you Philippians know, in the early days of your acquaintance with the gospel, when I set out from Macedonia, not one church shared with me in the matter of giving and receiving, except you only.*
PHILIPPIANS 4:14–15 NIV

As our lives become more hectic and crowded, finding a way to help others—and be helped by them—can open the door to blessings for everyone, including more time with our family and friends, and more rest for our minds, bodies, and souls. God never meant for us to face our days alone.

*Father God, You have brought so many good people into my life. Help me remember to offer my help to them and to ask for help when I need it. Amen.*

## *Evening*

*The one who blesses others is abundantly blessed; those who help others are helped.*
PROVERBS 11:25 MSG

*We loved you so much that we shared with you not only God's Good News but our own lives, too.*
1 THESSALONIANS 2:8 NLT

Unbelievers may hear Christians talk about Jesus. What they may not experience is unconditional love from those who call themselves Christ followers. Practice sharing your life with those around you. Reach out in friendship.

*God, help me share my life with others. Let others see Jesus in the way I live and the way I love. Amen.*

# DAY 17 – *Sin*

*He himself bore our sins in his body on the tree, that we might die to sin
and live to righteousness. By his wounds you have been healed.*
1 PETER 2:24 ESV

*The next day he saw Jesus coming toward him, and said, "Behold, the Lamb of God,
who takes away the sin of the world!"*
JOHN 1:29 ESV

The wage of sin is death. A wise person avoids life-threatening situations at
any cost. That is what we should do as Christians. We should do everything
in our power to avoid sin, which should be as odious to us as death itself.

*Lord God, I want my life to be pleasing to You. Guide me through the power
of Your Holy Spirit. Amen.*

*The wages of the righteous is life, the income of the wicked, punishment.*
PROVERBS 10:16 NASB

*Therefore, just as sin came into the world through one man, and death through sin,
and so death spread to all men because all sinned—for sin indeed was in the world
before the law was given, but sin is not counted where there is no law.*
ROMANS 5:12–13 ESV

Throughout scripture, God's promises and humanity's sin run together in
entwined messages. God's merciful thread runs through our pain-filled,
erroneous lives, too. God calls us to leave behind the darkness of sin and
live in His holiness. His love strips evil from us and brings us into a close
relationship with Him.

*Lord, thank You for calling me out of sin and into Yourself.
I want to glorify You. Amen.*

# DAY 18 – *Contentment*

*You make my life pleasant, and my future is bright.*
PSALM 16:6 CEV

*But godliness with contentment is great gain.*
1 TIMOTHY 6:6 KJV

How can we learn to be content? We must start looking to Jesus. If we take hold of all we have as joint heirs with Christ and as partakers of grace, we will have no desire for the world's riches. We need a fresh vision for who we are in Christ. Therein we will find contentment.

*Father, I am so foolish. I have everything in You, yet I try to find more*
*in the world and in myself. Thank You for the true riches*
*I have found through Jesus Christ. Amen.*

*Better is the little that the righteous has than the abundance of many wicked.*
PSALM 37:16 ESV

*All my longings lie open before you, Lord; my sighing is not hidden from you. . . .*
*My soul thirsts for God, for the living God.*
PSALM 38:9, 42:2 NIV

Our souls thirst for the living God. We need more of Him—more of His presence, His Word, His consolation, His hope. Nothing material or relational can fill the void in our hearts—just the living God, breathing fresh life into an aching soul.

*Lord, fill my deepest longings with Your quenching presence.*
*Keep me looking only to You for soul satisfaction. Amen.*

# DAY 19 - *Laziness*

*The path of lazy people is overgrown with briers;*
*the diligent walk down a smooth road.*
PROVERBS 15:19 MSG

*No matter how much you want, laziness won't help a bit,*
*but hard work will reward you with more than enough.*
PROVERBS 13:4 CEV

The Bible gives us a simple solution to conquer the sin of sloth. Namely, God admonishes us to do our best in whatever task we undertake, no matter how large or menial the JOB. As we give our best, God returns the gesture. He blesses us with a centered life and a more meaningful, productive existence.

*Dear Jesus, please forgive me for the times I have been lazy. Empower and remind*
*me to give my best in everything I do, just as You give Your best to me. Amen.*

*Laziness leads to a sagging roof; idleness leads to a leaky house.*
ECCLESIASTES 10:18 NLT

*My dear friends, in the name of the Lord Jesus, I beg you not to have anything to do with*
*any of your people who loaf around and refuse to obey the instructions we gave you.*
2 THESSALONIANS 3:6 CEV

We shine a negative light on God when we are lazy or slothful. Christians should be proud to do their best in all things, as a sign to others that being a Christian is something special.

*During the times when I get lazy, help me remember that my actions reflect not only*
*upon myself, but also upon You, O Lord. Amen.*

# DAY 20 – *Rest*

## *Morning*

*"Consider the lilies of the field, how they grow: they neither toil nor spin."*
MATTHEW 6:28 NKJV

*I will both lay me down in peace, and sleep: for thou, LORD,*
*only makest me dwell in safety.*
PSALM 4:8 KJV

Don't let thoughts of days past and in the future keep you from catching those forty winks. Fall asleep in God's Word, rest easy, and rise refreshed.

*God, with Your Word in my thoughts, I can lie down in peace and sleep. You will keep me safe, now and forever, as I rest and then rise in Your power. Amen.*

## *Evening*

*And he said, "My presence will go with you, and I will give you rest."*
EXODUS 33:14 ESV

*For anyone who enters God's rest also rests from their works, just as God did from his. Let us, therefore, make every effort to enter that rest, so that no one will perish by following their example of disobedience.*
HEBREWS 4:10–11 NIV

Imagine a busy person's calendar. More often than not, it is bursting with reminders. Seldom is there an opening in the day's schedule for unexpected things that may arise, let alone a few minutes set aside for rest. But God instructs us to plan for rest in our schedule and to leave ourselves some breathing room.

*Lord, correct my thinking and clear my clutter. Let me not be so busily focused on my own agenda that I miss Yours. Amen.*

# DAY 21 – *Peace*

## *Morning*

*Therefore, since we have been justified by faith, we have peace with God through our Lord Jesus Christ.*
ROMANS 5:1 ESV

*For to us a child is born, to us a son is given, and the government will be on his shoulders. And he will be called Wonderful Counselor, Mighty God, Everlasting Father, Prince of Peace.*
ISAIAH 9:6 NIV

Peace with God does not always mean a calm time of happiness. The salvation that Jesus brought comes with a price: conflict against evil. But in the end, all who trust in Him experience the peace of eternal life.

*While life on earth may be rocky, Lord, nothing can upset the peace I have found in You. Amen.*

## *Evening*

*"The LORD bless you, and keep you; the LORD make His face shine on you, and be gracious to you."*
NUMBERS 6:24–25 NASB

*For the mind set on the flesh is death, but the mind set on the Spirit is life and peace.*
ROMANS 8:6 NASB

Much as we seek peace in our lives, we cannot find it until we have peace with God, the source of all peace. Real spiritual peace only comes through the Savior.

*Heavenly Father, be my peace today. Let me rest in Your unfailing love. Amen.*

# DAY 22 – *Perseverance*

## *Morning* —————————————————

*Keep on asking and it will be given you; keep on seeking and you will find;*
*keep on knocking [reverently] and [the door] will be opened to you.*
MATTHEW 7:7 AMP

*For if we are faithful to the end, trusting God just as firmly as when*
*we first believed, we will share in all that belongs to Christ.*
HEBREWS 3:14 NLT

God calls for persistence, also known as perseverance, over a dozen times in the New Testament. He means for the trials that come our way to increase our perseverance. When we successfully pass small hurdles, He may put bigger ones in our way. Why? Because He loves us. Persistence results in faith that is pure, molten gold.

*Lord, we can only persist because You are unchanging. We pray that we will*
*keep our eyes fixed on You and keep moving forward. Amen.*

## *Evening* —————————————————

*And I am certain that God, who began the good work within you, will continue his*
*work until it is finally finished on the day when Christ Jesus returns.*
PHILIPPIANS 1:6 NLT

*Blessed is the one who perseveres under trial because, having stood the test, that*
*person will receive the crown of life that the Lord has promised to those who love him.*
JAMES 1:12 NIV

Perseverance means staying in life's fight and refusing to give up. This attitude empowers us and makes the victim mentality dissipate. It builds confidence, one fight at a time. Keep on keeping on—it's a powerful life tool.

*Lord, give me the strength to get up from the mat and continue.*
*I choose to believe in Your promises. Amen.*

# DAY 23 – *Healing*

## *Morning*

*"See now that I myself am he! There is no god besides me. I put to death and I bring to life, I have wounded and I will heal, and no one can deliver out of my hand."*
DEUTERONOMY 32:39 NIV

*Let all that I am praise the LORD; may I never forget the good things he does for me. He forgives all my sins and heals all my diseases.*
PSALM 103:2–3 NLT

Our heavenly Father patiently waits for us to come to Him with the fragments of our shattered lives. When we bring our brokenness to the foot of the cross, He provides a life-giving transfusion, healing the hurt and shaping His children into healthy, whole vessels.

*Lord, I bring my shattered remnants and broken dreams to You. Bring healing and wholeness to my life. Amen.*

## *Evening*

*Christ carried the burden of our sins. He was nailed to the cross, so that we would stop sinning and start living right. By his cuts and bruises you are healed.*
1 PETER 2:24 CEV

*He heals the brokenhearted and binds up their wounds.*
PSALM 147:3 NASB

No matter how dark your circumstances, God can redeem them. He can weave your pain into the tapestry of your life and provide hope, help, and healing. Open your heart to God today and receive the gift of healing.

*Father, thank You for offering me hope and healing. Help me let the pain go so that it does not define me. Amen.*

# DAY 24 – *God's Love*

## *Morning*

"For God so loved the world that He gave His only begotten Son, that whoever believes in Him should not perish but have everlasting life."
JOHN 3:16 NKJV

"Understand, therefore, that the LORD your God is indeed God. He is the faithful God who keeps his covenant for a thousand generations and lavishes his unfailing love on those who love him and obey his commands."
DEUTERONOMY 7:9 NLT

Many things in life are pricey. Name-brand clothing, cars—even phones. But they will wear out or be used up before long, no matter what the price tag. By contrast, God's preserving, unfailing love is priceless. His amazing love was costly, but it's not pricey.

*Thank You, Father, that no price tag can be put on Your lavish love for me. Amen.*

## *Evening*

Thank GOD! He deserves your thanks. His love never quits. Thank the God of all gods, His love never quits. Thank the Lord of all lords. His love never quits.
PSALM 136:1–3 MSG

Give thanks to the LORD, for he is good; his love endures forever.
PSALM 107:1 NIV

When the sea of life batters us, it's easy to forget the Lord's goodness. We may even doubt the Lord whom we serve. That's a good time to stop and give thanks to God, who never stops being good or ends His love for us. Our situations change, our love fails, but God never varies.

*Thank You, Lord, that Your love never changes. I can depend on it, though my life seems to be crashing around me. Nothing is larger than You. Amen.*

# DAY 25 – *Creation*

*Morning* ————————————————————————————

> *Does not the potter have the right to make out of the same lump of clay*
> *some pottery for special purposes and some for common use?*
> ROMANS 9:21 NIV

> *God has set up his kingdom in heaven, and he rules the whole creation.*
> PSALM 103:19 CEV

God has created a glorious world, and He has freely given it to us. The early quiet of the day is a beautiful time to encounter the Lord. Give Him your early hours, and He will give you all the blessings you can hold.

> *I raise my voice to You in the morning, Lord. Help me appreciate Your*
> *new day and use it to the fullest. Amen.*

*Evening* ————————————————————————————

> *"God sets out the entire creation as a science classroom,*
> *using birds and beasts to teach wisdom."*
> JOB 35:11 MSG

> *Let all creation rejoice before the LORD, for he comes, he comes to judge the earth.*
> PSALM 96:13 NIV

God's creation. In a world where such glory exists, why do we continually allow worldly concerns to occupy so much of our attention? Let God be our glory, and indeed, when we find ourselves most down, He will lift our heads up and show us all the wonders of His magnificent creation.

> *Lord, protect me from those things that turn my attention from You. Clear the eyes of*
> *my heart so they can focus on the splendor of Your creation. Amen.*

# DAY 26 – *Trials*

*Consider it a sheer gift, friends, when tests and challenges come at you from all sides.*
JAMES 1:2 MSG

*Weeping may endure for a night, but joy cometh in the morning.*
PSALM 30:5 KJV

Some trials are short lived. Others are more complex. As believers, we can find joy in the Lord even as certain trials remain a backdrop in our lives. Your loving heavenly Father has not forgotten you. You may feel that relief will never come, but take courage. It will.

*God, where there is anguish in my life, may Your joy enter in. I ask for grace to face my trials, knowing that in time You will replace weeping with joy. Amen.*

*He said to his disciples, "Hard trials and temptations are bound to come, but too bad for whoever brings them on! Better to wear a millstone necklace and take a swim in the deep blue sea than give even one of these dear little ones a hard time!"*
LUKE 17:1–2 MSG

*And though the Lord give you the bread of adversity, and the water of affliction. . . thine ears shall hear a word behind thee, saying, This is the way, walk ye in it.*
ISAIAH 30:20–21 KJV

There are times when God allows us to experience trials. These are hard times, when the Christian walk is tough. Sometimes we may want to give up, saying the path is too rough. But if we call on God for help, the path may not be easier, but we will be strengthened in our faith and our fellowship with God.

*Thank You, Lord, for allowing hardships and tests that make me stronger as a Christian. Help me trust You when the path becomes difficult. Amen.*

DAY 27 – *Reflecting Christ*

## *Morning*

*Look at [this obvious fact] which is before your eyes. If anyone is confident that he is Christ's, let him reflect and remind himself that even as he is Christ's, so too are we.*
2 CORINTHIANS 10:7 AMP

*If you're abused because of Christ, count yourself fortunate. It's the Spirit of God and his glory in you that brought you to the notice of others. . . . Be proud of the distinguished status reflected in that name!*
1 PETER 4:14–16 MSG

When you gave your heart to God, His light came on inside your heart. Christianity lives from the inside out. Your life should reflect the character and nature of the One who created you. As you point others to God, your light shines, repelling darkness and giving comfort to everyone God brings across your path.

*Jesus, show me what I can do and say to let my light shine brightly. Amen.*

## *Evening*

*And also for me, that words may be given to me in opening my mouth boldly to proclaim the mystery of the gospel, for which I am an ambassador in chains, that I may declare it boldly, as I ought to speak.*
EPHESIANS 6:19–20 ESV

*Because we understand our fearful responsibility to the Lord, we work hard to persuade others. God knows we are sincere, and I hope you know this, too.*
2 CORINTHIANS 5:11 NLT

We have to weigh our options carefully when we mingle with worldly people. On one hand, we want to be a godly inspiration; on the other, we don't want our actions to reflect God in a negative light. We must pray that the light of Christ shines through us so that we reflect God in all situations.

*Lord, please help me to glorify You always. Let me consider You first before myself, and help me be the right kind of witness to those around me. Amen.*

# DAY 28 - *False Teaching*

*Then the L*ORD *said to me, "The prophets are prophesying falsehood in My name. I have neither sent them nor commanded them nor spoken to them; they are prophesying to you a false vision, divination, futility and the deception of their own minds."*
JEREMIAH 14:14 NASB

*For of this sort are they which creep into houses, and lead captive silly women laden with sins, led away with divers lusts, ever learning, and never able to come to the knowledge of the truth.*
2 TIMOTHY 3:6–7 KJV

We are silly when we are so open minded that we believe things we know are too good to be true—a slick sales pitch, the false teaching of a charismatic leader, or the unexamined claims of someone offering us something larger, better, or easier. If we are to be truly strong, we must listen to God alone and settle our hearts in the truth of His Word.

*Father, I have been confused by many voices in this world. Open my ears to Your voice alone. Settle my heart in Your Word, because I know it is truth. Amen.*

*"When a prophet speaks in the name of the L*ORD*, if the thing does not come about or come true, that is the thing which the L*ORD *has not spoken."*
DEUTERONOMY 18:22 NASB

*Anyone who runs ahead and does not continue in the teaching of Christ does not have God; whoever continues in the teaching has both the Father and the Son.*
2 JOHN 1:9 NIV

Spiritual ideas abound, but not all are sound. How can we tell meat from mush? Compare the message to Christ's words. Jesus gave us strong doctrines and good teaching to lead us into His truth. Faithful expositors cling to His Word.

*Keep me aware of Your truth, Lord. I want to live on it, not on mush. Amen.*

DAY 29 – *God's Promises*

*Morning* ───────────────────────────────

*I have ruled this way, and God will never break his promise to me. God's promise is
complete and unchanging; he will always help me and give me what I hope for.*
2 SAMUEL 23:5 CEV

*In hope of eternal life which God, who cannot lie, promised before time began.*
TITUS 1:2 NKJV

God always keeps His word. The Bible is filled with the promises of God—
vows to us that we can trust will be completed. God never lies. Lying is not
in Him. He sees us as worthy of His commitment.

*God, thank You that Your Word is trustworthy and true.
Praise You for Your many promises. Amen.*

*Evening* ───────────────────────────────

*So God's promise is given to us because we put our trust in Him.
We can be sure of it. It is because of His loving-favor to us.*
ROMANS 4:16 NLV

*Through these he gave us the very great and precious promises. With these gifts you
can share in God's nature, and the world will not ruin you with its evil desires.*
2 PETER 1:4 NCV

How wonderful that God never forgets His promises. If He says it, He means
it. And if He means it, He does it. Talk about keeping your word!

*Lord, I want to be trustworthy like You. Remind me of the commitments I've made,
just as You remember Your commitments to me. Amen.*

# DAY 30 – *God's Presence*

*Morning* ——————————————————————————

*Know therefore this day, and consider it in thine heart, that the L*ORD *he is God in heaven above, and upon the earth beneath: there is none else.*
DEUTERONOMY 4:39 KJV

*And he said, My presence shall go with thee, and I will give thee rest.*
EXODUS 33:14 KJV

It is not so important that we feel God's presence with us as it is that we have faith in His being with us always. Feelings come and go, but the presence of God in our lives never changes.

*Let me sense Your loving arms around me, Lord; but when I don't, help me to remember that You are there, anyway. Amen.*

*Evening* ——————————————————————————

*Be humble in the presence of God's mighty power, and he will honor you when the time comes.*
1 PETER 5:6 CEV

*"Good people will prosper like palm trees, grow tall like Lebanon cedars; transplanted to G*OD*'s courtyard, they'll grow tall in the presence of God, lithe and green, virile still in old age."*
PSALM 92:12–14 MSG

When we think that God is watching us, we are on our best behavior, but when we forget that He is there, we misbehave. It is as we grow in our knowledge of God's presence in our lives that it is easier to walk in the path of righteousness.

*Lord God, grant me special insight that I might recognize Your presence in my life and follow You always. Amen.*

# DAY 31 - *Laughter*

## *Morning*

*"He will yet fill your mouth with laughter, and your lips with shouting."*
JOB 8:21 ESV

*All you saints! Sing your hearts out to GOD! Thank him to his face! He gets angry once in a while, but across a lifetime there is only love. The nights of crying your eyes out give way to days of laughter.*
PSALM 30:4–5 MSG

When Satan bombards us with lies—"God's not real"; "You'll never get that job"; "You're unlovable"—it's time to look back to God's Word. Imbed in your mind the truth that with God, nothing is impossible. And then, in the midst of the storm, laugh, letting the joy of God's truth be your strength.

*I trust in Your Word, Lord. Help me rest in that assurance. Amen.*

## *Evening*

*On your feet now—applaud GOD! Bring a gift of laughter, sing yourselves into his presence.*
PSALM 100:1–2 MSG

*Our mouths were filled with laughter, our tongues with songs of joy.*
PSALM 126:2 NIV

As children of the Creator Himself, we were made to laugh—to experience great joy. Our design didn't include for us to carry the stress, worry, and heaviness every day. Go ahead! Ask God to give you a really good laugh today.

*Lord, help me rediscover laughter. Help me take every opportunity You bring to see the joy in life and the comedy that it brings to my world every day. Amen.*

# DAY 32 – *Christian Life*

*Christian brothers, we ask you, because of the Lord Jesus, to keep on living in a way that will please God. I have already told you how to grow in the Christian life.*
1 THESSALONIANS 4:1 NLV

*He found Saul and brought him to Antioch, where they met with the church for a whole year and taught many of its people. There in Antioch the Lord's followers were first called Christians.*
ACTS 11:26 CEV

As hard as we might try to live as God would want, we find that we can't quite do it. We need help. God gives us that help if we only seek it. Prayer, scripture, and the support of fellow believers makes living the Christian life much easier and more fulfilling.

*When I struggle with life, Lord, grant me Your wisdom to lead me through. Amen.*

*"If your sons pay close attention to their way, to walk before me in faithfulness with all their heart and with all their soul, you shall not lack a man on the throne of Israel."*
1 KINGS 2:4 ESV

*You're no longer wandering exiles. This kingdom of faith is now your home country. You're no longer strangers or outsiders. You belong here, with as much right to the name Christian as anyone.*
EPHESIANS 2:19 MSG

What seems impossible on our own becomes a pleasure when we have help. We are never alone in our Christian journey. We are given one another, and we are even in touch with God's Holy Spirit.

*O Lord, show me how You want me to be. Open my eyes, my heart, my spirit. Amen.*

## *Morning*

*For this they willfully forget: that by the word of God the heavens were of old, and the earth standing out of water and in the water, by which the world that then existed perished, being flooded with water.*
2 PETER 3:5–6 NKJV

*The Word was first, the Word present to God, God present to the Word. The Word was God, in readiness for God from day one.*
JOHN 1:1–2 MSG

Without God's Word, how would we know about God? God's Word helps us know Jesus, whom the Bible also calls the Word. Through the written Word and His Son, God has shown us the way to Himself.

*Lord, let me see You through Your Word. My desire is to know You more every day. Amen.*

## *Evening*

*The Son is the radiance of God's glory and the exact representation of his being, sustaining all things by his powerful word.*
HEBREWS 1:3 NIV

*For the word of the LORD is right and true; he is faithful in all he does.*
PSALM 33:4 NIV

The only true stabilizing force we have in this life is the Word of God. God's Word will be our shield and our strength in the most troubled of times. Turn to it daily, and you will be renewed.

*Heavenly Father, calm my soul, place Your peace within my heart. When things look most dismal, shine Your light upon me. Amen.*

## *Morning*

*The path of right-living people is level. The Leveler evens the road for
the right-living. We're in no hurry, GOD. We're content to linger
in the path sign-posted with your decisions.*
ISAIAH 26:7–8 MSG

*I press on to reach the end of the race and receive the heavenly prize
for which God, through Christ Jesus, is calling us.*
PHILIPPIANS 3:14 NLT

As humans, we often want to cover our bases, assuring ourselves that our
decisions are right, but we must not lose ourselves in the analysis. Find your
strength in the leadership of the Holy Spirit and move forward with confidence.

*Lord, help me trust You in the decisions I make throughout my day. Help me to stop
second-guessing myself and trust who You created me be. Amen.*

## *Evening*

*Without good advice everything goes wrong—
it takes careful planning for things to go right.*
PROVERBS 15:22 CEV

*I will instruct thee and teach thee in the way which thou shalt go:
I will guide thee with mine eye.*
PSALM 32:8 KJV

God tells us that whenever we have a decision to make, He will instruct and
teach us. He will not let us flounder, but as we seek His face, He will provide
direction, understanding, wisdom, and insight. He will teach us the way—
the road or journey we need to take that is in our best interest.

*All-knowing Lord, I praise You that regardless of the decision, You know what is best
for me and will direct me in the path I should take. Amen.*

## *Morning*

*I tell you that any sinful thing you do or say can be forgiven. Even if you speak against the Son of Man, you can be forgiven. But if you speak against the Holy Spirit, you can never be forgiven, either in this life or in the life to come.*
MATTHEW 12:31–32 CEV

*"If you then, being evil, know how to give good gifts to your children, how much more will your heavenly Father give the Holy Spirit to those who ask Him?"*
LUKE 11:13 NASB

Christ died to heal our relationship with God, but the Holy Spirit enables us to live for Him. Our relationship is with the Father, Son, and Holy Spirit, and in our lives, each works in concert with the other persons of the Trinity.

*Lord, without Your Holy Spirit helping me, I would never be able to live for You. Thank You! Amen.*

## *Evening*

*"Therefore go and make disciples of all nations, baptizing them in the name of the Father and of the Son and of the Holy Spirit, and teaching them to obey everything I have commanded you. And surely I am with you always, to the very end of the age."*
MATTHEW 28:19–20 NIV

*"When you are brought before synagogues, rulers and authorities, do not worry about how you will defend yourselves or what you will say, for the Holy Spirit will teach you at that time what you should say."*
LUKE 12:11–12 NIV

The Holy Spirit dwells in us, as Christians, and makes us able to live for God in a sin-filled world. With the Spirit's guidance, God sends us on a heavenly mission on earth: to share His good news with the world. Only by living in the Spirit do we have success in our mission for our Lord.

*Holy Spirit, direct my path so that I may share the wonderful news of salvation. Be with me; guide me, I pray. Amen.*

# DAY 36 - *Wealth*

*I have seen another evil under the sun, and it weighs heavily on mankind: God gives some people wealth, possessions and honor, so that they lack nothing their hearts desire, but God does not grant them the ability to enjoy them, and strangers enjoy them instead. This is meaningless, a grievous evil.*
ECCLESIASTES 6:1–2 NIV

*"Sell your possessions and give to those in need. This will store up treasure for you in heaven! And the purses of heaven never get old or develop holes. Your treasure will be safe; no thief can steal it and no moth can destroy it."*
LUKE 12:33 NLT

Though possessions are gifts from God, they can also distract believers from the fact that all in this life is temporary. However many possessions God gives us, we need to share them generously and store up treasures in heaven.

*Father, I have been blessed with many things; help me share them with others. Amen.*

*All the believers lived in a wonderful harmony, holding everything in common. They sold whatever they owned and pooled their resources so that each person's need was met.*
ACTS 2:44–45 MSG

*You suffered along with those who were thrown into jail, and when all you owned was taken from you, you accepted it with joy. You knew there were better things waiting for you that will last forever.*
HEBREWS 10:34 NLT

If people would pursue God with the same energy that they pursue the glitter of gold, the result would be Christians who give themselves completely to the loving will of God, and the world would begin to be more the way God intended it to be from the beginning.

*Be my strength, Lord, that I might be able to give myself completely over to Your will. Amen.*

# DAY 37 - *Forgiveness*

## *Morning*

*Who is a God like you, who pardons sin and forgives the transgression of the remnant*
*of his inheritance? You do not stay angry forever but delight to show mercy.*
*You will again have compassion on us; you will tread our sins underfoot*
*and hurl all our iniquities into the depths of the sea.*
MICAH 7:18-19 NIV

*But if ye do not forgive, neither will your Father which is in*
*heaven forgive your trespasses.*
MARK 11:26 KJV

When we knowingly sin against God, we're often hesitant to seek His face
for forgiveness. Even in those rare instances when we sin in ignorance, we
must still humble ourselves before Him. But we never need fear that He'll
turn away from us. Such total forgiveness should bring us running back to
Him on a daily basis.

*Heavenly Father, forgive me for both secret and presumptuous sins.*
*Help me live constantly. Amen.*

## *Evening*

*"The LORD is slow to anger, abounding in love and forgiving sin and rebellion.*
*Yet he does not leave the guilty unpunished."*
NUMBERS 14:18 NIV

*Judge not, and ye shall not be judged: condemn not, and ye shall not be condemned:*
*forgive, and ye shall be forgiven.*
LUKE 6:37 KJV

Some things we need to remember. Others we need to forget. When we
can put away past hurts, we look more like our forgiving Father. When the
Lord provides unexpected healing in a fractured relationship, we can thank
Him for such marvelous grace.

*Lord God, I praise You for the blessedness of forgotten and forgiven hurts. Amen.*

# DAY 38 – *God's Faithfulness*

## *Morning*

*And we know that all things work together for good to them that love God,
to them who are the called according to his purpose.*
ROMANS 8:28 KJV

*"I will not leave you as orphans; I will come to you."*
JOHN 14:18 NIV

God never, ever abandons us. No matter how busy we are, He never forgets us. He promised His followers that He would always help and support them, a promise He still keeps today.

*Lord, You sent Your Holy Spirit as a helper and guide. No matter how tough our world becomes, let us remember Your presence in our lives. Amen.*

## *Evening*

*If we believe not, yet he abideth faithful: he cannot deny himself.*
2 TIMOTHY 2:13 KJV

*Know therefore that the LORD thy God, he is God, the faithful God,
which keepeth covenant and mercy with them that love him and keep his
commandments to a thousand generations.*
DEUTERONOMY 7:9 KJV

Never does the Lord forsake His own. The only distance that is ever between us is the distance that we put there.

*Father, let me feel Your gentle weight upon my heart, and keep me ever mindful of Your presence in my life. You are always faithful. Amen.*

*Morning* ────────────────────────────────

*His lord said unto him, Well done, thou good and faithful servant:*
*thou hast been faithful over a few things, I will make thee ruler over*
*many things: enter thou into the joy of thy lord.*
MATTHEW 25:21 KJV

*Though you have not seen him, you love him; and even though you do not see him*
*now, you believe in him and are filled with an inexpressible and glorious joy, for you*
*are receiving the end result of your faith, the salvation of your souls.*
1 PETER 1:8–9 NIV

God's joy isn't based on our circumstances; rather, its roots begin with the
seed of God's Word planted in our hearts. Suddenly, our hearts spill over
with joy, knowing that God loves us and that He has complete control of
our lives. Joy is Jesus.

*Dear Jesus, knowing You surpasses anything and everything else the world offers.*
*Never allow the joy in my heart to evaporate in the desert of difficulties. Amen.*

*Evening* ────────────────────────────────

*And an angel of the Lord appeared to them, and the glory of the Lord shone around*
*them, and they were filled with great fear. And the angel said to them, "Fear not, for*
*behold, I bring you good news of great joy that will be for all the people. For unto you*
*is born this day in the city of David a Savior, who is Christ the Lord."*
LUKE 2:9–11 ESV

*"Do not grieve, for the joy of the LORD is your strength."*
NEHEMIAH 8:10 NIV

Not to be confused with happiness, joy is not dependent on external
circumstances. It's a Holy Spirit–inspired mystery that defies all reason.
Living joyfully is not denying reality. But in the midst of our parched desert
times, our heavenly Father reaches to lift and sustain us.

*Giver of strength, fill me with joy in the midst of sorrow like a desert flower. Amen.*

# DAY 40 – *Evil*

## *Morning*

The LORD is watching everywhere, keeping his eye on both the evil and the good.
PROVERBS 15:3 NLT

And He was saying, "That which proceeds out of the man, that is what defiles the
man. For from within, out of the heart of men, proceed the evil thoughts."
MARK 7:20–21 NASB

Evil people are not to be hated, but pitied. They are our mission in life.
Lives devoid of the good news are lives not worth living. Reach out to
people who do wrong through your prayers. They need them most of all.

*Lord, show me how to love even the most unlovable people. Instead of anger, let me
show compassion. Fill my heart with a love that will overcome evil. Amen.*

## *Evening*

For our struggle is not against flesh and blood, but against the rulers, against the
powers, against the world forces of this darkness, against the spiritual forces of
wickedness in the heavenly places. Therefore, take up the full armor of God, so that
you will be able to resist in the evil day, and having done everything, to stand firm.
EPHESIANS 6:12–13 NASB

This is the verdict: Light has come into the world, but people loved
darkness instead of light because their deeds were evil. Everyone who does
evil hates the light, and will not come into the light.
JOHN 3:19–20 NIV

The Lord despises evil, and one day all evil will be erased. As kingdom people,
we can rejoice in the promise of peace and harmony that God is sure to supply.

*Father, when this world seems consumed by evil, remind me of
Your promise of peace to come. Amen.*

# DAY 41 – *Children*

*I have no greater joy than to hear that my children walk in truth.*
3 JOHN 1:4 KJV

*And again, I will put my trust in him. And again, Behold I
and the children which God hath given me.*
HEBREWS 2:13 KJV

How can our children learn to be quiet and meditate on God's Word when their schedules are hectic and every minute is committed? It's easy to crowd out the things that matter most to God: worshiping Him, listening to Him, and seeking His presence.

*Heavenly Father, as my children grow up, I pray they will learn not just how to stay busy but how to stay still. And within that stillness to hear Your quiet voice. Amen.*

*Start children off on the way they should go, and even when
they are old they will not turn from it.*
PROVERBS 22:6 NIV

*Discipline your son, and he will give you rest; he will give delight to your heart.*
PROVERBS 29:17 ESV

As our to-do list grows, it becomes harder to engage in child's play. But spending time with a special child in our lives affords us the opportunity to influence him or her for God's kingdom. So don't waste another moment: seize the day and play!

*Father, help me learn to play and enjoy time with the children You have brought
into my life. Bless them and use me today. Amen.*

# DAY 42 – *Forgiveness*

## *Morning*

*For thou, Lord, art good, and ready to forgive;*
*and plenteous in mercy unto all them that call upon thee.*
PSALM 86:5 KJV

*"They refused to listen and failed to remember the miracles you performed among them. . . . But you are a forgiving God, gracious and compassionate, slow to anger and abounding in love. Therefore you did not desert them."*
NEHEMIAH 9:17 NIV

The Lord desires for us to have relationships founded on kindness, tenderheartedness, and forgiveness. As we, through the Holy Spirit in us, are able to live this kind of life, we model Christ to others. Our purpose in life is to become more like Him. Why not begin today living a life of forgiveness?

*Forgiving Lord, I desire to be more like You. Enable me to forgive those who have hurt me and live a life of forgiveness. Amen.*

## *Evening*

*To him who is able to keep you from stumbling and to present you before his glorious presence without fault and with great joy.*
JUDE 1:24 NIV

*"Therefore, I tell you, her many sins have been forgiven—as her great love has shown. But whoever has been forgiven little loves little."*
LUKE 7:47 NIV

Often we feel we fall short in our walk with God. We plunge into the trap of measuring ourselves by another's yardstick. God desires that we fall at His feet and worship Him. When sin enters our lives, as it will, we turn to Him for forgiveness. He's there in the darkest hours.

*Dear heavenly Father, pour out Your love into my heart this day. I need forgiveness. Amen.*

# DAY 43 – *Prayer*

*Pray in the Spirit at all times and on every occasion. Stay alert and be persistent in your prayers for all believers everywhere.*
EPHESIANS 6:18 NLT

*I want everyone everywhere to lift innocent hands toward heaven and pray, without being angry or arguing with each other.*
1 TIMOTHY 2:8 CEV

Nothing draws us closer to other people than praying for them. Asking for God's intervention in their lives is an awesome privilege. We experience matchless rejoicing when our prayers are answered. Let's not just promise to pray for someone. Let's be faithful to do it!

*Dear Lord, often I have good intentions to pray for others but fail to follow through. Help me be faithful in prayer so that I may see Your power at work. Amen.*

 *Evening* ——————————————————

*Answer me when I call to you, my righteous God. Give me relief from my distress; have mercy on me and hear my prayer.*
PSALM 4:1 NIV

*I call on you, my God, for you will answer me; turn your ear to me and hear my prayer.*
PSALM 17:6 NIV

Our God can be reached any hour of the day or night and every day of the year—including weekends and holidays! When we pray, we don't have to worry about disconnections, poor reception, or being put on hold. The Bible assures us that God is eager to hear our petitions and that He welcomes our prayers of thanksgiving.

*Dear Lord, thank You for always being there for me. Whether I am on a mountaintop and just want to praise Your name or I am in need of Your comfort and encouragement, I can count on You. Amen.*

DAY 44 – *Truth*

*Morning* —————————————————————————

> God can't stomach liars; he loves the company of those who keep their word.
> PROVERBS 12:22 MSG

> If you do the right thing, honesty will be your guide. But if you are crooked,
> you will be trapped by your own dishonesty.
> PROVERBS 11:3 CEV

When we are honest, we take hold of the truth of Christ and spread it to others we meet. It is by living honest, straightforward lives that we move closer to God in all His glory.

> *I wish that I could be the person You want me to be, almighty God.*
> *Empower me with the spirit of truth, that I might always live honestly*
> *and openly in Your sight. Amen.*

*Evening* —————————————————————————

> My hope is in you, so may goodness and honesty guard me.
> PSALM 25:21 NCV

> "They taught the true teachings and spoke no lies. With peace and honesty they did
> what I said they should do, and they kept many people from sinning."
> MALACHI 2:6 NCV

There is nothing wrong with pulling someone's leg, so long as it isn't a way of life and that we don't do damage by our untruth. We need to be able to trust others. We need real honesty.

> *Help me never undermine the faith that others have in me, Lord. Amen.*

# DAY 45 - *Work*

You have six days each week for your ordinary work, but the seventh day
is a Sabbath day of rest dedicated to the LORD your God.
On that day no one in your household may do any work.
EXODUS 20:9-10 NLT

"Be strong and courageous, and do the work. Don't be afraid or discouraged,
for the LORD God, my God, is with you. He will not fail you or forsake you."
1 CHRONICLES 28:20 NLT

Are you feeling disheartened by the sheer size of your responsibilities? Be
strong and courageous! Do the work! Don't be afraid or discouraged by the
size of the task. The Lord God is with you, and He will not fail or forsake you!

*Dear Lord, give me strength and courage to do the work You have called me to do.
Take away my fear and discouragement, and help me to lean on You. Amen.*

You will again obey the LORD and follow all his commands I am
giving you today. Then the LORD your God will make you most
prosperous in all the work of your hands.
DEUTERONOMY 30:8-9 NIV

If you plan and work hard, you will have plenty;
if you get in a hurry, you will end up poor.
PROVERBS 21:5 CEV

A key factor behind our work is not our identity but our motivation. When
Adam and Eve worked, they were working for God. Just because sin
entered the world doesn't mean we have a different boss. Our projects and
daily tasks are a reflection of what we can give back to Him.

*Lord, thank You for giving me the work I have.
Give me a passion for reflecting You in it. Amen.*

## *Morning*

*And he said unto them, Which of you shall have a friend, and shall go unto him at midnight, and say unto him, Friend, lend me three loaves; for a friend of mine in his journey is come to me, and I have nothing to set before him? And he from within shall answer and say, Trouble me not: the door is now shut, and my children are with me in bed; I cannot rise and give thee. I say unto you, Though he will not rise and give him, because he is his friend, yet because of his importunity he will rise and give him as many as he needeth.*
LUKE 11:5–8 KJV

*The righteous choose their friends carefully,
but the way of the wicked leads them astray.*
PROVERBS 12:26 NIV

Some friends are not worth having: the kind who deceive us and lead us astray. Friendships should sharpen faith, not destroy it.

*Father, open my eyes to the damaging friendships in my life. Let nothing harm my relationship with You. Amen.*

## *Evening*

*You can trust a friend who corrects you, but kisses from an enemy are nothing but lies.*
PROVERBS 27:6 CEV

*Don't make friends with anyone who has a bad temper.*
PROVERBS 22:24 CEV

God offers His people advice on their friendships, which are an important part of spiritual life. Our friendships, and how we treat our friends, can tell a lot about our faith. We need to choose our friends wisely and treat them well.

*Lord, build strong friendships in my life, and help me be a good friend in turn. Amen.*

# DAY 47 - *Anxiety*

## *Morning*

*Anxiety in the heart of man causes depression, but a good word makes it glad.*
PROVERBS 12:25 NKJV

*Without the help of the LORD it is useless to build a home or to guard a city.*
*It is useless to get up early and stay up late in order to earn a living.*
*God takes care of his own, even while they sleep.*
PSALM 127:1–2 CEV

Stress can make you feel like a grape in a winepress. The good news is that God has given you everything you need, but it's up to you to utilize the wisdom He has provided. Alleviate pressure where you can and then know that God's power will make up for the rest.

*Lord, help me to do what I can do, and I'll trust You to do for me*
*those things that I can't do. Amen.*

## *Evening*

*"The seed cast in the weeds represents the ones who hear the kingdom news but are*
*overwhelmed with worries about all the things they have to do and all the things they*
*want to get. The stress strangles what they heard, and nothing comes of it."*
MARK 4:18–19 MSG

*A twinkle in the eye means joy in the heart,*
*and good news makes you feel fit as a fiddle.*
PROVERBS 15:30 MSG

God does not want His kids to be worn out and stressed out. We need time to recreate—to revive and refresh our bodies and minds. A little relaxation, recreation—and yes—fun are essential components of a balanced life.

*Lord, You are the One who gives balance to my life.*
*Help me find time for a little relaxation. Amen.*

# DAY 48 - *God's Love*

*"The LORD your God is with you, the Mighty Warrior who saves.*
*He will take great delight in you; in his love he will no longer rebuke you,*
*but will rejoice over you with singing."*
ZEPHANIAH 3:17 NIV

*"For the Father Himself loves you, because you have loved Me and have believed*
*that I came forth from the Father."*
JOHN 16:27 NASB

Those who are lucky enough to find someone to share their lives with enjoy
a special gift from God. But for every person, the love of God is very real,
and very much freely given. We can be happy because we know we are
loved.

*O Lord, giver of life and giver of love, though I am unworthy, I thank You for loving*
*me so much. Help me know Your love at all times. Amen.*

*Nothing in all creation can separate us from God's love*
*for us in Christ Jesus our Lord!*
ROMANS 8:39 CEV

*The way of the wicked is an abomination unto the LORD:*
*but he loveth him that followeth after righteousness.*
PROVERBS 15:9 KJV

God sends light into our lives in many ways. The greatest light of all is love,
and we know love through His greatest gift, Jesus Christ.

*Fill me with Your blessed warmth and glow, Lord. Shine through me for others to see.*
*Let me be Your love in this world. Amen.*

# DAY 49 - *Comfort*

*Shout for joy, you heavens; rejoice, you earth; burst into song, you mountains!*
*For the LORD comforts his people and will have compassion on his afflicted ones.*
ISAIAH 49:13 NIV

*In the multitude of my thoughts within me thy comforts delight my soul.*
PSALM 94:19 KJV

The world hardly knows the meaning of comfort. But the Spirit of God
offers the best there is to have. When we come to Him in pain and faith, He
touches our hearts in tender ways that no human can. He offers a shoulder
to cry on.

*Thank You, heavenly Father, for Your loving care.*
*Comfort me when I hurt, I pray. Amen.*

*Remember the word to Your servant, in which You have made me hope.*
*This is my comfort in my affliction, that Your word has revived me.*
PSALM 119:49–50 NASB

*I serve you, LORD. Comfort me with your love, just as you have promised.*
PSALM 119:76 CEV

Cry out to God in times of affliction, and He will comfort you and lift you
above the fear of evil things. Truly, our help is in the Lord.

*There is nothing in this life, Lord, that I cannot face*
*as long as You are with me. Amen.*

# DAY 50 - *Guilt*

*Morning* ─────────────────────────────────────

*If we confess our sins, he is faithful and just to forgive us our sins,*
*and to cleanse us from all unrighteousness.*
1 JOHN 1:9 KJV

*Let the wicked forsake his way, and the unrighteous man his thoughts:*
*and let him return unto the LORD, and he will have mercy upon him;*
*and to our God, for he will abundantly pardon.*
ISAIAH 55:7 KJV

Ask forgiveness from the Lord, receive it, and move forward in the glory of God's grace. Your sins are forgiven, indeed!

*Cleanse me and prepare me for the wonderful life that is to come, Jesus. May I learn*
*from my mistakes and grow from them without allowing them to control my life.*
*Amen.*

*Evening* ─────────────────────────────────────

*Fools make fun of guilt, but the godly acknowledge it and seek reconciliation.*
PROVERBS 14:9 NLT

*As far as the east is from the west, so far hath he removed our transgressions from us.*
PSALM 103:12 KJV

We too often let guilt determine what our actions will be, rather than living as forgiven people. The Lord is more than willing to shower His children with mercy and grace. All we need to do is ask with a penitent heart.

*Thank You for Your gracious, forgiving love, Lord. Hear me when I call out to You,*
*Father, and remove my guilt as You forgive my sins. Amen.*

# DAY 51 – *Work*

## *Morning*

*"But as for you, be strong and do not give up, for your work will be rewarded."*
2 CHRONICLES 15:7 NIV

*"The LORD repay your work, and a full reward be given you by the LORD God of Israel, under whose wings you have come for refuge."*
RUTH 2:12 NKJV

God has given each of us work to do. Sometimes the labor is new and exciting. Sometimes the JOB is repetitive. Both types are given to us for His purpose. We can look forward to the reward God has for us when we complete the tasks He has set before us.

*Thank You, Lord, for the work I can do. Give me joy as I serve. Amen.*

## *Evening*

*The LORD helps the fallen and lifts those bent beneath their loads.*
PSALM 145:14 NLT

*The LORD will protect you now and always wherever you go.*
PSALM 121:8 CEV

God does not guarantee that we will never lose a JOB. He does promise that He will shield us from our first day on the JOB to the day we walk out the door for the last time. God goes behind and before us in all our comings and goings.

*Lord, You watch every path that we take. You lead us to and away from our places of employment. We trust You to shield us in the process. Amen.*

## *Morning*

"And these words that I command you today shall be on your heart."
DEUTERONOMY 6:6 ESV

The words of the LORD are pure words; as silver tried in a furnace
on the earth, refined seven times.
PSALM 12:6 NASB

We've all experienced moments when words are out of our mouths before
we know it. If we would stop and think before speaking, we wouldn't hurt
the feelings of others as often as we do. Weigh your words carefully before
using them. And if you've said something you cannot take back, be quick to
ask forgiveness.

*Dear Lord, I want to glorify You and edify others, not cut them down. Help me think
before I speak, and may my words be filled with compassion and love. Amen.*

## *Evening*

Let the words of my mouth, and the meditation of my heart, be acceptable
in thy sight, O LORD, my strength, and my redeemer.
PSALM 19:14 KJV

Do not let any unwholesome talk come out of your mouths, but only what is helpful
for building others up according to their needs, that it may benefit those who listen.
EPHESIANS 4:29 NIV

Learning to tame the tongue is a difficult task. First we must acknowledge
the destruction our tongues are capable of. Although our tongues are a tiny
part of the body, they can do great harm to us and others if left unchecked.

*Dear Lord, help me win the battle of the tongue by dwelling on Your truth. Amen.*

# DAY 53 – *Heaven*

*There will be no more night. They will not need the light of a lamp or the light of the sun, for the Lord God will give them light. And they will reign for ever and ever.*
REVELATION 22:5 NIV

*And God called the expanse Heaven. And there was evening and there was morning, the second day.*
GENESIS 1:8 ESV

Christ Himself spent a good deal of His life preparing for His ministry and work. Like Him, we are growing, maturing, and preparing for the kingdom of God, which awaits us. We are being made ready for our heavenly home.

*Lord, create in me a real hunger for Your truth that I may be more like You here on earth and forever in heaven. Amen.*

*"Know therefore today, and take it to your heart, that the LORD, He is God in heaven above and on the earth below; there is no other."*
DEUTERONOMY 4:39 NASB

*And I heard a sound from heaven like the roar of rushing waters and like a loud peal of thunder. The sound I heard was like that of harpists playing their harps.*
REVELATION 14:2 NIV

As family members embrace when they meet, so we are able to look forward to a day when we will be welcomed as family of Jesus Christ in heaven. He awaits us in love and care, and we will one day be united. In fact, we are already united through the Holy Spirit of God.

*Welcome, dear Lord, into the depths of my heart. Dwell there in love, and never leave me. Amen.*

DAY 54 - *Doubt*

*"Truly I tell you, if anyone says to this mountain, 'Go, throw yourself into the sea,'
and does not doubt in their heart but believes that
what they say will happen, it will be done for them."*
MARK 11:23 NIV

*If any of you lacks wisdom, you should ask God, who gives generously
to all without finding fault, and it will be given to you. But when you ask,
you must believe and not doubt, because the one who doubts is like
a wave of the sea, blown and tossed by the wind.*
JAMES 1:5–6 NIV

It's good to know that God is there for us when we turn to Him with our
doubts and questions. Prayer is the direct connection that we have with
God. When we find ourselves faced with new and different beliefs, it is wise
to take them to God.

*God, I think that I know what to believe, but new things come up almost every day.
Help me sort out what is right and good to believe and what is not. Amen.*

*Evening* ——————————————————————————

*And you must show mercy to those whose faith is wavering.*
JUDE 1:22 NLT

*But Abraham never doubted or questioned God's promise.
His faith made him strong, and he gave all the credit to God.*
ROMANS 4:20 CEV

God wants us to come to believe in Him with as few doubts as possible.
He will always help us learn as much as we can when our Christian faith is
challenged.

*Lord God, when my faith is unsteady, let me bring my concerns
to You so that I may see the truth. Amen.*

# DAY 55 - *Rest*

God will speak to this people, to whom he said, "This is the resting place, let the weary rest"; and, "This is the place of repose"—but they would not listen.
ISAIAH 28:11–12 TNIV

For thus saith the Lord GOD, the Holy One of Israel; In returning and rest shall ye be saved; in quietness and in confidence shall be your strength: and ye would not.
ISAIAH 30:15 KJV

We are called to be God's work, His hands and feet in this world. But we are also called to rest and pray. Jesus put a priority on this, frequently leaving the crowd to seek solitude. Make time to rest. Find a place that is quiet where you can pray. Jesus modeled this for us. He wants us to find rest in Him.

*Father, show me the importance of rest. Allow me to say no to something today in order that I might say yes to some quiet time with You. Amen.*

The LORD is my shepherd; I shall not want. He maketh me to lie down in green pastures: he leadeth me beside the still waters. He restoreth my soul: he leadeth me in the paths of righteousness for his name's sake.
PSALM 23:1–3 KJV

I will find my rest in God alone. He is the One who gives me hope.
PSALM 62:5 NIrV

God Himself started the work-rest pattern before the earth was a week old. God didn't rest because He was tired; He rested because His work of creation was finished. But our work is never done! How can we rest? It's not easy. There are always more things that can be done. But most of those things can wait a day while you recharge.

*Father, help me rest from my labor as You rested from Yours. Refresh me this day. Amen.*

# DAY 56 – *Motives*

## *Morning*

*We justify our actions by appearances; GOD examines our motives.*
PROVERBS 21:2 MSG

*People may be pure in their own eyes, but the LORD examines their motives.*
PROVERBS 16:2 NLT

The Lord examines the motives of the heart. That can be both a blessing and a challenge. We all make mistakes, so errors made with a pure motive will be seen as such. However, good actions made with an impure motive will not be rewarded.

*Heavenly Father, forgive me for the dishonesty behind impure motives.*
*Thank You for leading me into all truth. Amen.*

## *Evening*

*Therefore do not go on passing judgment before the time, but wait until the Lord comes who will both bring to light the things hidden in the darkness and disclose the motives of men's hearts; and then each man's praise will come to him from God.*
1 CORINTHIANS 4:5 NASB

*When you ask, you do not receive, because you ask with wrong motives, that you may spend what you get on your pleasures.*
JAMES 4:3 NIV

Even though we can't always judge another person's motives, we can always take stock of our own. Even right behaviors can become wrong when the motive is impure. Ask Jesus to reveal your true motives to you before you fall into sin.

*Lord, please help me recognize the truth behind my motives before I*
*hurt others or cause myself to sin. Amen.*

# DAY 57 – *Sharing the Gospel*

## *Morning*

*Also pray for us that God will give us an opportunity to tell people his message.
Pray that we can preach the secret that God has made known about Christ.
This is why I am in prison.*
COLOSSIANS 4:3 NCV

*He said to them, "Go into all the world. Preach the good news to everyone."*
MARK 16:15 NIrV

So many people have no idea what it means to have the Spirit of Christ in their hearts. It is our JOB, as the voice and hands of God, to let people know the truth of Christ, so they, too, might come to put their trust in Him.

*Help me teach others by the example of my life what it means to be Christian.
I will put my trust in You. Help me share that trust with others. Amen.*

## *Evening*

*Jesus went to every town and village. He taught in their meeting places
and preached the good news about God's kingdom.*
MATTHEW 9:35 CEV

*And how are they to preach unless they are sent? As it is written,
"How beautiful are the feet of those who preach the good news!"*
ROMANS 10:15 ESV

To be truly in love with God is a consuming passion. We can't wait to tell the world of the wonderful truth we know. The Spirit of God enters into our hearts, and our lives are never the same again. Praise the Lord with your whole heart, and show forth all His wonderful works.

*Lord, each day brings new wonders, and I am reminded of Your great love for me.
Make me an agent of Your will and Word to others. Amen.*

# DAY 58 – *Loving Others*

 *Morning* ─────────────────────────────

*Jesus replied: " 'Love the Lord your God with all your heart and with all your soul and with all your mind.' This is the first and greatest commandment. And the second is like it: 'Love your neighbor as yourself.' "*
MATTHEW 22:37–39 NIV

*Dear children, let's not merely say that we love each other; let us show the truth by our actions.*
1 JOHN 3:18 NLT

People say love is a decision. Sounds simple enough, right? The fact is that telling others we love them and showing that love are two very different realities. Jesus is the embodiment of active love. He loved those who were thought most unlovable. And we are called to do the same.

*Lord, let me be intentional, active, and willing to put aside my own desires so that I can love others better. Amen.*

*Evening* ─────────────────────────────

*Be completely humble and gentle; be patient, bearing with one another in love. Make every effort to keep the unity of the Spirit through the bond of peace.*
EPHESIANS 4:2–3 NIV

*And let us consider how to stir up one another to love and good works, not neglecting to meet together, as is the habit of some, but encouraging one another, and all the more as you see the Day drawing near.*
HEBREWS 10:24–25 ESV

An attitude can be as damaging as an unkind word or a forceful blow. We wield great power in the way we treat other people. If we think that we are better than other people, it will show in our manner, our looks, our words, and our actions.

*Lord God, transform my actions toward others. Help me be humble and loving always. Amen.*

# DAY 59 – *God's Correction*

*Morning* ────────────────────────────

*For whom the Lord loveth he correcteth; even as a father*
*the son in whom he delighteth.*
PROVERBS 3:12 KJV

*Thou shalt also consider in thine heart, that, as a man chasteneth his son, so the*
*Lord thy God chasteneth thee. Therefore thou shalt keep the commandments of the*
*Lord thy God, to walk in his ways, and to fear him.*
DEUTERONOMY 8:5-6 KJV

Often God tries to gently lead us along the path of goodness, but we resist.
Many times the only way to get our attention is through a stinging blow. It
is never out of anger, but always out of love.

*Break my spirit of defiance, no matter what it takes, so that I might openly receive*
*every instruction that You give. Amen.*

*Evening* ────────────────────────────

*For which cause we faint not; but though our outward man perish, yet the inward*
*man is renewed day by day. For our light affliction, which is but for a moment,*
*worketh for us a far more exceeding and eternal weight of glory.*
2 CORINTHIANS 4:16-17 KJV

*"For whom the Lord loves He chastens, and scourges every son whom He receives."*
*If you endure chastening, God deals with you as with sons;*
*for what son is there whom a father does not chasten?*
HEBREWS 12:6-7 NKJV

God's judgments are righteous and true, and He will always help us make
the changes that allow us to clean up our lives, if we will only ask Him to.

*I need to be reminded that Your way is the only way, Lord, so that I won't be tempted*
*to stray. Be with me to correct me and guide me. Amen.*

## *Morning*

*And Jesus said to him, "'If you can'! All things are possible for one who believes."*
MARK 9:23 ESV

*For we did not follow cleverly devised stories when we told you about the coming of our Lord Jesus Christ in power, but we were eyewitnesses of his majesty.*
2 PETER 1:16 NIV

It's not uncommon to run into people who claim the Bible is a collection of fairy tales. But remember, you, like the apostles, are an eyewitness. You were there when Jesus saved you. And you have testimonies from those who observed Jesus' ministry. When people wonder why you believe, tell them.

*When others act as if I'm crazy to believe in You, help me not take offense, Lord. Instead, help me show them Your truth. Amen.*

## *Evening*

*"And all things you ask in prayer, believing, you will receive."*
MATTHEW 21:22 NASB

*"I tell you the truth, whoever believes has eternal life."*
JOHN 6:47 NCV

Jesus encouraged us to believe in Him so there would be an overflowing of the Spirit upon others. If we harbor destructive emotions, it's not flowing out of us. While our circumstances might not be perfect, we're still asked to believe.

*Dear heavenly Father, help me ferret out anything that would hinder belief. Thank You, Lord. Amen.*

# DAY 61 – *Helping Others*

## *Morning*

> Don't get tired of helping others. You will be rewarded
> when the time is right, if you don't give up.
> GALATIANS 6:9 CEV

> "I tell you, use the riches of this world to help others. In that way, you will make
> friends for yourselves. Then when your riches are gone,
> you will be welcomed into your eternal home in heaven."
> LUKE 16:9 NIrV

We are given so many opportunities to help others. Jesus said that every time we help any person in need, it is as if we have done it for Christ Himself. Let us always reach out and take hold of the chances we have for serving others.

*Lord, so often I turn my head from those in need. Open my eyes and my heart
that I might extend the hand of Christ to them. Amen.*

## *Evening*

> They must stick to the true message they were taught, so that their
> good teaching can help others and correct everyone who opposes it.
> TITUS 1:9 CEV

> Do nothing out of selfish ambition or vain conceit. Rather, in humility value others above
> yourselves, not looking to your own interests but each of you to the interests of the others.
> PHILIPPIANS 2:3-4 NIV

When you start to look out for "number one," remember that your God is looking out for you. You are His precious child. As you allow Him to take care of you, it will free up space in your heart and allow you to look to the needs of others.

*Father, You have made me to be a part of something much larger than myself.
Focus my attention on those around me and not only on my own needs. Amen.*

# DAY 62 – *Guidance*

*And thine ears shall hear a word behind thee, saying, This is the way, walk ye in it,*
*when ye turn to the right hand, and when ye turn to the left.*
ISAIAH 30:21 KJV

*A man's heart deviseth his way: but the LORD directeth his steps.*
PROVERBS 16:9 KJV

In our lives, we need to learn to let the Lord rule. Giving God control is not a sign of weakness; it is the greatest show of strength we will ever make. Under the guidance of God, we become conquerors in a world that tries hard to break us down.

*Heavenly Father, do not let me be swayed from the path You have set me on.*
*Others may fail me, but You never will. Hallelujah! Amen.*

*The steps of a good man are ordered by the LORD: and he delighteth in his way.*
PSALM 37:23 KJV

*The righteousness of the perfect shall direct his way:*
*but the wicked shall fall by his own wickedness.*
PROVERBS 11:5 KJV

God wants only the best for us. He has given instruction, not to show His power or might, but to help us live the best life we possibly can. He only wants our peace and happiness. In turn, we should live in such a way that He is honored.

*Dear God, please assist us in our attempts to live as You have instructed.*
*May we do nothing to bring shame to Your holy name. Amen.*

# DAY 63 - *Wealth*

*But if anyone has the world's goods and sees his brother in need,*
*yet closes his heart against him, how does God's love abide in him?*
1 JOHN 3:17 ESV

*The more you have, the more people come to help you spend it. So what good is*
*wealth—except perhaps to watch it slip through your fingers!*
ECCLESIASTES 5:11 NLT

Making money doesn't result in financial stability. Wealth runs through our
fingers as we spend more than we make, and we wonder how we will pay
for everything. It's time for us to put the principles we know into action.
God gives us joy in our possessions. He only asks us to use them wisely.

*Jehovah Jireh, the Lord who provides, we thank You for Your provision.*
*Teach us to value the eternal over the temporal. Amen.*

*The blessing of the LORD makes one rich, and He adds no sorrow with it.*
PROVERBS 10:22 NKJV

*And thou say in thine heart, My power and the might of mine hand*
*hath gotten me this wealth. But thou shalt remember the LORD thy God:*
*for it is he that giveth thee power to get wealth.*
DEUTERONOMY 8:17–18 KJV

Sometimes we act as if financial accomplishments live and die with us. God
showers us with health, intelligence, education, and opportunity. Every
breath and heartbeat are gifts from Him! We never suspect the roles He
plays behind the scenes to encourage and prosper us.

*Father, please forgive me when I take credit for blessings You give because of Your*
*generous heart. Help me use them for Your glory. Amen.*

# DAY 64 – *Prayer*

## *Morning*

*I am the one who has seen the afflictions that come from the rod of the Lord's anger. . . . He has walled me in, and I cannot escape. He has bound me in heavy chains. And though I cry and shout, he has shut out my prayers. . . . Yet I still dare to hope when I remember this: The faithful love of the Lord never ends!*
LAMENTATIONS 3:1, 7–8, 21–22 NLT

*I will answer their prayers before they finish praying.*
ISAIAH 65:24 CEV

God alone knows what we need before we ask. He even knows what we need before we know the need. Life may take us by surprise, but never the Lord God who knows the end from the beginning. He knows what's behind, what's ahead, and what's now—and He will hear your prayers.

*I praise You, Lord, that You surround me through all of life.*
*Keep my eyes of faith on You, I pray. Amen.*

## *Evening*

*"This, then, is how you should pray: 'Our Father in heaven, hallowed be your name, your kingdom come, your will be done, on earth as it is in heaven. Give us today our daily bread. And forgive us our debts, as we also have forgiven our debtors. And lead us not into temptation, but deliver us from the evil one.' "*
MATTHEW 6:9–13 NIV

*I call on you, my God, for you will answer me; turn your ear to me and hear my prayer.*
PSALM 17:6 NIV

God answers all prayers. The answers can come in three forms: "yes," "no," or "wait." God's Word tells us that when we call or cry out to Him, He will answer us. God always hears our requests and responds in accordance with His will.

*Lord, thank You that I can cry out to You for all that is within my heart.*
*I praise You that You are a God who hears and answers. Amen.*

# DAY 65 – *Change*

## *Morning*

*When Pharaoh let the people go, God did not lead them on the road through the Philistine country, though that was shorter. For God said, "If they face war, they might change their minds and return to Egypt."*
EXODUS 13:17 NIV

*To everything there is a season, a time for every purpose under heaven.*
ECCLESIASTES 3:1 NKJV

Change is a regular part of modern life. JOBS shift or disappear. Friends move. Babies are born, and children graduate and marry. Only one thing in our lives never changes: God. When our world swirls and threatens to shift out of control, we can know that God is never surprised, never caught off guard by anything that happens.

*Lord, help me remember Your love and guidance when my life turns upside down. Grant me wisdom for the journey and a hope for the future. Amen.*

## *Evening*

*"He who is the Glory of Israel does not lie or change his mind; for he is not a human being, that he should change his mind."*
1 SAMUEL 15:29 NIV

*"Heaven and earth will pass away, but my words will never pass away."*
MATTHEW 24:35 NIV

The world and our lives are constantly changing. But there is one thing that is permanent. And that is Jesus Christ. No matter what changes are happening in our lives, we can rest assured that He remains the same—yesterday, today, and forever.

*Lord, what a relief to know that in this ever-changing world, You remain the same. You are always there. Amen.*

# DAY 66 – *God's Presence*

## *Morning*

*But now God has made you his friends again. He did this through Christ's death in the body so that he might bring you into God's presence as people who are holy, with no wrong, and with nothing of which God can judge you guilty.*
COLOSSIANS 1:22 NCV

*Then the LORD God Almighty will be with you, just as you say he is.*
AMOS 5:14 NIV

Sometimes we have trouble feeling God's presence, especially in troublesome situations. God has told us that He will never leave us. So if we feel as if God is not near, perhaps the distance is of our own choosing. Look into the goodness of God's Word. Seek His face. Proclaim that He is standing by your side. And He will be, just as you have said.

*Thank You, Lord, for always being with me. With You by my side, I will live! I will overcome all. Thank You for being immovable. Amen.*

## *Evening*

*May he be enthroned in God's presence forever; appoint your love and faithfulness to protect him.*
PSALM 61:7 NIV

*"Never will I leave you; never will I forsake you."*
HEBREWS 13:5 NIV

When God is silent, His love is still present. He wants us to abide in His presence. As we continue to trust Him amid the silence, we learn that His presence is all we need. God has promised that He will never leave us nor forsake us. Believe Him. His presence is enough.

*Dear Lord, help me trust You even when You choose to remain silent. May I learn how to be content in Your presence alone. Amen.*

# DAY 67 – *Recognition*

## *Morning*

*Solomon rode high on a crest of popular acclaim—it was all GOD's doing.*
*GOD gave him position and honor beyond any king in Israel before him.*
1 CHRONICLES 29:25 MSG

*"Your Father, who sees what is done in secret, will reward you."*
MATTHEW 6:6 NIV

Perhaps your behind-the-scenes sacrifices are going unnoticed by the world. Do not give up and think it doesn't matter. It matters to God. Seek to please Him above anyone else, and your life will honor Him.

*Lord, may what I do in secret bring glory to You. May I not seek*
*man's approval, but Yours alone. Amen.*

## *Evening*

*With one hand [Wisdom] gives long life, with the other she confers recognition.*
PROVERBS 3:16 MSG

*"What honor and recognition has Mordecai received for this?" the king asked.*
*"Nothing has been done for him," his attendants answered.*
ESTHER 6:3 NIV

When you are assured that God loves you and accepts you in Christ no matter what you have done, you will not need the praise of others. You may sometimes get worldly praise and receive it graciously, but you will not need it because your security rests firmly in your approval from God Himself.

*God, show me if I have become a slave to others' opinions of me. Amen.*

# DAY 68 – *Friendship*

———————————————————

*"And I tell you, make friends for yourselves by means of unrighteous wealth,
so that when it fails they may receive you into the eternal dwellings."*
LUKE 16:9 ESV

*Three of JOB's friends heard of all the trouble that had fallen on him. Each traveled from
his own country. . .and went together to JOB to keep him company and comfort him.*
JOB 2:11 MSG

We can become so wrapped up in the tasks we are trying to achieve that
we forget that life is about people—the relationships—God has put around
us. We need each other—as friends, family, or just passing acquaintances—
in order to live successful lives. God measures His wealth in souls. That
should be our focus, too.

*Lord, help me know when it's time to drop the task and run to the relationship. Amen.*

———————————————————

*You adulterous people, don't you know that friendship with the world means enmity
against God? Therefore, anyone who chooses to be a friend of the world
becomes an enemy of God.*
JAMES 4:4 NIV

*"My command is this: Love each other as I have loved you. Greater love has no one
than this: to lay down one's life for one's friends. You are my friends
if you do what I command."*
JOHN 15:12–14 NIV

Relationships take time to be nourished so they will develop into a
satisfying experience. Isn't the entire Bible an analogy of God's patience,
wooing us into a deeper relationship with Him? True friendship cannot be
rushed or scheduled or abbreviated or economized. It just takes time.

*Lord Jesus, show me how to be a friend. Help me love my friends
at all times, for Your glory. Amen.*

# DAY 69 – *Dreams*

*"For the vision is yet for the appointed time; it hastens toward the goal and it will not
fail. Though it tarries, wait for it; for it will certainly come, it will not delay."*
HABAKKUK 2:3 NASB

*What joy for those whose strength comes from the LORD, who have set their minds
on a pilgrimage to Jerusalem. When they walk through the Valley of Weeping, it will
become a place of refreshing springs. The autumn rains will clothe it with blessings.*
PSALM 84:5-6 NLT

Have you ever questioned God when your goals and plans were altered?
We all have disappointments and failures, but God never fails us. Our
disappointment will form pools of blessings when we continue on God's
path despite dashed dreams.

*Heavenly Father, help me surrender my dreams and goals to You. When my dreams
evaporate, please turn my weeping into blessings. Amen.*

*Evening* —————————————————————

*I have not yet reached my goal, and I am not perfect. But Christ has taken
hold of me. So I keep on running and struggling to take hold of the prize.*
PHILIPPIANS 3:12 CEV

*However, as it is written: "What no eye has seen, what no ear has heard,
and what no human mind has conceived"—the things God
has prepared for those who love him.*
1 CORINTHIANS 2:9 NIV

God knows the dreams He has placed inside of you. He created you and
knows what you can do—even better than you know yourself. Maintain your
focus—not on the dream but on the dream maker—and together you will
achieve your dream.

*God, thank You for putting dreams in my heart. I refuse to quit. I'm looking to You
to show me how to reach my dreams. Amen.*

# DAY 70 – *Compassion*

*Light shines in the darkness for the godly. They are generous,*
*compassionate, and righteous.*
PSALM 112:4 NLT

*Is there any encouragement from belonging to Christ? Any comfort from his love?*
*Any fellowship together in the Spirit? Are your hearts tender and compassionate?*
*Then make me truly happy by agreeing wholeheartedly with each other, loving one*
*another, and working together with one mind and purpose.*
PHILIPPIANS 2:1–2 NLT

People who suffer greatly need our compassion and love, but instead they
often receive our judgment and condemnation. Christ does not ask us to
accept sin, or the results of sin, but He commands us to love the one who sins.

*Lord, let compassion rule in my heart as I face a sinful world. I am a sinner, too,*
*and only through Your infinite love am I made whole. Amen.*

*Then the LORD passed by in front of him and proclaimed,*
*"The LORD, the LORD God, compassionate and gracious."*
EXODUS 34:6 NASB

*Remember, O LORD, Your compassion and Your lovingkindnesses,*
*for they have been from of old.*
PSALM 25:6 NASB

The Lord loves all His children, and we need to learn to love all our sisters
and brothers. No one need ever be alone, if we will extend our hands in
love to the sick, the lonely, and the poor.

*My God, there are so many suffering people in this world. Lead me to*
*where they are, that I may shower compassion on them. Amen.*

# DAY 71 – *Rejoicing*

## *Morning*

*God Most High, I will rejoice; I will celebrate and sing because of you.*
PSALM 9:2 CEV

*The LORD has done it this very day; let us rejoice today and be glad.*
PSALM 118:24 NIV

God made a glorious today for us. Now it's our responsibility to rejoice in it. What's holding you back from finding gladness in the dawn of each new morning?

*Father, help me always put my problems in perspective*
*with a giant dose of rejoicing in You. Amen.*

## *Evening*

*May the glory of the LORD endure forever; may the LORD rejoice in his works.*
PSALM 104:31 NIV

*"Fig trees may no longer bloom, or vineyards produce grapes; olive trees may be fruitless, and harvest time a failure; sheep pens may be empty, and cattle stalls vacant—but I will still celebrate because the LORD God saves me."*
HABAKKUK 3:17–18 CEV

Rejoicing in the Lord is not a matter of circumstances but of will. We can choose to remember the God of our salvation and be content with His love for us. No matter how much goes awry, we have so much more to be thankful for because of the grace of God.

*Thank You, God, that You have provided for my salvation and my joy. Help me look*
*to You instead of dwelling on my momentary troubles. Amen.*

# DAY 72 - *Comparison*

## *Morning*

*If we live in the Spirit, let us also walk in the Spirit. Let us not be desirous of vain glory, provoking one another, envying one another.*
GALATIANS 5:25–26 KJV

*It is obvious what kind of life develops out of trying to get your own way all the time. . .cutthroat competition. . .the vicious habit of depersonalizing everyone into a rival. . . . If you use your freedom this way, you will not inherit God's kingdom.*
GALATIANS 5:19–21 MSG

It is important to run your own race, at your own pace—not too fast, but not too slowly, either. Try not to compare yourself too closely with others. We are all at different stages on our own courses. You can learn from those who have gone before, and you have to privilege of teaching those who come behind.

*Lord, give me the strength I need to finish my race and the wisdom I need to run it well. And help me be an encouragement to others. Amen.*

## *Evening*

*But may it never be that I would boast, except in the cross of our Lord Jesus Christ, through which the world has been crucified to me, and I to the world.*
GALATIANS 6:14 NASB

*For we dare not class ourselves or compare ourselves with those who commend themselves. But they, measuring themselves by themselves, and comparing themselves among themselves, are not wise.*
2 CORINTHIANS 10:12 NKJV

Today could be better than yesterday. Yet that hope is nothing compared to the hope the Christian holds in the Lord. Rest easy and content in the Lord.

*Father, thank You for being my All in life. I have no need to compare. My life is complete in You. Amen.*

## *Morning*

God's plan was to make me a servant of his church and to send me
to preach his complete message to you.
COLOSSIANS 1:25 CEV

[God] has made everything beautiful in its time. He has also set eternity in the human
heart; yet no one can fathom what God has done from beginning to end.
ECCLESIASTES 3:11 NIV

The more exhausted we are, the harder it is to remember that God has a
plan for us and that we are living that plan every day. We are unable to see
"the big picture" of our lives, what God has in store for us, and how what
we do every day fits into His plan. We have to trust in His wisdom and keep
on the journey He has set before us.

*Lord, guide my steps so that everything I do reveals my love*
*for You and my faith in Your plan for my life. Amen.*

## *Evening*

As Samuel came close, Saul called out, "GOD's blessings on you!
I accomplished GOD's plan to the letter!"
1 SAMUEL 15:13 MSG

O LORD, You are my God; I will exalt You, I will give thanks to Your name;
for You have worked wonders, plans formed long ago, with perfect faithfulness.
ISAIAH 25:1 NASB

The Lord desires that we have plans for our lives, but He wants us to
develop them in cooperation with His will for us. Our plans should be in line
with His plan.

*Lord, help me fully surrender to Your plan, knowing that Your plan*
*cannot be thwarted. Thank You that I don't need to worry*
*about my life when I'm in Your hands. Amen.*

# DAY 74 - *God's Word*

*"Have faith in me, and you will have life-giving water flowing from deep inside you, just as the Scriptures say."*
JOHN 7:38 CEV

*Above all, you must realize that no prophecy in Scripture ever came from the prophet's own understanding, or from human initiative. No, those prophets were moved by the Holy Spirit, and they spoke from God.*
2 PETER 1:20–21 NLT

God gave us the Bible to serve us much as an anchor serves a boat. God's Word can set your mind at peace and hold you steady through life's storms. It is assurance that no matter what you face in this battle of life, God will bring you safely home.

*God, I know the Bible is true and full of wisdom for my life. Help me grow in and understand what I read and apply it to my life. Amen.*

*Evening* —————————————————————

*I have written to you who are God's children because you know the Father. I have written to you who are mature in the faith because you know Christ, who existed from the beginning. I have written to you who are young in the faith because you are strong. God's word lives in your hearts, and you have won your battle with the evil one.*
1 JOHN 2:14 NLT

*Whoever says, "I know him," but does not do what he commands is a liar, and the truth is not in that person.*
1 JOHN 2:4 NIV

Drifting away from the Word of God can be unnervingly easy. We think we are just taking a break and suddenly we find ourselves entangled in a mass of sin. We must constantly be focused on the Word.

*Dear Lord, keep me from distractions. Help me pay attention to Your Word, and let me grow ever closer to You. Amen.*

*My son, attend to my words; incline thine ear unto my sayings. Let them not depart from thine eyes; keep them in the midst of thine heart. For they are life unto those that find them, and health to all their flesh. Keep thy heart with all diligence; for out of it are the issues of life.*
PROVERBS 4:20–23 KJV

*Don't you realize that your body is the temple of the Holy Spirit, who lives in you and was given to you by God? You do not belong to yourself, for God bought you with a high price. So you must honor God with your body.*
1 CORINTHIANS 6:19–20 NLT

We need to institute simple, physical disciplines like exercise, diet, and rest to properly care for the temple of the Holy Spirit—our bodies. While those actions will attend to the needs of the body, prayer, fasting, and fellowship will attend to the spirit.

*Father, forgive me for not caring for Your temple as I should. Help me to make time in my life for those simple disciplines that You require for a healthy body and spirit. Amen.*

*God be merciful unto us, and bless us; and cause his face to shine upon us; Selah. That thy way may be known upon earth, thy saving health among all nations.*
PSALM 67:1–2 KJV

*"But I will restore you to health and heal your wounds," declares the LORD, "because you are called an outcast, Zion for whom no one cares."*
JEREMIAH 30:17 NIV

Good stewardship includes good health practices. Sometimes, however, even when we do all the right things, illness occurs. Life holds no guarantees except one. Namely, God loves us enough to care for us when we cannot care for ourselves.

*Heavenly Father, thank You for caring for me in sickness and in health. Amen.*

# DAY 76 – *Pride*

*"Those who exalt themselves will be humbled, and those who*
*humble themselves will be exalted."*
MATTHEW 23:12 NIV

*Then [Jesus] said to them, "Whoever welcomes this little child in my name welcomes*
*me; and whoever welcomes me welcomes the one who sent me.*
*For it is the one who is least among you all who is the greatest."*
LUKE 9:48 NIV

Often people view themselves and their daily activities as more important
than someone else's. Jesus' mentality was the exact opposite. He promised
that the last would be first. Glorify Him today by humbling yourself.

*Lord, give me humility as I interact with people today. Amen.*

*The eyes of the arrogant will be humbled and human pride brought low;*
*the LORD alone will be exalted in that day.*
ISAIAH 2:11 NIV

*For by the grace given me I say to every one of you: Do not think of yourself more*
*highly than you ought, but rather think of yourself with sober judgment,*
*in accordance with the faith God has distributed to each of you.*
ROMANS 12:3 NIV

Some of our most embarrassing moments follow on the heels of something
we've said about ourselves. Mortifying moments can bring us back to
reality—and humility. Embarrassing lessons serve as painful reminders that
humility doesn't come easy.

*Lord, help me not to brag, but to be humble in my speech. Amen.*

# DAY 77 - *Gratitude*

## *Morning*

*That I may publish with the voice of thanksgiving, and tell of all thy wondrous works.*
PSALM 26:7 KJV

*Daniel answered and said: "Blessed be the name of God forever and ever,
for wisdom and might are His."*
DANIEL 2:20 NKJV

Though God is great, He doesn't appreciate being taken for granted any more than we would. When God brings us through a trial, do we worship Him with great thankfulness, or do we take that blessing as our due? And when He responds to ordinary situations, do we give thanks?

*Make me thankful, Lord, for all the ways in which You bless and care for me.
I don't want my life to become laden with ungratefulness. Amen.*

## *Evening*

*He that regardeth the day, regardeth it unto the Lord; and he that regardeth not the day,
to the Lord he doth not regard it. He that eateth, eateth to the Lord, for he giveth God
thanks; and he that eateth not, to the Lord he eateth not, and giveth God thanks.*
ROMANS 14:6 KJV

*Joyfully you'll pull up buckets of water from the wells of salvation. And as you do it,
you'll say, "Give thanks to GOD. Call out his name. Ask him anything! Shout to the
nations, tell them what he's done, spread the news of his great reputation!"*
ISAIAH 12:3-4 MSG

Every favor and earthly blessing that we experience is given to us by God. Give thanks to God today. It blesses Him to hear you express your gratitude, and it will do your heart good as well.

*God, I am thankful for all You have given me. Help me have a grateful
heart and express my appreciation to You in everything! Amen.*

# DAY 78 – *Trials*

## *Morning*

*So that no one would be unsettled by these trials.*
*For you know quite well that we are destined for them.*
1 THESSALONIANS 3:3 NIV

*God will bless you, if you don't give up when your faith is being tested. He will*
*reward you with a glorious life, just as he rewards everyone who loves him.*
JAMES 1:12 CEV

God never tests us beyond our level of endurance. He is faithful to see us
through each hardship and to bless us richly when our trial is through. The
nighttimes of our life may seem dismal and black, but there is always a
glorious morning on the rise.

*When times seem exceptionally difficult, Lord, help me remember that they will pass*
*away. No trial lasts forever, Lord, and the promise of good things to come is mine. Amen.*

## *Evening*

*"Many will be purified, cleansed, and refined by these trials. But the wicked will*
*continue in their wickedness, and none of them will understand.*
*Only those who are wise will know what it means."*
DANIEL 12:10 NLT

*After consulting the people, the king appointed singers to walk ahead of the army,*
*singing to the LORD and praising him for his holy splendor. This is what they sang:*
*"Give thanks to the LORD; his faithful love endures forever!"*
2 CHRONICLES 20:21 NLT

So often in this world, we come face-to-face with experiences that are
overwhelming to us. Believe that God will not allow you to be overcome by
your trials; instead, He will faithfully and lovingly bring you through to the
other side.

*Dear Lord, when I am overwhelmed, help me trust and depend on You always. Amen.*

# DAY 79 - *Anger*

*"You must not worship any of the gods of neighboring nations, for the L<small>ORD</small> your God, who lives among you, is a jealous God. His anger will flare up against you, and he will wipe you from the face of the earth."*
D<small>EUTERONOMY</small> 6:14–15 <small>NLT</small>

*We wither beneath your anger; we are overwhelmed by your fury. You spread out our sins before you—our secret sins—and you see them all. We live our lives beneath your wrath, ending our years with a groan.*
P<small>SALM</small> 90:7–9 <small>NLT</small>

God tells us it is okay to be angry, but we are not to sin. We need to have a spirit of reconciliation, making amends and compromising. When we don't have this perspective of quickly resolving conflict, our anger festers. We end up making room for the devil, allowing Satan to have a foothold in our lives.

*Forgiving Lord, I surrender my anger to You. Please give me a spirit of reconciliation and the opportunity to make amends. Amen.*

*For his anger lasts only a moment, but his favor lasts a lifetime!*
P<small>SALM</small> 30:5 <small>NLT</small>

*The L<small>ORD</small> is compassionate and merciful, slow to get angry and filled with unfailing love.*
P<small>SALM</small> 103:8 <small>NLT</small>

Anger is a natural, human response. Yet the Bible warns us not to become angry too quickly. Quick anger leads to foolish actions. Instead, take a couple of deep breaths and remember that you can place all burdens at the feet of Christ.

*Lord, guide me as I find the right path and hold on tightly to my tongue— and my temper. Amen.*

# DAY 80 – *Spiritual Refreshment*

## *Morning*

*Therefore we have been comforted in your comfort. And we rejoiced exceedingly more for the joy of Titus, because his spirit has been refreshed by you all.*
2 Corinthians 7:13 nkjv

*Do not be wise in your own eyes; fear the Lord and shun evil. This will bring health to your body and nourishment to your bones.*
Proverbs 3:7–8 niv

Just as we exercise to strengthen our bodies, we must use our spiritual muscles to attain the strength and peace we all need and desire. As we pray, read, and meditate on God's Word, we increase our spiritual stamina. Although our circumstances may not change, the Lord gives us a new perspective filled with hope.

*Dear Lord, please help me out of my spiritual rut. As I seek Your strength, revive my soul, I pray. Amen.*

## *Evening*

*Each of us is now a part of his resurrection body, refreshed and sustained at one fountain—his Spirit—where we all come to drink.*
1 Corinthians 12:13 msg

*Like a snow-cooled drink at harvest time is a trustworthy messenger to the one who sends him; he refreshes the spirit of his master.*
Proverbs 25:13 niv

Some days spiritual dryness seems to fill our souls. That's just when we need to seek Jesus for a time of spiritual refreshment. A relationship with Him that is growing closer will not remain dry too long.

*Father, when my soul cries for refreshment, lead me to You. Amen.*

# DAY 81 – *Commitment*

*"Remember, Lord, how I have walked before you faithfully and with wholehearted devotion and have done what is good in your eyes." And Hezekiah wept bitterly.*
2 Kings 20:3 niv

*Let us hold unswervingly to the hope we profess, for he who promised is faithful.*
Hebrews 10:23 niv

Sometimes just a whisper from Satan, the father of lies, can cause shakiness where once there was steadfastness. Place your hope in Christ alone. He will help you resist the lies of this world. Hold unswervingly to your Savior today. He is faithful!

*Jesus, You are the object of my hope. There are many distractions in my life, but I pray that You will help me keep my eyes on You. Amen.*

*Evening* —————————————————————————

*And let us not be weary in well doing: for in due season we shall reap, if we faint not.*
Galatians 6:9 kjv

*Joyful are those who obey his laws and search for him with all their hearts. They do not compromise with evil, and they walk only in his paths.*
Psalm 119:2–3 nlt

Most people don't set out to fall into a pattern of sin. It happens gradually—often with one compromise at a time. This is why we must continually be on guard and committed to our faith. Many small compromises can lead to devastation. Be on guard and live wisely.

*Father, help me stay on the wise path, wholly committed to You in all I do. Amen.*

# DAY 82 - *Temptation*

*Don't blame God when you are tempted! God cannot be tempted by evil, and he doesn't use evil to tempt others. We are tempted by our own desires that drag us off and trap us. Our desires make us sin, and when sin is finished with us, it leaves us dead.*
JAMES 1:13–15 CEV

*Because he himself suffered when he was tempted,*
*he is able to help those who are being tempted.*
HEBREWS 2:18 NIV

God gives us the reason to say no. So many people would lead us from the path of God. Ask the Lord for guidance. In the face of our strongest temptations, God will give us strength and the reason to resist.

*O God, help me free myself from those things I know displease You.*
*Guide me, strengthen me, liberate me, I pray. Amen.*

*"Watch and pray, lest you enter into temptation.*
*The spirit indeed is willing, but the flesh is weak."*
MATTHEW 26:41 NKJV

*No temptation has overtaken you except what is common to mankind. And God is faithful; he will not let you be tempted beyond what you can bear. But when you are tempted, he will also provide a way out so that you can endure it.*
1 CORINTHIANS 10:13 NIV

As we feel God's presence in our lives, we become able to rely on His strength to resist temptation when our strength is not enough. Our choice is not so much whether to give in to temptation, but whether we will allow God to strengthen us when we need it most.

*Lord, lift me above the temptations of this world, and set me onto*
*a new path of righteousness and grace. Amen.*

# DAY 83 – *Salvation*

*"The LORD is my strength and song, and He has become my salvation."*
EXODUS 15:2 NKJV

*The Spirit and the bride say, "Come!" And let the one who hears say, "Come!"*
*Let the one who is thirsty come; and let the one who wishes*
*take the free gift of the water of life.*
REVELATION 22:17 NIV

As we drink deeply of the water of life, we recognize God's great gift.
Grateful, we seek out ways to serve Him. But even if we gave all we had, we
could never repay God. His gift of salvation would still be free.

*Thank You, Lord, for giving me the free gift of salvation—*
*the best gift anyone could offer. Amen.*

*Evening* ———————————————————

*"My God is my rock, in whom I find protection. He is my shield, the power that*
*saves me, and my place of safety. He is my refuge, my savior."*
2 SAMUEL 22:3 NLT

*He said to me: "It is done. I am the Alpha and the Omega, the Beginning and the*
*End. To the thirsty I will give water without cost from the spring of the water of life."*
REVELATION 21:6 NIV

God's life-giving message, one we must have at any price, and one to which
we cannot assign value, costs us nothing. Jesus loves us so much that He
gave up His life that we might partake of these invigorating waters. So drink
up; the water of life is free.

*Dear Lord, thank You for letting me drink for free from the spring of the water of life.*
*Help me remember Your sacrifice and Your love for me. Amen.*

# DAY 84 - *Generosity*

## *Morning*

*It is well with the man who deals generously and lends. . . . He has distributed freely;*
*he has given to the poor; his righteousness endures forever;*
*his horn is exalted in honor.*
PSALM 112:5, 9 ESV

*Honor the LORD from your wealth and from the first of all your produce; so your*
*barns will be filled with plenty and your vats will overflow with new wine.*
PROVERBS 3:9–10 NASB

The truth is that everything we have comes from God. The Bible calls us to
cheerfully give back to the Lord one-tenth of all we earn. Giving to God has
great reward. When believers honor God by giving to Him, we can trust that
He will provide for our needs.

*Lord, remind me not to separate my finances from my faith. All that I have comes from*
*Your hand, and I should give generously from what You have entrusted to me. Amen.*

## *Evening*

*Jesus said to him, "If you wish to be complete, go and sell your possessions and give*
*to the poor, and you will have treasure in heaven; and come, follow Me."*
MATTHEW 19:21 NASB

*Those who give to the poor will lack nothing, but those who close their*
*eyes to them receive many curses.*
PROVERBS 28:27 NIV

Though we think of giving in financial terms, God doesn't. He calls on us to
live generously, not just giving our finances or our goods but sharing our
whole lives with others. Whether it is forgiveness or a good meal, we are to
withhold nothing from others in need.

*Father, help me expand my idea of generosity. May I give generously of my time*
*and talents, as well as my resources. Amen.*

# DAY 85 – *Helping Others*

"Be sure you do not do good things in front of others just to be seen by them.
If you do, you have no reward from your Father in heaven."
MATTHEW 6:1 NLV

*Knowledge makes us proud of ourselves, while love makes us helpful to others.*
1 CORINTHIANS 8:1 CEV

We all need help. We can't do life alone. And perhaps that is a great
blessing to realize. God never meant for us to do it alone! He designed us
to live in community—family, friends, and church—helping and serving and
meeting one another's needs.

*Lord, You promise never to leave us nor forsake us. Thank You for
providing helpers to come alongside of me. Amen.*

*Joanna, the wife of Chuza who was one of Herod's helpers, was another one.
Susanna and many others also cared for Jesus by using what they had.*
LUKE 8:3 NLV

*We should help others do what is right and build them up in the Lord.*
ROMANS 15:2 NLT

We may not be called to literally lay down our lives for someone, but we all
are called to lay down our lives in sacrificing our needs and desires for others.
Whatever the acts of love are, you can be assured that you are modeling
Jesus' sacrificial life by laying down your own life for the good of others.

*Lord Jesus, in an effort to follow Your example, show me someone I can help. Amen.*

# DAY 86 – *Faith*

## *Morning*

*For verily I say unto you, That whosoever shall say unto this mountain,
Be thou removed, and be thou cast into the sea; and shall not doubt in his heart,
but shall believe that those things which he saith shall come to pass;
he shall have whatsoever he saith.*
MARK 11:23 KJV

*[Jesus] replied, "If you have faith as small as a mustard seed, you can say to this
mulberry tree, 'Be uprooted and planted in the sea,' and it will obey you."*
LUKE 17:6 NIV

The Lord understands the limitations of our humanity. Surely it was not
happenstance that Christ chose a seed as His example when teaching
about faith. A mustard seed is one of the tiniest of all seeds, yet even
mustard seed faith can accomplish great things.

*Father, I cannot see You with my eyes, but I know You are there.
Increase my faith, I pray. Amen.*

## *Evening*

*By faith the walls of Jericho fell down, after they were compassed about seven days.*
HEBREWS 11:30 KJV

*Then the LORD said to Moses, "I will rain down bread from heaven for you. The
people are to go out each day and gather enough for that day. In this way I will test
them and see whether they will follow my instructions."*
EXODUS 16:4 NIV

Our faith is a living, breathing organism that needs to be fed every day.
Christ, His Word, and His presence are our daily manna. He has been
rained down upon us, given to us by God. All we have to do is take Him
into our lives.

*Christ, I come to You needing nourishment to renew my faith. Amen.*

# DAY 87 – *Rest*

—————————————————————

*"Come to Me, all you who labor and are heavy laden, and I will give you rest.
Take My yoke upon you and learn from Me, for I am gentle and lowly in heart,
and you will find rest for your souls."*
MATTHEW 11:28–29 NKJV

*I know that nothing is better for them than to rejoice, and to do good in their lives,
and also that every man should eat and drink and enjoy the good
of all his labor—it is the gift of God.*
ECCLESIASTES 3:12–13 NKJV

Constant work is not what God intended for our lives. We should work hard,
yes, but not to the exclusion of rest and times of renewal for our minds and
souls. Our food, homes, and friendships are gifts that God meant for us to
enjoy.

*Lord, thank You for the gifts You've bestowed on me.
Help me find moments to enjoy them. Amen.*

—————————————————————

*Six days may work be done; but in the seventh is the sabbath of rest, holy to the
LORD: whosoever doeth any work in the sabbath day, he shall surely be put to death.*
EXODUS 31:15 KJV

*Have compassion on me, LORD, for I am weak. Heal me, LORD, for my bones are
in agony. I am sick at heart. How long, O LORD, until you restore me? . . .
The LORD has heard my plea; the LORD will answer my prayer.*
PSALM 6:2–3, 9 NLT

We have not all broken a bone. But we do all know the deep-down pain of
troubled bones. Illness and exhaustion. Broken relationships. Debt. The next
time troubled bones keep us awake at night, we can take them to God in
prayer.

*Lord, our bones are troubled. We ask that You will give us peaceful rest. Amen.*

# DAY 88 – *Fear*

*Yea, though I walk through the valley of the shadow of death, I will fear no evil:
for thou art with me; thy rod and thy staff they comfort me.*
PSALM 23:4 KJV

*The LORD is my light and my salvation; whom shall I fear? The LORD is the defense of
my life; whom shall I dread? When evildoers came upon me to devour my flesh,
my adversaries and my enemies, they stumbled and fell. Though a host
encamp against me, my heart will not fear; though war arise against me,
in spite of this I shall be confident.*
PSALM 27:1–3 NASB

Fear is a paralyzing thing. The specific thing that frightens is as individual
and unique as people, but we all struggle with fear at some time in our
lives. As Christians, we can take the admonition "Fear not" to heart. God
knows our fears and encourages us to turn fear into faith.

*Thank You, Lord, for Your faithfulness and love that casts out fear. Amen.*

*I sought the LORD, and He heard me, and delivered me from all my fears.*
PSALM 34:4 NKJV

*O death, where is thy sting? O grave, where is thy victory?*
1 CORINTHIANS 15:55 KJV

We can either live life in fear or live life by faith. Fear and faith cannot
coexist. Jesus Christ has conquered our greatest fear—death. Knowing this
truth enables us to courageously face our fears. There is no fear that cannot
be conquered by faith.

*Lord, You alone know my fears. Help me trust You more. May I walk in the victory
You have purchased for me on the cross. Amen.*

# DAY 89 – *Worry*

*Morning* —

*"Therefore I tell you, do not worry about your life, what you will eat or drink; or about your body, what you will wear. Is not life more than food, and the body more than clothes?"*
MATTHEW 6:25 NIV

*But stop worrying! Just remember what the LORD your God did to Egypt and its king.*
DEUTERONOMY 7:18 CEV

Although heaven and earth may pass away, God's words—the anchor of our spirit, the bread of our lives, that which gives us peace beyond understanding—will remain forever.

*Lord, thank You for being my Rock, my Refuge, and my Rest. Amen.*

*Evening* —

*Dear friend, guard Clear Thinking and Common Sense with your life; don't for a minute lose sight of them. They'll keep your soul alive and well, they'll keep you fit and attractive. You'll travel safely, you'll neither tire nor trip. You'll take afternoon naps without a worry, you'll enjoy a good night's sleep. No need to panic over alarms or surprises, or predictions that doomsday's just around the corner, because GOD will be right there with you; he'll keep you safe and sound.*
PROVERBS 3:21–26 MSG

*Cast your burden upon the LORD and He will sustain you;*
*He will never allow the righteous to be shaken.*
PSALM 55:22 SASB

God desires that we help bear one another's burdens. The trouble is that in doing so, we often fail to take our burdens to the One who can do something about them. We are called to release our cares to our heavenly Father. If you cast your burdens on Him, then He will sustain you.

*Lift the worries that weigh on my mind and heart today, Father. I can't bear them alone any longer. Thank You for Your promise to sustain me. Amen.*

# DAY 90 – *Priorities*

## *Morning*

If you make Insight your priority, and won't take no for an answer, searching for it
like a prospector panning for gold, like an adventurer on a treasure hunt,
believe me, before you know it Fear-of-GOD will be yours;
you'll have come upon the Knowledge of God.
PROVERBS 2:3–5 MSG

"But seek first the kingdom of God and his righteousness,
and all these things will be added to you."
MATTHEW 6:33 ESV

Jesus asks for the unexpected. He may ask us for our things, our time, or
our talents. He asks us to align our use of what He has given us with His
priorities. What does the Master need? That should become our priority.

*Master of all, we invite You to be the Master of our hearts, of everything we possess
and are. Teach us to make Your priorities our own. Amen.*

## *Evening*

But if a widow has children or grandchildren, these should learn first of all to put their
religion into practice by caring for their own family and so repaying their parents and
grandparents, for this is pleasing to God.
1 TIMOTHY 5:4 NIV

I observed everything going on under the sun, and really,
it is all meaningless—like chasing the wind.
ECCLESIASTES 1:14 NLT

There will always be things that need to be done. But Christ Jesus wants
our time. He doesn't want us to feel overburdened. Ask God to help you
see what things in your life are necessary and important as you let Him help
you focus on the best things that He desires for you.

*Dear God, help me to prioritize the tasks in my life. Amen.*

# DAY 91 – *Aging*

*"Honor your father and your mother, that your days may be long in the land
that the LORD your God is giving you."*
EXODUS 20:12 ESV

*Gray hair is a crown of splendor; it is attained in the way of righteousness.*
PROVERBS 16:31 NIV

As we age physically, our spiritual growth should correspond. The seed of
faith planted in our hearts is meant to germinate, bud, and bloom over the
natural course of time. And gray hair—the evidence that God has been
cultivating us both physically and spiritually—is the crowning touch.

*Father, as I age, teach me to wear spiritual maturity as a crown. Physically, help me
learn to rejoice in what is remaining rather than lament what is lost. Amen.*

*"You will go to the grave at a ripe old age, like a sheaf of grain
harvested at the proper time!"*
JOB 5:26 NLT

*And even to your old age I am he; and even to hoar hairs will I carry you:
I have made, and I will bear; even I will carry, and will deliver you.*
ISAIAH 46:4 KJV

God is the strength of our souls. Even if no other human being is there to
help, He will give us boldness to face whatever is before us, whether it is
loneliness or added responsibilities and challenges as we age. Our strength
is in His constant companionship.

*Lord Jesus, help me trust You to supply all my needs and embolden me for
whatever lies ahead. Amen.*

DAY 92 - *Death*

*Morning* ─────────────────────────────────

*"I am the ressurection and the life: be that believeth in me,*
*though he were dead, yet shall he live."*
JOHN 11:25 KJV

*The life of mortals is like grass, they flourish like a flower of the field; the wind blows*
*over it and it is gone, and its place remembers it no more.*
PSALM 103:15–16 NIV

Our lives begin and end in the blink of an eye. The things that we think are
so important may one day be merely trivial. All that will matter is that we
told others about Christ. Our mission is to do the will of God, to go where
God is working, and to make a difference for Him.

*Lord, I am willing to make an eternal difference for You. Amen.*

*Evening* ─────────────────────────────────

*"I will deliver this people from the power of the grave; I will redeem them from death.*
*Where, O death, are your plagues? Where, O grave, is your destruction?"*
HOSEA 13:14 NIV

*My flesh and my heart fail; but God is the strength of my heart*
*and my portion forever.*
PSALM 73:26 NKJV

When death takes someone dear, the world's very foundation seems to
shake. We question God, asking why He couldn't stop the situation causing
our pain. His Word doesn't always answer our questions, but it is a place we
can run to for comfort.

*Father, thank You for Your words of comfort when I am wracked with grief and pain.*
*Help me never forget that You are there for me.*

DAY 93 – *Loving Others*

*Morning* ───────────────────────

*For this very reason, make every effort to add to your faith goodness;
and to goodness, knowledge; and to knowledge, self-control; and to self-control,
perseverance; and to perseverance, godliness; and to godliness, mutual affection;
and to mutual affection, love.*
2 PETER 1:5–7 NIV

*But if anyone has the world's goods and sees his brother in need, yet closes his heart
against him, how does God's love abide in him?*
1 JOHN 3:17 ESV

Because of God's love, Jesus paid an overwhelming debt He didn't owe
through His death on the cross. The apostle Paul admonishes us to incur a
debt we can never pay—the debt of continuing love. Love is the only debt
God encourages. In this instance, we can never owe enough.

*Dear Lord, thank You for the price You paid for me. May I increase the debt
of love I owe to others. Amen.*

*Evening* ───────────────────────

*"But here is what I tell you. Love your enemies. Pray for those who hurt you."*
MATTHEW 5:44 NIrV

*Don't just pretend to love others. Really love them. Hate what is wrong.
Hold tightly to what is good.*
ROMANS 12:9 NLT

We should never underestimate the power of touch. Touching communicates
our affection but also our affirmation and sympathy. You can encourage
people—or comfort them—with a simple touch. So hold those you love
close. Hug them, and let them see a bit of Jesus' love in you every day.

*Lord, I turn to You when I need comfort. Let me also offer those around me
the comfort of a loving embrace. Amen.*

# DAY 94 - *Peace*

## *Morning*

*These things I have spoken unto you, that in me ye might have peace. In the world ye shall have tribulation: but be of good cheer; I have overcome the world.*
JOHN 16:33 KJV

*Those who love Your law have great peace, and nothing causes them to stumble.*
PSALM 119:165 NASB

God's desire is not to overwhelm you. He recommends that you do your very best to lead a quiet, simple life while you work hard at the things you need to do. Find peace as you release yourself from self-imposed requirements and surrender to God's will.

*Heavenly Father, please help me order my life in a way that brings peace to my life and to the lives of those around me. Amen.*

## *Evening*

*The LORD gives strength to his people; the LORD blesses his people with peace.*
PSALM 29:11 NIV

*The peace of God, which surpasses all understanding, will guard your hearts and minds through Christ Jesus.*
PHILIPPIANS 4:7 NKJV

The peace of God cannot be explained. It cannot be bought. The world cannot give it to us. But when we release our cares to the Lord in prayer, His peace washes over us and fills our hearts and minds. What a comfort is the peace of God when we find ourselves in the valley.

*Sovereign God, You are with me through the good and the bad. Draw near to me and replace my worry with Your peace. Amen.*

*Morning* —————————————————————————

> Then the LORD God said, "It is not good for the man to be alone;
> I will make him a helper suitable for him."
> GENESIS 2:18 NASB

> God. . .gives the desolate a home in which to dwell.
> PSALM 68:6 AMP

The Lord made people to have relationships with Himself and others, and
He recognizes and provides for our need for human companionship. His
best prescription for loneliness: relationships with Him and with His people.

*Father, sometimes I struggle with feeling alone. In those times, help me reach out to
Your love and to the companionship of fellow believers. Amen.*

*Evening* —————————————————————————

> Just thinking of my troubles and my lonely wandering makes me miserable. . . . Then
> I remember something that fills me with hope. The LORD's kindness never fails!
> LAMENTATIONS 3:19, 21–22 CEV

> You are close beside me. Your rod and your staff protect and comfort me.
> PSALM 23:4 NLT

Our world can be a lonely place when everyone's too busy to give time to
one another. We need the Lord in our lives so we never have to worry about
being alone. When the pace of life threatens to bury you, reach out to God.
He will not leave you lonely.

*Lord, I am reaching out to You. When I feel most alone, be close to me.
Help me always be aware of Your presence. Amen.*

## *Morning*

*"When I was in my prime, God's friendship was felt in my home."*
JOB 29:4 NLT

*"I no longer call you slaves, because a master doesn't confide in his slaves. Now you are my friends, since I have told you everything the Father told me."*
JOHN 15:15 NLT

One of the first casualties of a busy life is friendship. Often we don't even realize it is missing, because the more activities we have, the more people that surround us. We all have a need for close friendships. We need others in our lives who will challenge us to make us sharper, bolder, gentler, and more Christlike.

*Dear Jesus, I know You are a friend who sticks closer than a brother, yet sometimes I need the comfort of friends I can see and touch. Help me invest in friends. Amen.*

## *Evening*

*The LORD would speak to Moses face to face, as one speaks to a friend.*
EXODUS 33:11 NIV

*Two are better than one, because they have a good return for their labor: if either of them falls down, one can help the other up. But pity anyone who falls and has no one to help them up.*
ECCLESIASTES 4:9–10 NIV

We need friends. Jesus sent the disciples out two by two because He knew how important it was to have someone to share with and to support. Standing alone, we feel like our strength is limited, but with someone else by our side, new reserves of strength surface.

*Lord, be with me this day. Guide me toward friends who will support me in my faith and the things I desire to do. Amen.*

DAY 97 – *Prayer*

## *Morning*

*Epaphras, who is one of you and a servant of Christ Jesus, sends greetings.
He is always wrestling in prayer for you, that you may stand firm
in all the will of God, mature and fully assured.*
COLOSSIANS 4:12 NIV

*"I looked for someone among them who would build up the wall and stand before me in
the gap on behalf of the land so I would not have to destroy it, but I found no one."*
EZEKIEL 22:30 NIV

It's easy in the busyness of life to overlook a prayer request someone else
has made. Take time right when you receive a request to talk to the Lord on
the requester's behalf. Be the bridge that carries that person through the
valley of darkness back to the mountaintop of joy.

*Heavenly Father, help me have a heart of compassion. Help me never be too busy to
pray for those I know and even those I don't know
who need Your comfort. Amen.*

## *Evening*

*"And all things you ask in prayer, believing, you will receive."*
MATTHEW 21:22 NASB

*Yet the LORD will command his lovingkindness in the day time, and in the night his
song shall be with me, and my prayer unto the God of my life.*
PSALM 42:8 KJV

So often we are our own worst enemy. This is true of our prayers. Too often
we come before God asking His help, but when He doesn't respond to us
the way we think He should, we reject Him.

*Please help me open my heart and soul to Your will, Lord. Amen.*

# DAY 98 – *False Teaching*

## *Morning*

But there were also false prophets in Israel, just as there will be false teachers among you. They will cleverly teach destructive heresies and even deny the Master who bought them. In this way, they will bring sudden destruction on themselves.
2 PETER 2:1 NLT

Dear friends, do not believe every spirit, but test the spirits to see whether they are from God, because many false prophets have gone out into the world. This is how you can recognize the Spirit of God: Every spirit that acknowledges that Jesus Christ has come in the flesh is from God.
1 JOHN 4:1–2 NIV

We know false teaching is out there, but how can we identify it and avoid wrong theology? When we know God's Word well, false teaching will jump out at us. Anything that does not agree with scripture is in the wrong.

*Father, my desire is to learn Your Word well, so that I
remain faithful to Your teaching. Amen.*

## *Evening*

Anyone who teaches something different disagrees with the correct and godly teaching of our Lord Jesus Christ. Those people who disagree are proud of themselves, but they don't really know a thing. . . . They have wicked minds and have missed out on the truth.
1 TIMOTHY 6:3–5 CEV

"It is useless for you to worship me, when you teach rules made up by humans."
MATTHEW 15:9 CEV

The world, which is the stomping ground of the devil, is quick to turn us away from God, offering a hundred false gods in His place. When we lose God, we've lost everything.

*O Lord, You are every good thing. Be with me in everything I do. Amen.*

# DAY 99 - *Repentance*

*If a man does not repent, God will whet his sword; he has bent and readied his bow.*
PSALM 7:12 ESV

*Return to the LORD your God, for he is merciful and compassionate, slow to get*
*angry and filled with unfailing love. He is eager to relent and not punish.*
JOEL 2:13 NLT

When God commands us to repent, He doesn't want a mumbled apology.
He doesn't even want demonstrative tears—unless they come from a
repentant heart. Repentance from sinning against God involves a willful
action, a changing of direction.

*Forgive me, Lord. Help me turn from my sin. Amen.*

*I came not to call the righteous, but sinners to repentance.*
LUKE 5:32 KJV

*Let us test and examine our ways, and return to the LORD!*
LAMENTATIONS 3:40 ESV

Taking time to reflect, to think, and to examine oneself is a necessary step
in moving toward intimacy with God. He will show us the sins we need to
confess and give us the grace of repentance.

*Lord, speak to me through Your Holy Spirit of what is wrong in my life.*
*Bless me with the gift of repentance and allow me to enjoy*
*the sweetness of Your forgiveness. Amen.*

# DAY 100 – *Miracles*

## *Morning*

*Our Lord, no other gods compare with you—Majestic and holy!*
*Fearsome and glorious! Miracle worker!*
EXODUS 15:11 CEV

*"God does wonders that cannot be understood; he does so many miracles*
*they cannot be counted."*
JOB 5:9 NCV

The word *miracle* sounds strange in this day and age. If only people would open their hearts and begin looking more deeply than they are able with their eyes alone. A beautiful sunset, the wonder of human life: all of these are miracles in a sense, and all of them are evidence of the wonder of God.

*Make me a believer, Lord. Show me the multitude of miracles*
*You have created and are creating. Amen.*

## *Evening*

*Tell the nations of his glory; tell all peoples the miracles he does.*
PSALM 96:3 NCV

*So each generation should set its hope anew on God, not forgetting his glorious*
*miracles and obeying his commands.*
PSALM 78:7 NLT

It is a special joy to see the world with eyes open to miracles, and to feel life with a heart attuned to God's love. If we understand God, then we must believe in His miracles.

*Heavenly Father, let me understand creation the way You intended it,*
*miraculous and beautiful. Amen.*

*Morning* ——————————————————————————

*Make a careful exploration of who you are and the work you have been given,
and then sink yourself into that. Don't be impressed with yourself.
Don't compare yourself with others. Each of you must take responsibility
for doing the creative best you can with your own life.*
GALATIANS 6:4–5 MSG

*Because of the transgression of a land, many are its princes; but by a man of
understanding and knowledge right will be prolonged.*
PROVERBS 28:2 NKJV

God raises up individuals in families, at work, at church, and in government
to become leaders. Whatever our JOBS are, we are responsible. How we
behave and what we believe not only influences us but also those we come
into contact with.

*Lord, give me seeing eyes and hearing ears to guide others. Amen.*

*Evening* ——————————————————————————

*And they lodged all around the house of God because they had the responsibility,
and they were in charge of opening it every morning.*
1 CHRONICLES 9:27 NKJV

*Then God said to Abraham, "Your responsibility is to obey the terms of the covenant.
You and all your descendants have this continual responsibility."*
GENESIS 17:9 NLT

When we fail to take responsibility for our choices, we tend to make the
same bad ones over and over again. Accepting responsibility for our actions
tells God that we want to learn from our mistakes so they don't happen
again.

*Lord, as hard as it is to admit when I am wrong, teach me to humbly accept
responsibility for my choices. Amen.*

# DAY 102 – *Addiction*

## Morning

*Do not join those who drink too much wine or gorge themselves on meat, for
drunkards and gluttons become poor, and drowsiness clothes them in rags.*
PROVERBS 23:20–21 NIV

*Let us behave decently, as in the daytime, not in carousing and drunkenness, not in
sexual immorality and debauchery, not in dissension and jealousy.*
ROMANS 13:13 NIV

Struggling with addiction is tough. Don't do it alone. Having someone
to hold you accountable could be the extra support necessary to remain
steadfast.

*Father, I wish to be free from addiction. Help me to seek out trusted friends and
counselors to hold my hand and keep me accountable. Amen.*

## Evening

*"But if you do not do what is right, sin is crouching at your door;
it desires to have you, but you must rule over it."*
GENESIS 4:7 NIV

*There hath no temptation taken you but such as is common to man: but God is
faithful, who will not suffer you to be tempted above that ye are able; but will with
the temptation also make a way to escape, that ye may be able to bear it.*
1 CORINTHIANS 10:13 KJV

The word addiction often brings to mind alcohol and drugs. But the truth
is, addiction can take many forms. Sugar. Social media. Shoes. Be on the
lookout for any harmful, have-to-have areas in your life.

*Lord, help me spot addiction in my life. Even small things. Be my guide
as I pursue a life of devotion to You alone. Amen.*

# DAY 103 - *Rest*

*Morning* ———————————————————————————

*When thou liest down, thou shalt not be afraid: yea, thou shalt lie down,*
*and thy sleep shall be sweet.*
PROVERBS 3:24 KJV

*For he spake in a certain place of the seventh day on this wise, and God*
*did rest the seventh day from all his works. . . . There remaineth*
*therefore a rest to the people of God.*
HEBREWS 4:4, 9 KJV

It takes more than a quiet place or a time away to bring true rest. We must
jump into God's everlasting arms and dive into His Word. Rest is found
in knowing Christ and understanding that through His sacrifice, we are at
peace. As we allow God's peace to fill us, we will find real rest.

*Father God, there are many days when I don't have time to sit.*
*In all these times, remind me that peace comes from knowing You*
*and resting in the work You have done. Amen.*

*Evening* ———————————————————————————

*Whenever the evil spirit from God bothered Saul, David would play his harp.*
*Saul would relax and feel better, and the evil spirit would go away.*
1 SAMUEL 16:23 CEV

*By the seventh day God had finished the work he had been doing; so on the seventh*
*day he rested from all his work. Then God blessed the seventh day and made it holy,*
*because on it he rested from all the work of creating that he had done.*
GENESIS 2:2-3 NIV

When we overextend ourselves every single day, we run the risk of burning
out—and forgetting why God created the Sabbath. Our bodies, minds, and
emotions need rest. The Sabbath gives us a chance to take a breather.

*God, help me slow down my schedule and quiet my heart. Amen.*

*Morning*

"*Do not worry then, saying, 'What will we eat?' or 'What will we drink?' or 'What will we wear for clothing?' For the Gentiles eagerly seek all these things; for your heavenly Father knows that you need all these things. But seek first His kingdom and His righteousness, and all these things will be added to you.*"
MATTHEW 6:31–33 NASB

*What is more, I consider everything a loss because of the surpassing worth of knowing Christ Jesus my Lord, for whose sake I have lost all things.*
*I consider them garbage, that I may gain Christ.*
PHILIPPIANS 3:8 NIV

Ask the Lord to help you control your spending by leading you into wise decisions. He wants you to enjoy the beautiful things He created, but only after you have learned that they mean nothing compared to the treasure found in knowing Christ.

*Father, thank You for all the wonderful blessings You have given me. Help me spend wisely and remain focused on the greatest treasure—You. Amen.*

*Evening*

*How joyful are those who fear the LORD and delight in obeying his commands. . . .*
*They themselves will be wealthy, and their good deeds will last forever.*
PSALM 112:1, 3 NLT

*And this same God who takes care of me will supply all your needs from his glorious riches, which have been given to us in Christ Jesus.*
PHILIPPIANS 4:19 NLT

Searching for wisdom for your situation and asking God to direct you in the right decisions will lead you down a path of financial success.

*Lord, show me the wisdom of making good decisions financially. Help me choose wisely when and where to spend or save. Amen.*

# DAY 105 – *Sin*

*For He made Him who knew no sin to be sin for us, that we might
become the righteousness of God in Him.*
2 CORINTHIANS 5:21 NKJV

*For a man's ways are before the eyes of the LORD, and he ponders all his paths.
The iniquities of the wicked ensnare him, and he is held fast in the cords of his sin.*
PROVERBS 5:21–22 ESV

It is not enough to try not to sin, but we should do everything in our power
to avoid it, turn from it, move as far away from it as possible, and leave it as
far behind as we can.

*May I choose the right path, almighty God, turning from what
I know You would not have me do. Amen.*

*Although I don't do what I know is right, I agree that the Law is good. So I am not
the one doing these evil things. The sin that lives in me is what does them. I know
that my selfish desires won't let me do anything that is good. Even when I want to do
right, I cannot. Instead of doing what I know is right, I do wrong.*
ROMANS 7:16–19 CEV

*No one who abides in him keeps on sinning; no one who keeps on sinning
has either seen him or known him.*
1 JOHN 3:6 ESV

Sin is like a web. As we become occupied with the things we should not be
doing, we become oblivious to the dangers that surround us. We feel that
we are in control, when in fact we are in a very precarious position.

*Lord, I turn my attention to so many things that I should not.
Forgive me when I stray. Amen.*

## *Morning*

*"I have come as a light into the world, that whoever believes in Me
should not abide in darkness."*
JOHN 12:46 NKJV

*"If you abide in Me, and My words abide in you, you will ask what you desire,
and it shall be done for you."*
JOHN 15:7 NKJV

Abiding is an active service of trust in God that demands much of us but
also provides us with untold blessings.

*Heavenly Father, strengthen me to abide in You. I cannot do it on my own,
but only with Your support. Amen.*

## *Evening*

*Whoever transgresses and does not abide in the doctrine of Christ does not have God.
He who abides in the doctrine of Christ has both the Father and the Son.*
2 JOHN 1:9 NKJV

*"As the Father loved Me, I also have loved you; abide in My love. If you keep
My commandments, you will abide in My love, just as I have kept My Father's
commandments and abide in His love."*
JOHN 15:9–10 NKJV

Abiding in God changes our relationship with our fellow humans. We
cannot keep our heads in the clouds as we walk with Jesus on earth. We
must deal day by day with others and, through our actions, show them the
love we have received.

*Father, lead me in my interactions with others. Show Your love through me. Amen.*

# DAY 107 – *God's Plan*

*For we are God's masterpiece. He has created us anew in Christ Jesus,*
*so we can do the good things he planned for us long ago.*
EPHESIANS 2:10 NLT

*"I know what I'm doing. I have it all planned out—plans to take care of you,*
*not abandon you, plans to give you the future you hope for."*
JEREMIAH 29:10–11 MSG

We humans have such limited vision. God sees the big picture. Be open. Be flexible. Allow God to change your plans in order to accomplish His divine purposes. Instead of becoming frustrated, look for ways the Lord might be working.

*Dear Lord, forgive me when I become so rigidly locked in my own agenda that*
*I miss Yours. Give me Your eternal perspective so that I may be*
*open to divine interruptions. Amen.*

*God's plan looked foolish to men, but it is wiser than the best plans of men.*
*God's plan which may look weak is stronger than the strongest plans of men.*
1 CORINTHIANS 1:25 NLV

*And we know that all things work together for good to them that love God,*
*to them who are the called according to his purpose.*
ROMANS 8:28 KJV

God can take any bad experience and turn it into something good— something that will fulfill His plan. He has called you and has a divine purpose for your life. Thank Him for His mighty plan today!

*Dear God, thank You for working all things according to*
*Your purpose and for my good. Amen.*

# DAY 108 – *Family*

─────────────────────────────────

Then the LORD God made a woman from the rib he had taken out of the man, and he brought her to the man. The man said, "This is now bone of my bones and flesh of my flesh; she shall be called 'woman,' for she was taken out of man." That is why a man leaves his father and mother and is united to his wife, and they become one flesh.

GENESIS 2:22–24 NIV

I will instruct you and teach you in the way you should go;
I will counsel you with my loving eye on you.
PSALM 32:8 NIV

Even good things, like enjoying your work, can crowd out the best things, like loving your family. When God rings a warning bell that we are neglecting areas of importance, we need to listen, gratefully, and hasten to make changes before it's too late.

*Fix my attention, Lord! Help me identify my imbalances and areas of neglect. Amen.*

─────────────────────────────────

Though my father and mother forsake me, the LORD will receive me.
PSALM 27:10 NIV

You must be very careful not to forget the things you have seen God do for you.
Keep reminding yourselves, and tell your children and grandchildren as well.
DEUTERONOMY 4:9 CEV

God created families, and it was His plan that we share His workings in our lives with generations to come.

*Rock of Ages, help us always remember Your loving-kindness and pass the word on to those who share our genes, blood, and even our knobby knees. Amen.*

# DAY 109 - *Forgiveness*

## *Morning* ———————————————————

*If my people, which are called by my name, shall humble themselves, and pray,*
*and seek my face, and turn from their wicked ways; then will I hear from heaven,*
*and will forgive their sin, and will heal their land.*
2 Chronicles 7:14 kjv

*"He who is not with Me is against Me; and he who does not gather with Me scatters.*
*'Therefore I say to you, any sin and blasphemy shall be forgiven people,*
*but blasphemy against the Spirit shall not be forgiven.'"*
Matthew 12:30-31 nasb

If we are not humbled by the greatness of God's forgiveness, we need to
question whether we have a relationship with Him or not.

*Lord, thank You for forgiveness. I am unworthy, yet You love me. Amen.*

## *Evening* ———————————————————

*Bless the Lord, O my soul, and forget not all His benefits: who forgives all your*
*iniquities, who heals all your diseases, who redeems your life from destruction,*
*who crowns you with lovingkindness and tender mercies.*
Psalm 103:2-4 nkjv

*If we confess our sins, he is faithful and just and will forgive us our sins*
*and purify us from all unrighteousness.*
1 John 1:9 niv

We may give up on each other, but God never gives up on us. His offer of
forgiveness is open to us today and every day to come. He asks us daily to
follow Him, until the day we finally do.

*Though I push the patience of others to the limit, I am glad to know that I have not*
*pushed Yours, Lord. Continue to forgive me. I am weak, and only*
*Your great love keeps me going. Amen.*

# DAY 110 - *God's Presence*

## *Morning*

*"The LORD your God goes with you; he will never leave you nor forsake you."*
DEUTERONOMY 31:6 NIV

*My dear friends, if our hearts do not make us feel guilty, we can come without fear into God's presence.*
1 JOHN 3:21 NCV

While we're doing life on our own, we can forget that God is standing there waiting to do life every day with us. If you feel distant from God today, look up. He's waiting for you to find your rightful place with Him.

*God, I never want to become so busy that I lose sight of You. Amen.*

## *Evening*

*And this is the boldness we have in God's presence: that if we ask God for anything that agrees with what he wants, he hears us.*
1 JOHN 5:14 NCV

*The LORD is close to the brokenhearted; he rescues those whose spirits are crushed.*
PSALM 34:18 NLT

When others turn away from us, we know we can always rely on our eternal Father, the One who will never leave or forsake us. He is close to us in the best and the worst of times. He rescues us when we are crushed. Take His hand. Rest in His presence.

*God, thank You for always being there. With every breath I take, may I know You are right here beside me, loving me. Amen.*

# DAY 111 – *God's Word*

*After he was raised from the dead, his disciples recalled what he had said. Then they believed the scripture and the words that Jesus had spoken.*
JOHN 2:22 NIV

*Then Jesus spoke to them again, saying, "I am the light of the world. He who follows Me shall not walk in darkness, but have the light of life."*
JOHN 8:12 NKJV

We can be thankful for the light that illuminates our path—the Word of God. Without it we would stumble along through life not knowing which paths to take in a world that sometimes looks dark and scary.

*Heavenly Father, thank You for Your Word that is a lamp unto my feet and a light unto my path. Amen.*

*Evening* ⸺

*For, "All people are like grass, and all their glory is like the flowers of the field; the grass withers and the flowers fall, but the word of the Lord endures forever." And this is the word that was preached to you.*
1 PETER 1:24–25 NIV

*All Scripture is inspired by God and profitable for teaching, for reproof, for correction, for training in righteousness; so that the man of God may be adequate, equipped for every good work.*
2 TIMOTHY 3:16–17 NASB

It is important that we spend time in God's Word. We are to participate in Bible studies, worship God with fellow believers, and have a daily time of prayer and devotions. It is through these activities that we will become equipped for the good work God has planned for us.

*Lord, I praise You that Your Word can mold me into a being capable of carrying out Your good works. Help me consistently study Your Word. Amen.*

DAY 112 – *Spiritual Fruit*

*Morning* —————————————————————

*Blessed is the one who does not walk in step with the wicked. . .but whose delight is in the law of the LORD, and who meditates on his law day and night.*
PSALM 1:1–2 NIV

*You did not choose me. I chose you and sent you out to produce fruit, the kind of fruit that will last. Then my Father will give you whatever you ask for in my name.*
JOHN 15:16 CEV

Whether or not we expect to be, we are spiritual fruit producers. As we live day by day, others can see the love, faith, and goodness that flow from our lives as we serve Jesus. As we grow in Him, our lives testify to His greatness and the work He's doing in our lives.

*Father, help me cultivate spiritual fruit in my life so that I can declare Your greatness to those I meet. Amen.*

*Evening* —————————————————————

*"Remain in me, as I also remain in you. No branch can bear fruit by itself; it must remain in the vine. Neither can you bear fruit unless you remain in me. I am the vine; you are the branches. If you remain in me and I in you, you will bear much fruit; apart from me you can do nothing."*
JOHN 15:4–5 NIV

*For you were once darkness, but now you are light in the Lord. Live as children of light (for the fruit of the light consists in all goodness, righteousness and truth) and find out what pleases the Lord.*
EPHESIANS 5:8–10 NIV

It is wise to ask God's help as we weigh in our hearts what is good and fruitful to do. With His help, we may hope to walk in the paths of righteousness.

*O Lord, please guide my steps as I seek to live a fruitful life. Amen.*

# DAY 113 - *Guidance*

*And I will bring the blind by a way that they knew not; I will lead them in paths that they have not known: I will make darkness light before them, and crooked things straight. These things will I do unto them, and not forsake them.*
ISAIAH 42:16 KJV

*When Jesus spoke again to the people, he said, "I am the light of the world. Whoever follows me will never walk in darkness, but will have the light of life."*
JOHN 8:12 NIV

Jesus said His followers will never have to walk in darkness again but will have a life in the light. No more stumbling—we have His guidance. His light of life is a vibrant life lived confidently because we can see the path before us through eyes of faith.

*Light of life, thank You that we do not hover in darkness any longer. In You we walk boldly in the light of life, forgiven, free, and vibrant. Amen.*

*Nevertheless I am continually with thee: thou hast holden me by my right hand. Thou shalt guide me with thy counsel, and afterward receive me to glory.*
PSALM 73:23–24 KJV

*Good and upright is the LORD; therefore He instructs sinners in the way. He leads the humble in justice, and He teaches the humble His way. . . . He will instruct him in the way he should choose.*
PSALM 25:8–9, 12 NASB

God wants us to live life His way. Our good and upright God tells us that when we come before Him as humble, meek, needy, or afflicted, He will teach us what is right and just. God will teach us His way of living.

*God, please don't let me be distracted in this world but instead let me focus on You. Guide me in Your way, I humbly pray. Amen.*

# DAY 114 – *Comfort*

## *Morning*

*Even though I walk through the darkest valley, I will fear no evil, for you are with me; your rod and your staff, they comfort me.*
PSALM 23:4 NIV

*You have allowed me to suffer much hardship, but you will restore me to life again and lift me up from the depths of the earth. You will restore me to even greater honor and comfort me once again.*
PSALM 71:20–21 NLT

Worldly pleasures bring a temporary comfort, but the problem still remains when the pleasure or comfort fades. However, the words of God are soothing and provide permanent hope and peace. Through God's Word, you will be changed, and your troubles will dim in the bright light of Christ.

*Thank You, Father, for the rich comfort Your Word provides. Help me remember to find my comfort in scripture rather than in earthly things. Amen.*

## *Evening*

*God blesses those people who grieve. They will find comfort!*
MATTHEW 5:4 CEV

*God our Father loves us. He is kind and has given us eternal comfort and a wonderful hope. We pray that our Lord Jesus Christ and God our Father will encourage you and help you always to do and say the right thing.*
2 THESSALONIANS 2:16-17 CEV

Comfort is God's cure for disappointment. Maybe we don't understand exactly what our friends are going through, but we can offer comfort by being honest—letting them know we have never experienced their situation, but we are there to walk with them through the storm.

*Lord, help me be aware of the needs of others and help me to find the words to reach out to them. Amen.*

# DAY 115 – *Strength*

*Depend on the LORD and his strength; always go to him for help.*
PSALM 105:4 NCV

*The Spirit of God, who raised Jesus from the dead, lives in you.*
*And just as God raised Christ Jesus from the dead, he will give life to your*
*mortal bodies by this same Spirit living within you.*
ROMANS 8:11 NLT

Whatever we face—wherever we go—whatever dreams we have for our
lives, take courage and know that anything is possible when we draw on the
power of God.

*Father, help me remember that You are always with me,*
*ready to help me do all things. Amen.*

*Incline Your ear to me, rescue me quickly; be to me a rock of strength,*
*a stronghold to save me.*
PSALM 31:2 NASB

*"Be strong and courageous. Do not be afraid or discouraged because of the king of*
*Assyria and the vast army with him, for there is a greater power with us than with*
*him. With him is only the arm of flesh, but with us is the LORD our God to help us*
*and to fight our battles." And the people gained confidence from*
*what Hezekiah the king of Judah said.*
2 CHRONICLES 32:7–8 NIV

Whenever your energy is lagging, whenever you are discouraged or afraid,
look to your source of power. Call on Jesus to give you strength, and you
will have confidence and victory.

*Jesus, fill me with Your power. Provide me with confidence, strength, and fearlessness*
*as I go throughout my days, walking in Your will. Amen.*

DAY 116 – *Worship*

## *Morning*

Because of your great mercy, I come to your house, LORD, and I am filled with
wonder as I bow down to worship at your holy temple.
PSALM 5:7 CEV

All the earth shall worship thee, and shall sing unto thee;
they shall sing to thy name. Selah.
PSALM 66:4 KJV

Only God is worthy to be praised. In all we do and all we are, our lives
should pay tribute to God. Nothing else is good enough. Offer God
worship and praise, for He alone is deserving.

*Thank You for the gifts You give, almighty God. From the rise of the sun to its setting
in the night, I will praise You for all that You have done.
Glory is Yours, Father. Amen.*

## *Evening*

"Where is He who has been born King of the Jews? For we saw His star in the east
and have come to worship Him."
MATTHEW 2:2 NASB

Thy graven images also will I cut off, and thy standing images out of the midst of
thee; and thou shalt no more worship the work of thine hands.
MICAH 5:13 KJV

God loves music and the spirit from which music springs. The quality is
not nearly as important as the intention of the heart. Sing out to God and
worship Him!

*Speak to me through the beauty of music, Lord, and may I always
sing to You in worship. Amen.*

*Morning*

We are therefore Christ's ambassadors, as though God were making his appeal
through us. We implore you on Christ's behalf: Be reconciled to God.
2 CORINTHIANS 5:20 NIV

"I will make you a light for all nations to show people
all over the world the way to be saved."
ISAIAH 49:6 NCV

We are called to be Christ's representatives, His ambassadors. Humility, not
arrogance, should be observed in our lives. Forgiveness and love should
be readily displayed. Peace should shine forth. When nonbelievers observe
your life, do they receive an accurate picture of Jesus?

*Dear Lord, help me realize the responsibility I have as Your ambassador. May I
correctly represent You to others so that they will be drawn to You. Amen.*

*Evening*

Instead, you must worship Christ as Lord of your life. And if someone asks about
your hope as a believer, always be ready to explain it. But do this in a gentle and
respectful way. Keep your conscience clear. Then if people speak against you, they
will be ashamed when they see what a good life you live because you belong to Christ.
1 PETER 3:15–16 NLT

As long as I am in the world, I am the world's Light.
JOHN 9:5 AMP

Every day we are being watched—both by the Father and by the people
around us. Our attitudes and speech often are weighed against beliefs we
profess. Take time to search your heart. If your speech and attitude aren't
Christ centered, re-aim your heart to hit the mark.

*Lord, help me be a good representation of You. Amen.*

# DAY 118 – *God's Protection*

## *Morning*

*But the LORD is my defence; and my God is the rock of my refuge.*
PSALM 94:22 KJV

*Those who live in the shelter of the Most High will find rest in the
shadow of the Almighty. This I declare about the LORD: he alone is my refuge,
my place of safety; he is my God, and I trust him.*
PSALM 91:1–2 NLT

If you are abiding in Christ, moment by moment, you are constantly safe
under His protection. In that secret place, that hidden place in Him, you can
maintain holy serenity, a peace of mind that surpasses all understanding. If
you are trusting in God, nothing can move you or harm you.

*God, You are my Refuge. Your Word is the truth on which I rely. Amen.*

## *Evening*

*He shall cover thee with his feathers, and under his wings shalt thou trust:
his truth shall be thy shield and buckler.*
PSALM 91:4 KJV

*Be thou my strong habitation, whereunto I may continually resort: thou hast given
commandment to save me; for thou art my rock and my fortress.*
PSALM 71:3 KJV

Christ Himself is our sanctuary. The world's offerings, its counsel and its
substances, have nothing to sustain us. Safety can only be found in our
relationship with Jesus Christ. Christ Himself is the sanctuary, the place of
protection and shelter.

*Lord Jesus, thank You for being my protection. Amen.*

# DAY 119 – *Ambition*

## *Morning*

*Lazy people want much but get little, but those who work hard will prosper.*
PROVERBS 13:4 NLT

*A heart at peace gives life to the body, but envy rots the bones.*
PROVERBS 14:30 NIV

If ambition means wanting to do well at your job, then ambition is good. But, if ambition means you want to compete against your neighbor, destroy his reputation, and rejoice when you do better than your colleague does, then ambition is destructive.

*Lord, help my only ambition be to do my best and become like You. Amen.*

## *Evening*

*I realized that it's good and proper for a man to eat and drink. It's good for him to be satisfied with his hard work on this earth. That's what he should do during the few days of life God has given him. That's what God made him for.*
ECCLESIASTES 5:18 NIrV

*We're not, understand, putting ourselves in a league with those who boast that they're our superiors. We wouldn't dare do that. But in all this comparing and grading and competing, they quite miss the point.*
2 CORINTHIANS 10:12 MSG

Nowhere does scripture condemn the drive to achieve a worthy goal. Ambition, in itself, is not a problem. It is how ambition manifests itself. Are we striving to better ourselves for God? Or has the goal become winning? Are we looking for worldly admiration only?

*Father God, Your standards are what I need to hold before me. Grant me the wisdom to keep Your values in mind as I aim for any higher goal. Amen.*

# DAY 120 - *Blessings*

 *Morning* ──────────────────────

*Those who live only to satisfy their own sinful nature will harvest decay and death from that sinful nature. But those who live to please the Spirit will harvest everlasting life from the Spirit.*
GALATIANS 6:8–10 NLT

*"I am coming to you now, but I say these things while I am still in the world, so that they may have the full measure of my joy within them."*
JOHN 17:13 NIV

God longs to bestow His richest blessings on us. He loves us, so He desires to fill our cup to overflowing with the things that He knows will bring us pleasure and growth.

*Dear Jesus, forgive me for not accepting the fullness of Your blessings and Your joy. Help me to see the ways that I prevent my cup from being filled to overflowing. Amen.*

*Evening* ──────────────────────

*Says the LORD of Heaven's Armies, "I will open the windows of heaven for you. I will pour out a blessing so great you won't have enough room to take it in! Try it! Put me to the test!"*
MALACHI 3:10 NLT

*"I thank You and praise You, O God of my fathers; You have given me wisdom and might, and have now made known to me what we asked of You, for You have made known to us the king's demand."*
DANIEL 2:23 NKJV

God blesses us every day in both great and simple ways. Family, friends, work, faith—all these things from a bountiful buffet of gifts, and caring for them isn't always enough. We need to spend a little time with the One who has granted us the blessings.

*Father God, You have given us so much to be grateful for. Show me a way to spend more time with You. Amen.*

# DAY 121 – *Work*

*For even when we were with you, we used to give you this order: if anyone is not willing to work, then he is not to eat, either. For we hear that some among you are leading an undisciplined life, doing no work at all, but acting like busybodies.*
2 Thessalonians 3:10–11 NASB

*Who can find a virtuous and capable wife? She is more precious than rubies. . . .*
*She is energetic and strong, a hard worker.*
Proverbs 31:10, 17 NLT

Although it may be tempting to do just enough to get by, we put forth our best effort when we remember we represent God to the world. A Christian's character on the Job should be a positive reflection of the Lord.

*Father, help me to represent You well through my work.*
*I want to reflect Your love in all I do. Amen.*

*Evening* ───────────────────────────────

*"Be strong, all you people of the land," declares the Lord, "and work.*
*For I am with you," declares the Lord Almighty.*
Haggai 2:4 NIV

*Work with enthusiasm, as though you were working for the Lord rather than for people. Remember that the Lord will reward each one of us for the good we do, whether we are slaves or free.*
Ephesians 6:7–8 NLT

God tells us that whatever our task, we are to do it in the name of the Lord Jesus. We are to work as though Jesus were our supervisor, glorifying Him in thought, word, and deed. We are to give thanks to God for the work He has commissioned us to do.

*Lord, please help me do everything in Your name and with*
*thanksgiving to God the Father. Amen.*

DAY 122 – *Terrorism*

*Morning*

> Do justice to the fatherless and the oppressed, so that man who
> is of the earth may strike terror no more.
> PSALM 10:18 ESV

> In righteousness shalt thou be established: thou shalt be far from oppression;
> for thou shalt not fear: and from terror; for it shall not come near thee.
> ISAIAH 54:14 KJV

Today terrorism is a real fear that often threatens to overwhelm us. No
matter what we experience, nothing is larger than God. He protects and
encourages us, just as He calls the terrorist to give up his ways and turn
instead to Him.

*Heavenly Father, it's hard to take in all the horrific things that happen in this life.
Keep my eyes focused on You. Amen.*

*Evening*

> There they are in great terror, for God is with the generation of the righteous.
> PSALM 14:5 ESV

> "My God, my rock, in whom I take refuge, my shield and the horn of my salvation,
> my stronghold and my refuge; my savior, You save me from violence."
> 2 SAMUEL 22:3 NASB

Those who experience the damages of terrorism can be certain that God
has not forgotten them. He is the just Judge who does not excuse terrorists'
actions.

*Lord, when I become discouraged by terrorism, remind me that You reign
and Your justice will be done. Amen.*

# DAY 123 – *Poverty*

*Giving to the poor will keep you from poverty, but if you close your eyes
to their needs, everyone will curse you.*
PROVERBS 28:27 CEV

*Whoever oppresses the poor to increase his own wealth,
or gives to the rich, will only come to poverty.*
PROVERBS 22:16 ESV

Contrary to popular belief, the poor have not been deserted by God. He
often uses people to help supply the impoverished person's needs and calls
on Christians to aid those who lack money.

*Lord, use me to help those who are struggling. Turn my selfishness to love for others,
that I might share what I have been given. Amen.*

*"They are blessed who realize their spiritual poverty,
for the kingdom of heaven belongs to them."*
MATTHEW 5:3 NCV

*A rich man's wealth is his strong city; the poverty of the poor is their ruin.*
PROVERBS 10:15 ESV

God will provide for His poorer children through the grace of His richer
ones. We are called to give from our blessed abundance, that others less
fortunate might live.

*Heavenly Father, remind me today that all my wealth comes from You
and that my call is to help others. Amen.*

# DAY 124 - *Worry*

*"Don't be like this people, always afraid somebody is plotting against them.
Don't fear what they fear. Don't take on their worries."*
ISAIAH 8:12 MSG

*Give all your worries and cares to God, for he cares about you.*
1 PETER 5:7 NLT

Give Christ your concerns, worries, what-ifs. Put all those cares on Him, for His shoulders are broad enough to carry them. And the amazing thing is that He actually wants them!

*God, I come to You today with all my burdens. They are rolling off my shoulders and onto Yours. Thank You for sharing Your strength. Amen.*

*"You will stand trial before governors and kings because you are my followers.
But this will be your opportunity to tell the rulers and other unbelievers about me.
When you are arrested, don't worry about how to respond or what to say.
God will give you the right words at the right time."*
MATTHEW 10:18–19 NLT

*Do not be anxious about anything, but in every situation, by prayer and petition,
with thanksgiving, present your requests to God.*
PHILIPPIANS 4:6 NIV

Today's world does not make worry-free living easy. Instead of putting things into perspective, we let our anxieties spiral out of control. The apostle Paul urges his readers not to be worried about anything. Instead, he writes that we should present all our requests—with expressions of gratitude—to God.

*Dear Lord, teach me to look to You in times of worry. Let me always
give thanks for my experiences. Amen.*

# DAY 125 – *Wealth*

*Don't trust in money you have taken from others. Don't be proud of things you have stolen. Even if your riches grow, don't put your trust in them.*
PSALM 62:10 NIrV

*But don't forget to help others and to share your possessions with them. This too is like offering a sacrifice that pleases God.*
HEBREWS 13:16 CEV

Money cannot buy happiness, nor can it bring us life. Christ brings us life, and He brings it most abundantly. He is the real treasure, and as long as our hearts remain with Him, our lives will truly be rich.

*Help me keep my eyes focused on Your truth, Lord. Enable me to show others that You are the real treasure in life. Amen.*

*Evening* ────────────────────────────────

*Don't let it bother you when others get rich and live in luxury. Soon they will die and all of their wealth will be left behind.*
PSALM 49:16–17 CEV

*Honor the LORD from your wealth.*
PROVERBS 3:9 NASB

Christ said that no one could be the servant of two masters. When we become enthralled by money and all it can buy, we cannot fully devote our attention to God.

*Father, I pray that I might learn to pursue You with every energy of my heart and soul. Amen.*

*Morning* ————————————————————————————

Your righteousness is like the mighty mountains, your justice like the ocean depths.
You care for people and animals alike, O LORD.
PSALM 36:6 NLT

And the word of the LORD came again to Zechariah: "This is what the LORD
Almighty said: 'Administer true justice; show mercy and compassion to one another.
Do not oppress the widow or the fatherless, the foreigner or the poor.
Do not plot evil against each other.' "
ZECHARIAH 7:8–10 NIV

Our object lesson in justice is the cross, for through it, the Father exacted
justice for the sins of the world. Jesus was punished for our sins, to make
us right with our loving Father. We must pass justice on to others, as it has
been given to us.

*Father, when I am tempted to be unfair, bring me to the cross.*
*You have paid the price. Amen!*

*Evening* ————————————————————————————

"But let justice roll down like waters and righteousness like an ever-flowing stream."
AMOS 5:24 NASB

"You shall do no injustice in judgment; you shall not be partial to the poor nor defer to
the great, but you are to judge your neighbor fairly."
LEVITICUS 19:15 NASB

Things don't always work so well in real life. And yet God has promised
that in the end, justice will always carry the day. God knows every heart and
every situation. He will set all things right if we will only trust His wisdom.

*Injustice seems to rule, God. But I know better. You rule today,*
*and will tomorrow. I rest in You. Amen.*

DAY 127 – *Trials*

*Morning* ————————————————————————

*"I have done the Lord's work humbly and with many tears. I have endured the trials
that came to me from the plots of the Jews."*
ACTS 20:19 NLT

*Keep your eyes on Jesus, who both began and finished this race we're in.*
HEBREWS 12:2 MSG

In the face of trouble, we often try to run away, or we turn to worldly
solutions. These can never be enough. Instead, we must turn to God and
rely on His strength to get us through. He is greater than any trial this world
can produce.

*O Lord, receive me into Your loving care. Help me place You,
and You alone, at the center of my life. Amen.*

*Evening* ————————————————————————

*We can rejoice, too, when we run into problems and trials,
for we know that they help us develop endurance.*
ROMANS 5:3 NLT

*Dear friends, don't be surprised at the fiery trials you are going through, as if
something strange were happening to you. Instead, be very glad—for these trials
make you partners with Christ in his suffering, so that you will have the wonderful
joy of seeing his glory when it is revealed to all the world.*
1 PETER 4:12–13 NLT

When we experience trials, we often do not have the good sense to listen
to those who have walked our road before us. There is nothing wrong with
relying on the help of others.

*Heavenly Father, help me seek guidance when life gets hard.
I can't rely on myself alone. Amen.*

# DAY 128 – *Faith*

*Let love and faithfulness never leave you; bind them around your neck,
write them on the tablet of your heart.*
PROVERBS 3:3 NIV

*But you cannot make God accept you because of something you do.
God accepts sinners only because they have faith in him.*
ROMANS 4:5 CEV

If we will learn to accept a God who is greater and more powerful than the limits our minds can grasp, we will begin to experience God more fully. Faith is not without reason, but it is always beyond reason.

*Help me, Father, accept what I do not understand, believe that which I cannot see,
and trust that which is beyond my comprehension. Amen.*

*For we live by believing and not by seeing.*
2 CORINTHIANS 5:7 NLT

*I have been crucified with Christ; and it is no longer I who live, but Christ lives in
me; and the life which I now live in the flesh I live by faith in the Son of God,
who loved me and gave Himself up for me.*
GALATIANS 2:20 NASB

Arguments against the existence of God can sound good, but they amount to nothing more than opinion in the face of fact. We walk by faith, not by sight.

*All around me are people who attack my faith. Be with me, Lord. Amen.*

# DAY 129 – *Spiritual Fruit*

## *Morning*

*So that you may live a life worthy of the Lord and please him in every way:*
*bearing fruit in every good work, growing in the knowledge of God.*
COLOSSIANS 1:10 NIV

*"A good tree cannot bear bad fruit, and a bad tree cannot bear good fruit."*
MATTHEW 7:18 NIV

How people spend their time and money, how much they help the needy,
whether they are patient when wronged, whether they gossip. . .every action
bears fruit, revealing whether individuals are true disciples of Jesus Christ.
The lives we lead shout whether Christ is front and center in our lives.

*Lord, may my every action bear witness to Your Holy Spirit's work,*
*leading people to a direct knowledge of the truth. Amen.*

## *Evening*

*May you always be filled with the fruit of your salvation—the righteous character*
*produced in your life by Jesus Christ—for this will bring much glory and praise to God.*
PHILIPPIANS 1:11 NLT

*But the fruit of the Spirit is love, joy, peace, patience, kindness, goodness,*
*faithfulness, gentleness, self-control; against such things there is no law.*
GALATIANS 5:22–23 NASB

We are told in Galatians that the marks of the Holy Spirit are love, joy,
peace, patience, kindness, goodness, faithfulness, gentleness, and self-
control. It takes constant growth, through a consistent pursuit of godliness,
to acquire these character traits. Ask your Father which areas in your
Christian walk need the most growth.

*Lord, please show me which milestones of Christian living I need to focus on in order*
*to have the full markings of the Holy Spirit in my life. Amen.*

# DAY 130 – *Fearing God*

## Morning

*"Oh, that they had such a heart in them that they would fear Me and always keep all My commandments, that it might be well with them and with their children forever!"*
DEUTERONOMY 5:29 NKJV

*"And now, Israel, what does the LORD your God require of you, but to fear the LORD your God, to walk in all His ways and to love Him, to serve the LORD your God with all your heart and with all your soul?"*
DEUTERONOMY 10:12 NKJV

When we think about our fears, our minds and bodies almost always tense. Why does the Bible say we should "fear" God? In reality, to fear God is not the same as fearing the creepy-crawly spider inching up the living room wall. Instead, we fear God when we have a deep respect and reverence for Him.

*Lord, help my daily actions and speech reflect my respect for You. Amen.*

## Evening

*And fear not them which kill the body, but are not able to kill the soul: but rather fear him which is able to destroy both soul and body in hell.*
MATTHEW 10:28 KJV

*The fear of the LORD leads to life; then one rests content, untouched by trouble.*
PROVERBS 19:23 NIV

To fear the Lord is to respect Him and acknowledge that His ways are best for us. Our Abba Father, a gracious and loving God, is also a just and mighty God who is saddened, and even angered, when we continually turn from Him.

*Lord, I respect You. Help me acknowledge that You are God, You know best, and You have given me guidelines by which to live. Amen.*

# DAY 131 – *Forgiveness*

## *Morning*

*And forgive us our sins; for we also forgive every one that is indebted to us.*
*And lead us not into temptation; but deliver us from evil.*
LUKE 11:4 KJV

*"For if you forgive other people when they sin against you, your heavenly Father will*
*also forgive you. But if you do not forgive others their sins,*
*your Father will not forgive your sins."*
MATTHEW 6:14–15 NIV

In the Sermon on the Mount, Jesus encouraged His listeners to forgive offenders, but He didn't mention whether the offenders sought forgiveness. Jesus was only concerned about believers' obligations. We forgive because we are forgiven!

*Lord, how often I ask You for forgiveness—and how readily You give it.*
*May I never take for granted the gift of Your forgiveness. Amen.*

## *Evening*

*"And when you stand praying, if you hold anything against anyone, forgive them,*
*so that your Father in heaven may forgive you your sins."*
MARK 11:25 NIV

*For you were called to freedom, brethren; only do not turn your freedom into an*
*opportunity for the flesh, but through love serve one another.*
GALATIANS 5:13 NASB

We need to love and forgive others as God loves and forgives us. Always keep in mind that, although we may not like to admit it, we have all said and done some pretty awful things ourselves. Yet God has forgiven us and continues to love us. Stand tall in the freedom of love and forgiveness.

*Father, help me love and forgive others as You love and forgive me. Amen.*

## *Morning*

*But without faith it is impossible to please him: for he that cometh to God must believe that he is, and that he is a rewarder of them that diligently seek him.*
HEBREWS 11:6 KJV

*But that no man is justified by the law in the sight of God, it is evident: for, The just shall live by faith.*
GALATIANS 3:11 KJV

It has been said that faith is the bird that sings to greet the dawn while it is still dark. Faith assures us that daylight will dawn in our darkest moments, affirming God's presence so that even when positive feelings fade, our moods surrender to song.

*Heavenly Father, I pray for balance in my hide-under-the-covers days, so that I might surrender to You in song. Amen.*

## *Evening*

*Don't let anyone look down on you because you are young, but set an example for the believers in speech, in conduct, in love, in faith and in purity.*
1 TIMOTHY 4:12 NIV

*He replied, "Because you have so little faith. Truly I tell you, if you have faith as small as a mustard seed, you can say to this mountain, 'Move from here to there,' and it will move. Nothing will be impossible for you."*
MATTHEW 17:20 NIV

However small our faith, God can move mountains. When we drop the seed of our faith into the ground of His will, He will show us the direction He wants us to take. He may move the mountain; or He may carry us over, around, or through it.

*God, we trust You to move the mountains of our lives and to move us through them. Amen.*

# DAY 133 – *Argument*

*"For as churning cream produces butter, and as twisting the nose produces blood, so stirring up anger produces strife."*
PROVERBS 30:33 NIV

*Abram said to Lot, "Let's not have fighting between us, between your shepherds and my shepherds. After all, we're family. Look around. Isn't there plenty of land out there? Let's separate. If you go left, I'll go right; if you go right, I'll go left."*
GENESIS 13:8–9 MSG

When faced with disagreements, do we dig our feet into the ground and refuse to budge? Or do we put our desires second? Much bitterness among Christians could be avoided if we said, "You choose first. I will accept your decision."

*Heavenly Father, You have adopted us into Your family. Teach us to live together as brothers and sisters, united in Your love. Amen.*

*"But I say, if you are even angry with someone, you are subject to judgment! If you call someone an idiot, you are in danger of being brought before the court. And if you curse someone, you are in danger of the fires of hell."*
MATTHEW 5:22 NLT

*A gentle answer turns away wrath, but a harsh word stirs up anger.*
PROVERBS 15:1 NIV

Responding in anger is a natural thing for fallen humanity. But God calls us to end arguing by returning fury with love. It's not easy to speak the first peaceful word, but as we follow God's advice, amazing things happen. Instead of escalating the argument, we allow tensions to die down.

*Lord, help me dial down anger and spread Your love instead. Amen.*

# DAY 134 – *Strength*

*Morning*

*Our LORD, you break the bows of warriors, but you give strength*
*to everyone who stumbles.*
1 SAMUEL 2:4 CEV

*Goodness and fairness will give him strength, like a belt around his waist.*
ISAIAH 11:5 NCV

When you don't think you can take another step—don't! Just hold on. Tomorrow will give you a fresh start and the strength you need to go a little further and hold on a little longer. You've gotten this far in your faith believing that God will keep His promises and help you reach your destination.

*Lord, help me hold fast to You. With You by my side, I can make it through all circumstances of life no matter how tough they seem. Amen.*

*Evening*

*Lift up your eyes and look to the heavens: Who created all these? He who brings out the starry host one by one and calls forth each of them by name. Because of his great power and mighty strength, not one of them is missing.*
ISAIAH 40:26 NIV

*"Your sandals shall be iron and bronze; as your days, so shall your strength be."*
DEUTERONOMY 33:25 NKJV

For those particularly dark seasons of your life, you don't have to look to the east to find the morning star, but instead find that morning star in your heart. A new day is dawning and with it, new strength for the journey forward.

*Heavenly Father, help me hold tightly to Your strength, knowing the daybreak is on its way. Amen.*

# DAY 135 – *Serving God*

*People of Israel, what does the L*ORD *your God want from you? The L*ORD *wants you to respect and follow him, to love and serve him with all your heart and soul.*
DEUTERONOMY 10:12 CEV

*"God will show his mercy forever and ever to those who worship and serve him."*
LUKE 1:50 NCV

As we go about our day, doing whatever exciting or mundane activities we do, it is easy to lose focus and forget that our first priority is to serve God. In each action, our service and attitudes can reflect Christ—the Beginning and the End.

*God, help me serve You in all I do. Amen.*

*Evening* ───────────────────

*Everything will be destroyed. So you should serve and honor God by the way you live.*
2 PETER 3:11 CEV

*"For I was hungry, and you fed me. I was thirsty, and you gave me a drink. I was a stranger, and you invited me into your home. . . . And the King will say, 'I tell you the truth, when you did it to one of the least of these my brothers and sisters, you were doing it to me!' "*
MATTHEW 25:35, 40 NLT

Sometimes we can become so concerned with serving God that we forget that God is served when we serve people. It's all too easy to overlook people. Sometimes they don't even look like they need help. Although we cannot force someone to accept our help, we can make a point to offer it.

*Lord, open my eyes to see those who need care, and in helping them, serve You. Amen.*

# DAY 136 – *Wealth*

*"I love those who love me; and those who diligently seek me will find me. Riches and honor are with me, enduring wealth and righteousness. My fruit is better than gold, even pure gold, and my yield better than choicest silver."*
PROVERBS 8:17–19 NASB

*Command those who are rich in this present world not to be arrogant nor to put their hope in wealth, which is so uncertain, but to put their hope in God, who richly provides us with everything for our enjoyment.*
1 TIMOTHY 6:17 NIV

God desires to bless us with possessions we can enjoy. But it displeases Him when His children strain to attain riches in a worldly manner out of pride or a compulsion to flaunt. Riches are uncertain, but faith in God to meet our needs is indicative of the pure of heart.

*Heavenly Father, my hope is in You for my needs. I surrender my desire to attain earthly wealth. May I be rich in godliness and righteousness. Amen.*

*Let no man seek his own, but every man another's wealth.*
1 CORINTHIANS 10:24 KJV

*"What good will it be for someone to gain the whole world, yet forfeit their soul? Or what can anyone give in exchange for their soul?"*
MATTHEW 16:26 NIV

Rich people aren't excluded from heaven. But rich, busy, or ambitious people are often so focused on material things that they can't maneuver through the mire of worldly pursuits. They lose sight of the eternal prize and risk handing the victory to the enemy by forfeit.

*Father, please help me keep my life balanced. Let my primary desire always be to remain in the center of Your will, that I never forfeit the prize of eternal life. Amen.*

# DAY 137 - *Sin*

## *Morning*

*When he died, he died once to break the power of sin. But now that he lives, he lives for the glory of God. So you also should consider yourselves to be dead to the power of sin and alive to God through Christ Jesus. Do not let sin control the way you live; do not give in to sinful desires. Do not let any part of your body become an instrument of evil to serve sin. Instead, give yourselves completely to God.*
ROMANS 6:10–13 NLT

*I have no greater joy than to hear that my children are walking in the truth.*
3 JOHN 1:4 NIV

While we remain on earth, sin easily tempts us. That's just why believers must continually resist sin's hold and draw near to Jesus. He has opened the doors of forgiveness for every believer who habitually confesses the sticky sin that pulls him or her away from God.

*Cleanse me, Lord, from the goop of sin and help me stick to You alone. Amen.*

## *Evening*

*But each of you had better tremble and turn from your sins.*
*Silently search your heart as you lie in bed.*
PSALM 4:4 CEV

*Therefore, having these promises, beloved, let us cleanse ourselves from all filthiness of the flesh and spirit, perfecting holiness in the fear of God.*
2 CORINTHIANS 7:1 NKJV

While Jesus Himself cleanses us from all unrighteousness, as believers we need to be on the lookout for situations that might cause us to fall into sin. As we pray daily, God shows us areas in our character or behaviors that are displeasing to Him.

*Father, reveal the sin in my life and create a purified heart in me, I pray. Amen.*

# DAY 138 – *Appearance*

## *Morning* ───────────────────────────

*We are not commending ourselves to you again but giving you cause
to boast about us, so that you may be able to answer those who boast about
outward appearance and not about what is in the heart.*
2 CORINTHIANS 5:12 ESV

*"Whenever you fast, do not put on a gloomy face as the hypocrites do, for they
neglect their appearance so that they will be noticed by men when they are fasting.
Truly I say to you, they have their reward in full."*
MATTHEW 6:16 NASB

Worldly standards of beauty change; God's standards never do. It is not our makeup but what we are made of that lets our true beauty shine.

*Lord, help me remember that I may be the only "scripture" some people ever see.
Let my heart and manner represent You as best I can. Amen.*

## *Evening* ───────────────────────────

*So Jesus spoke to them: "You are masters at making yourselves look good in front of
others, but God knows what's behind the appearance."*
LUKE 16:15 MSG

*But understand this, that in the last days there will come times of difficulty.
For people will be lovers of self. . .having the appearance of godliness,
but denying its power. Avoid such people.*
2 TIMOTHY 3:1–5 ESV

We must remember that as we grow as Christians, we take on the characteristics of Christ. The more we become like Him, the more attractive we are in our own eyes and to those around us. When God looks at us as Christians, He sees the reflection of Christ.

*O God, help me to see myself through Your eyes. Amen.*

## *Morning*

*For wisdom is more precious than rubies, and nothing you desire can compare with her.*
PROVERBS 8:11 NIV

*Who is wise and understanding among you? Let them show it by their good life,*
*by deeds done in the humility that comes from wisdom.*
JAMES 3:13 NIV

Wisdom. The very term sounds outdated. But biblical wisdom, crafted by God before the earth existed, remains as fresh and powerful as its Creator. Whoever heeds God's instruction gains more than silver, gold, or rubies. His truth and His directions lead listeners to new life.

*Father, help us shake off the hypnotizing effects of culture's values*
*and listen to Your wisdom. Amen.*

## *Evening*

*But the wisdom from above is first of all pure. It is also peace loving, gentle at all times, and willing to yield to others. It is full of mercy and the fruit of good deeds. It shows no favoritism and is always sincere.*
JAMES 3:17 NLT

*Let no man deceive himself. If any man among you seemeth to be wise in this world, let him become a fool, that he may be wise. For the wisdom of this world is foolishness with God.*
1 CORINTHIANS 3:18–19 KJV

When we compare our wisdom with God's, we find that we are simple and dull. His knowledge so far exceeds our own. Thankfully, God offers His wisdom and knowledge with no strings attached.

*Lord, thank You for caring enough to share Your wisdom with me. Amen.*

## *Morning*

*Your kindness and love will always be with me each day of my life,
and I will live forever in your house, Lord.*
PSALM 23:6 CEV

*Do not let kindness and truth leave you; bind them around your neck,
write them on the tablet of your heart.*
PROVERBS 3:3 NASB

Satan delights when we treat others in an unkind manner. However, God, upon request, will help us prioritize our commitments so that our "yes" is "yes" and our "no" is "no." Then in everything we do, we are liberated to do to others as we would have them do to us.

*Lord, enable me in everything to do to others as I would desire
for them to do to me. Amen.*

## *Evening*

*"He has told you, O man, what is good; and what does the Lord require of you but
to do justice, and to love kindness, and to walk humbly with your God?"*
MICAH 6:8 ESV

*The Lord is righteous in everything he does; he is filled with kindness.*
PSALM 145:17 NLT

Random acts of kindness are never planned and seldom rewarded by those around us at the time. They are secrets between two people and God. But God remembers them, and they will be rewarded.

*Father, show me simple ways to be kind to others. May Your great kindness
toward me be reflected in all I do. Amen.*

# DAY 141 - *Fear*

————————————————————————————

*Fear not, little flock; for it is your Father's good pleasure to give you the kingdom.*
LUKE 12:32 KJV

*But whoso hearkeneth unto me shall dwell safely, and shall be quiet from fear of evil.*
PROVERBS 1:33 KJV

When you become bewildered and petrified by fear, don't be afraid. Just stand still and watch the Lord rescue you today. Be persistent, and God will see you through.

*Lord, be my shield. Surround me with Your presence. Help me keep still in this situation and watch You see me through it. And I will praise You forever and ever, in Jesus' name. Amen.*

————————————————————————————

*When thou liest down, thou shalt not be afraid: yea, thou shalt lie down, and thy sleep shall be sweet.*
PROVERBS 3:24 KJV

*God is our refuge and strength, always ready to help in times of trouble. So we will not fear when earthquakes come and the mountains crumble into the sea. Let the oceans roar and foam. Let the mountains tremble as the waters surge!*
PSALM 46:1–3 NLT

Someone has calculated that the words *fear not* appear exactly 365 times in the Bible. How wonderful to have this affirmation available to us every day of the year! Praise God that with Christ the Deliverer in our lives, we are no longer threatened by the world around us.

*Lord, I will not fear. No matter what comes against me, I am strong and courageous, able to overcome any foe—because You are by my side! Amen.*

# DAY 142 – *Praise*

*Morning* ————————————————————————

*You are the living LORD! I will praise you!*
2 SAMUEL 22:47 CEV

*Why, my soul, are you downcast? Why so disturbed within me? Put your hope in God, for I will yet praise him, my Savior and my God.*
PSALM 42:11 NIV

Imagine how God feels when one of His children praises Him simply for who He is, even when circumstances are far from perfect. Don't you suppose it feels like a tight hug around His neck? Adore Him today, for He is God.

*Father, You are the great I Am, faithful and good. I adore You. I choose to praise You whether You alter my circumstances or not. Amen.*

*Evening* ————————————————————————

*Make a joyful noise to the LORD, all the earth; break forth into joyous song and sing praises!*
PSALM 98:4 ESV

*Bless the LORD, O my soul: and all that is within me, bless his holy name. Bless the LORD, O my soul, and forget not all his benefits: who forgiveth all thine iniquities; who healeth all thy diseases; who redeemeth thy life from destruction; who crowneth thee with lovingkindness and tender mercies.*
PSALM 103:1–4 KJV

Often our adverse circumstances sabotage our efforts to praise God in every situation. The Bible admonishes us to praise God in every circumstance. To bless the Lord in all things is to receive God's blessings. Begin the practice of praise today!

*Heavenly Father, You are worthy of all my praise. I thank and praise You for my current circumstances, knowing that You are at work on my behalf. Amen.*

# DAY 143 – *Words*

> *The L*ORD *answered, "I can do anything!*
> *Watch and you'll see my words come true."*
> NUMBERS 11:23 CEV

> *Jesus answered and said to him, "If anyone loves Me, he will keep My word; and My*
> *Father will love him, and We will come to him and make Our home with him."*
> JOHN 14:23 NKJV

Words of anger, frustration, confusion, and jealously take away from the spirit of man, but words of affirmation and gestures of kindness add to every heart. Consider your words before you speak. Will you be adding to that person or taking away with what you are about to say?

> *God, help me think before I speak so that I can have*
> *a positive influence on others. Amen.*

> *You are my portion, L*ORD; *I have promised to obey your words.*
> PSALM 119:57 NIV

> *The L*ORD *detests the thoughts of the wicked, but gracious*
> *words are pure in his sight.*
> PROVERBS 15:26 NIV

The gift of speech is a valuable one. It also carries with it great responsibility. We are commanded to avoid silly or coarse speech, but to always use words that uplift and praise.

> *Let the words of my mouth always produce what is pleasing*
> *in Your sight, O Lord. Amen.*

# DAY 144 – *Judging*

*Don't judge others, and God won't judge you. Don't be hard on others,
and God won't be hard on you.*
LUKE 6:37 CEV

*"For you will be treated as you treat others. The standard you use in judging is the
standard by which you will be judged."*
MATTHEW 7:2 NLT

Leaping to judgment. Many churchgoers fall into this trap. Standing near
God, an unbeliever may come to faith—if the people in His congregation
are loving and nurturing. We need not judge a casual acquaintance's
spiritual life—God can do that. All we need to do is love, and He will bring
blessings.

*Thank You, Lord, that Your first reaction to me was love, not condemnation.
Turn my heart in love to all who don't yet know You. Amen.*

*"In due season God will judge everyone, both good and bad, for all their deeds."*
ECCLESIASTIES 3:17 NLT

*For You have maintained my right and my cause;
You sat on the throne judging in righteousness.*
PSALM 9:4 NKJV

Our Father God urges us not to judge others. After all, He doesn't look at
our outward appearance. He looks at the heart and judges by whether we
have a personal relationship with Him.

*God, please forgive me for the times that I have judged others. Help me develop a
gentle spirit that can share Your love and hope in a nonjudgmental way. Amen.*

# DAY 145 – *God's Word*

*Morning* ─────────────────────────────

God's word is alive and working and is sharper than a double-edged sword. It cuts all the way into us, where the soul and the spirit are joined, to the center of our joints and bones. And it judges the thoughts and feelings in our hearts.
HEBREWS 4:12 NCV

God's kingdom isn't just a lot of words. It is power.
1 CORINTHIANS 4:20 CEV

A journey through the holy scriptures can be a thrilling experience. To hear the stories of God and His people is a joy.

*Indeed, Lord, You are great. Teach me new things
every day from Your Word. Amen.*

*Evening* ─────────────────────────────

For we are not, like so many, peddlers of God's word, but as men of sincerity, as commissioned by God, in the sight of God we speak in Christ.
2 CORINTHIANS 2:17 ESV

Blessed is the one who reads the words of God's message, and blessed are the people who hear this message and do what is written in it.
REVELATION 1:3 NCV

The Bible is just another book if we do not heed its teachings and apply them to our lives. If we claim to be Christians, we must take the Word of God seriously.

*Father, I admit that many times I simply read the Bible as if it were a storybook.
Remind me to apply its truths and commands to my life. Amen.*

# DAY 146 – *Loving Others*

## *Morning*

*The LORD has told you, human, what is good; he has told you what he wants from you: to do what is right to other people, love being kind to others.*
MICAH 6:8 NCV

*The LORD watches over those who do what is right. But he hates sinful people and those who love to hurt others.*
PSALM 11:5 NIrV

Our duty as Christians is to look at all individuals as equals, brothers and sisters whom we can reach out to. When we look down on others, we do not just withdraw our reach to them, but to Christ as well.

*Dear Jesus, help me see Your Spirit in all people I meet. Teach me to love those around me as You would love them. Amen.*

## *Evening*

*If I could speak all the languages of earth and of angels, but didn't love others, I would only be a noisy gong or a clanging cymbal.*
1 CORINTHIANS 13:1 NLT

*Dear friends, let us love one another, for love comes from God. Everyone who loves has been born of God and knows God.*
1 JOHN 4:7 NIV

The way we show that we've received God's love is by loving one another. God gave no better example of love than when He sent His Son to live a life of sacrifice for our sakes. We ought to put the feelings and needs of others before our own as we imitate Christ and His sacrificial love.

*Dear God, thank You that true love comes from You. Let me show it to others. Amen.*

# DAY 147 – *Backsliding*

## *Morning*

*"They will never again pollute themselves with their idols and vile images and rebellion, for I will save them from their sinful apostasy. I will cleanse them. Then they will truly be my people, and I will be their God."*
Ezekiel 37:23 nlt

*Return, ye backsliding children, and I will heal your backslidings. Behold, we come unto thee; for thou art the Lord our God.*
Jeremiah 3:22 kjv

Though God calls His people to a lifetime commitment to Him, sin so easily distracts us from our goal. But even as we're pulled away from Him by the lures of Satan, God calls us to return to Him and love Him with an undivided heart.

*Father, so often I stray from You. Guide me back to Your side, that I might love You above all. Amen.*

## *Evening*

*"Your own wickedness will correct you, and your backslidings will rebuke you. Know therefore and see that it is an evil and bitter thing that you have forsaken the Lord your God, and the fear of Me is not in you," says the Lord God of hosts.*
Jeremiah 2:19 nkjv

*"If my people, who are called by my name, will humble themselves and pray and seek my face and turn from their wicked ways, then I will hear from heaven, and I will forgive their sin and will heal their land."*
2 Chronicles 7:14 niv

When we wander far from God, He waits for us continually, standing ready with open arms to receive us back to Him. It is important that we know that we can always go back to God. Always.

*Thank You, Father, for extending Your loving arms to me. If I should stray from Your path, guide me back into Your sight and care. Amen.*

# DAY 148 – *God's Provision*

*The young lions do lack, and suffer hunger: but they that seek
the LORD shall not want any good thing.*
PSALM 34:10 KJV

*He hath given meat unto them that fear him: he will ever be mindful of his covenant.*
PSALM 111:5 KJV

God's providence is revealed in both the big and small: the timing of a call
from a friend, the helping hand of a coworker, the cheer of a sunny day.
There are no coincidences—just a loving God revealing Himself to those
who watch for Him.

*Loving God, remind me to watch for You in daily life. Help me recognize You
in people, nature, and circumstances. Amen.*

*Evening* ——————————————————————

*As for the rich in this present age, charge them not to be haughty,
nor to set their hopes on the uncertainty of riches, but on God,
who richly provides us with everything to enjoy.*
1 TIMOTHY 6:17 ESV

*And these all, having obtained a good report through faith,
received not the promise: God having provided some better thing for us,
that they without us should not be made perfect.*
HEBREWS 11:39–40 KJV

God always provides for us. But He only gives us what we need for today,
not for tomorrow. He knows that we need those benefits like a daily vitamin.
By tomorrow, we may forget all that God has done for us.

*Father, You give us bread daily. We praise You for Your constant care. Amen.*

# DAY 149 - *Hospitality*

*Morning* ———————————————————

*Be not forgetful to entertain strangers: for thereby some
have entertained angels unawares.*
HEBREWS 13:2 KJV

*Use hospitality one to another without grudging.*
1 PETER 4:9 KJV

Living lavishly doesn't mean the same thing to everyone. But in most
cultures, lavish living best translates as hospitality. Welcoming next-door
neighbors, coworkers, family, and friends gives Christians the God-ordained
privilege to live lavishly by extending genuine hospitality.

*Father, thank You for all that You've given me. Thank You for the privilege of
encouraging others with something as simple as a genuine welcome. Amen.*

*Evening* ———————————————————

*For whosoever shall give you a cup of water to drink in my name,
because ye belong to Christ, verily I say unto you, he shall not lose his reward.*
MARK 9:41 KJV

*"But when you give a banquet, invite the poor, the crippled, the lame,
the blind, and you will be blessed. Although they cannot repay you,
you will be repaid at the resurrection of the righteous."*
LUKE 14:13–14 NIV

Expanding our guest lists requires us to consider others, not just ourselves.
Reaching out to someone who looks or seems a bit different than you
will feel good. There is certainly reward in heaven for believers who
demonstrate this type of kindness.

*Lord, remind me to reach out to others and be a friend
to all types of people. Amen.*

# DAY 150 – *Regret*

## *Morning*

*When the LORD blesses you with riches, you have nothing to regret.*
PROVERBS 10:22 CEV

*For now we see only a reflection as in a mirror; then we shall see face to face.*
*Now I know in part; then I shall know fully, even as I am fully known.*
1 CORINTHIANS 13:12 NIV

We don't have to look back with regret. We can live today with tomorrow in mind. We can gain spiritual wisdom by keeping our eyes on the Lord today. Let today count for eternity!

*Dear Lord, help me live today in light of eternity. May Your will*
*be done in my life today. Amen.*

## *Evening*

*Distress that drives us to God does that. It turns us around. It gets us back*
*in the way of salvation. We never regret that kind of pain. But those who let*
*distress drive them away from God are full of regrets,*
*end up on a deathbed of regrets.*
2 CORINTHIANS 7:10 MSG

*Even if I caused you sorrow by my letter, I do not regret it. Though I did*
*regret it—I see that my letter hurt you, but only for a little while.*
2 CORINTHIANS 7:8 NIV

There is nothing in our relationship with the Lord that can possibly cause regret or remorse. A good relationship with God is the path to true well-being, and it is a richness that nothing can destroy.

*O Lord, You have made my life so wonderful. I praise You for giving me*
*Your love so freely. Amen.*

# DAY 151 - *Creation*

*They gave up the truth about God for a lie, and they worshiped God's creation*
*instead of God, who will be praised forever. Amen.*
ROMANS 1:25 CEV

*"You will go out in joy and be led forth in peace; the mountains and hills will burst*
*into song before you, and all the trees of the field will clap their hands."*
ISAIAH 55:12 NIV

We don't have to be outdoorsmen to appreciate and be inspired by the
wonders of God's creation. Wildflowers that grow alongside highways or
the cloud formations that dance in the sky inspire us to praise God, the
Creator of all things. Nature declares the glory of the Lord.

*Lord, the beauty in Your creation inspires me to sing Your praises.*
*Praise be to God. Amen.*

*Oh, visit the earth, ask her to join the dance! Deck her out in spring showers,*
*fill the God-River with living water. Paint the wheat fields golden.*
*Creation was made for this!*
PSALM 65:9 MSG

*Therefore, if anyone is in Christ, he is a new creation.*
*The old has passed away; behold, the new has come.*
2 CORINTHIANS 5:17 ESV

Your delight in God's creation is a gift from Him and an offering of praise
back to Him for what He has done. To be thankful for the interest God gives
you in creation brings glory to Him and leads to knowing and appreciating
Him more.

*Great God of all creation, giver of all good things, thank You for the endless beauty*
*and wisdom in the world around me that speaks of You. Amen.*

# DAY 152 – *Spiritual Growth*

## *Morning*

> But there's far more to life for us. We're citizens of high heaven! We're waiting the
> arrival of the Savior, the Master, Jesus Christ, who will transform our earthy bodies
> into glorious bodies like his own. He'll make us beautiful and whole with the same
> powerful skill by which he is putting everything as it should be, under and around him.
> PHILIPPIANS 3:20–21 MSG

> You have now become a new person and are always learning more about Christ.
> You are being made more like Christ. He is the One Who made you.
> COLOSSIANS 3:10 NLV

No one likes to hear negative comments, whether they are true or not. It
takes a special person to seek criticism and suggestions for improvement.
The Bible says that we should be humble and always trying to improve
ourselves.

*O Lord, help me be open to the comments of others. Let me face my shortcomings
with dignity and open-mindedness. Amen.*

## *Evening*

> The more you grow like this, the more productive and useful you will be
> in your knowledge of our Lord Jesus Christ.
> 2 PETER 1:8 NLT

> I want to see you and share with you the same blessings that God's Spirit
> has given me. Then you will grow stronger in your faith.
> ROMANS 1:11 CEV

The apostle Paul advised that Christians examine themselves to see that
they are truly living the way Christ would want them to live. It is not always
easy. Happily, God supports us through our self-examination, and He loves
us no matter how good or bad we might find ourselves to be.

*Lord, help me ever work to change myself for the better. Amen.*

# DAY 153 – *Decision Making*

*Mark well that GOD doesn't miss a move you make; he's aware of every step you take. The shadow of your sin will overtake you; you'll find yourself stumbling all over yourself in the dark. Death is the reward of an undisciplined life; your foolish decisions trap you in a dead end.*
PROVERBS 5:21–23 MSG

*For as many as are led by the Spirit of God, these are sons of God.*
ROMANS 8:14 NKJV

God has the whole world in His hands, but daily choices belong to you. Choose to live in His will, making decisions based on His direction. Knowing His will comes from a personal relationship and from time spent with Him in prayer and in the Word.

*Heavenly Father, I choose Your dream, Your destiny for my life. Help me make the right choices for my life as I follow You. Amen.*

*You guide me with your counsel, and afterward you will take me into glory.*
PSALM 73:24 NIV

*And the peace of God, which passeth all understanding, shall keep your hearts and minds through Christ Jesus.*
PHILIPPIANS 4:7 KJV

If you're facing a major decision, remember these words of wisdom: follow after peace. The precious peace of God will put your heart and mind in a state of tranquility and contentment.

*Dear God, help me always follow after peace in my decisions. Amen.*

# DAY 154 - *Temptation*

*Brethren, even if anyone is caught in any trespass, you who are spiritual,*
*restore such a one in a spirit of gentleness; each one looking to yourself,*
*so that you too will not be tempted.*
GALATIANS 6:1 NASB

*Run from temptations that capture young people. Always do the right thing.*
*Be faithful, loving, and easy to get along with.*
*Worship with people whose hearts are pure.*
2 TIMOTHY 2:22 CEV

Sin can quickly get a foothold in our lives. Beware of your temptations.
Know your areas of vulnerability and avoid them. Draw close to the Lord.
Allow Him to satisfy your deepest longings. When we cling to good, evil
loses its grip.

*Dear Lord, help me avoid temptation. May I draw close to You so I can cling*
*to good and avoid evil in my life. Amen.*

*For this reason, when I could no longer endure it, I sent to know your faith,*
*lest by some means the tempter had tempted you, and our labor might be in vain.*
1 THESSALONIANS 3:5 NKJV

*Submit yourselves therefore to God. Resist the devil, and he will flee from you.*
JAMES 4:7 KJV

The antidrug slogan "Just say no" sounds easy. Yet if that is the case, why
are so many people addicted to drugs? For the same reason we struggle
with sin. Temptation is great. We are weak. An adversary is out to destroy
us, but our hearts will be encouraged as we focus on greater truth.

*Lord, thank You for the truth of Your Word. Help me resist*
*the devil by embracing You. Amen.*

# DAY 155 – *Guilt*

## *Morning*

*For if our heart condemn us, God is greater than our heart, and knoweth all things.*
1 JOHN 3:20 KJV

*So I confessed my sins and told them all to you. I said, "I'll tell the LORD
each one of my sins." Then you forgave me and took away my guilt.*
PSALM 32:5 CEV

The apostle Paul's example shows the effect a clear conscience can have
in the life of a believer. Boldness! Boldness to live for Christ. Obedience,
readily confessing sin, and total reliance on God to replace that sin with
righteous living help create a clear conscience.

*Holy Spirit, reveal to me my sin, cleanse me, and empower me to walk obediently
with a clear conscience that I might live boldly and courageously for You. Amen.*

## *Evening*

*For I will be merciful to their unrighteousness, and their sins and their
iniquities will I remember no more.*
HEBREWS 8:12 KJV

*Do not rejoice over me, my enemy; when I fall, I will arise;
when I sit in darkness, the LORD will be a light to me.*
MICAH 7:8 NKJV

God has made all things new through your salvation. You may be
challenged with the consequences that remain from past life choices, but
God is busy turning past mistakes into future successes. The enemy of your
soul wants you to dwell on the past. But God wants you to look forward to a
new harvest of goodness and mercy.

*Lord, help me to not focus on the past but to look to You
every step of the way. Amen.*

# DAY 156 – *Dating and Marriage*

*Do not be unequally yoked together with unbelievers. For what fellowship has righteousness with lawlessness? And what communion has light with darkness?*
2 CORINTHIANS 6:14 NKJV

*"But those who are considered worthy to attain to that age and to the resurrection from the dead neither marry nor are given in marriage."*
LUKE 20:35 ESV

Loving families are part of God's earthly plan. But whether we are single or wed, our ultimate goal remains the same: to serve our Lord, not just a spouse. Married or single, you can do God's will. Just love Him best. That's all He asks.

*Lord, You love me just as I am. Make my life a witness to You. Amen.*

*Marriage should be honored by all, and the marriage bed kept pure, for God will judge the adulterer and all the sexually immoral.*
HEBREWS 13:4 NIV

*Run from anything that stimulates youthful lusts. Instead, pursue righteous living, faithfulness, love, and peace. Enjoy the companionship of those who call on the Lord with pure hearts.*
2 TIMOTHY 2:22 NLT

Of course there was nothing like dating in the biblical era. Marriages were generally arranged, and couples often had little contact beforehand. But God's standard of sexual purity is unmistakable in both the Old and New Testaments.

*Lord God, help me remain true to Your standards. Amen.*

# DAY 157 – *Pride*

*How blessed is the man who has made the L*ORD *his trust, and has not
turned to the proud, nor to those who lapse into falsehood.*
PSALM 40:4 NASB

*Believers in humble circumstances ought to take pride in their high position.
But the rich should take pride in their humiliation—since they
will pass away like a wild flower.*
JAMES 1:9–10 NIV

Pride is a dangerous sin that separates us from our all-powerful God. When
we focus on our own frail "power," we cannot truly see Him as Lord.

*Lord, when I turn my attention inward, I lose sight of who You want me to be.
Redirect my focus, please. Amen.*

*Finishing is better than starting. Patience is better than pride.*
ECCLESIASTES 7:8 NLT

*Where there is strife, there is pride, but wisdom is found in those who take advice.*
PROVERBS 13:10 NIV

Our faith in Christ is not to be a source of bragging and pride, but a source
of comfort and service. Being Christians doesn't make us better than other
people, just better off.

*Creator God, all that I am, and all that I can be, is a gift from You, and nothing that
I have done on my own. Forgive my foolish pride. Amen.*

# DAY 158 – *Adversity*

*So we may boldly say: "The LORD is my helper; I will not fear.*
*What can man do to me?"*
HEBREWS 13:6 NKJV

*Anyone who meets a testing challenge head-on and manages to stick it out is mighty*
*fortunate. For such persons loyally in love with God, the reward is life and more life.*
JAMES 1:12 MSG

Just because we have faith, hope, and trust in the Lord does not mean that
life will be easy. Instead, God's love for us means that He will provide a way
through, not around, adversity, resulting in His greater glory.

*Father God, I know that no matter how troubled my life is, You can provide me a*
*way to persevere. Help me trust Your guidance and love. Amen.*

*"If we are thrown into the blazing furnace, the God we serve is able to deliver us*
*from it, and he will deliver us from Your Majesty's hand."*
DANIEL 3:17 NIV

*The wall was finished—just fifty-two days after we had begun. When our enemies*
*and the surrounding nations heard about it, they were frightened and humiliated.*
*They realized this work had been done with the help of our God.*
NEHEMIAH 6:15–16 NLT

Too often we think that our faith should keep us out of the furnace: a health
crisis, financial worries, troubling situations with our family. But being in the
furnace doesn't mean that God has abandoned us. He will be right there in
the furnace with you.

*Lord God, thank You that I can count on You to be with me in every circumstance.*
*Though evil threatens, You hold me in Your loving hands. Amen.*

# DAY 159 – *Trials*

*Your faith will be like gold that has been tested in a fire. And these trials will prove that your faith is worth much more than gold that can be destroyed. They will show that you will be given praise and honor and glory when Jesus Christ returns.*
1 PETER 1:7 CEV

*These things I have spoken unto you, that in me ye might have peace. In the world ye shall have tribulation: but be of good cheer; I have overcome the world.*
JOHN 16:33 KJV

Expect trouble, but refuse to let it defeat you. Trials strengthen our faith and our character. No one gets excited about a trial, yet we can be assured that God is still in control even when trouble comes our way.

*Lord Jesus, be my strength as I face trouble in this life. Walk with me. Hold my hand. Assure me that in my weakness, You are strong. Amen.*

 *Evening* ——————————————

*You obeyed my message and endured. So I will protect you from the time of testing that everyone in all the world must go through.*
REVELATION 3:10 CEV

*Then all his brothers, sisters, and former friends came and feasted with him in his home. And they consoled him and comforted him because of all the trials the LORD had brought against him.*
JOB 42:11 NLT

If you're in a season of emotional testing—of heartbreak or disappointment— don't allow your heart to become hardened. Do your best to pass the test, even if it's a hard one. Let God do the work He wants to do in you.

*Lord, sometimes I feel like my heart is being tested by circumstances, relationship, or even by You. Help me make it through this testing period without falling apart, I pray. Amen.*

## *Morning*

A froward man soweth strife: and a whisperer separateth chief friends.
PROVERBS 16:28 KJV

Do not pay attention to every word people say, or you may hear your servant cursing you—for you know in your heart that many times you yourself have cursed others.
ECCLESIASTES 7:21–22 NIV

In an ideal world, no one would speak badly of us, and we would never gossip about someone else. But in the real world, it happens. The best defense against hurt feelings is an intentional ignorance. The next time you overhear your name, keep walking.

*Lord, teach me to put a guard on both my lips and my ears. Close my ears to gossip that swirls around me. Amen.*

## *Evening*

Where no wood is, there the fire goeth out: so where there is no talebearer, the strife ceaseth. As coals are to burning coals, and wood to fire; so is a contentious man to kindle strife.
PROVERBS 26:20–21 KJV

If anyone thinks himself to be religious, and yet does not bridle his tongue but deceives his own heart, this man's religion is worthless.
JAMES 1:26 NASB

When you see the warning signs of gossip, do not associate yourself with the situation or the person(s), lest you be drawn in by the allure of juicy information. Do not become part of a subgroup that makes its entertainment the downgrading of others.

*O Lord, help me bridle my tongue and associate with those who bridle theirs. Amen.*

# DAY 161 – *Friendship*

## *Morning*

> When Job prayed for his friends, the LORD restored his fortunes.
> In fact, the LORD gave him twice as much as before!
> JOB 42:10 NLT

> There are "friends" who destroy each other, but a real friend
> sticks closer than a brother.
> PROVERBS 18:24 NLT

Jesus sticks close by us at our most undesirable, least lovable moments. We can tell Him anything and He understands. Like a true friend, Jesus enhances our good qualities and, with a breath of kindness, blows the rest away.

*Dear Jesus, thank You for loving me even when I fail, encouraging me in my discouragement, and sticking close to me during tough times.*
*May I be as good a friend as You are. Amen.*

## *Evening*

> Dear friends, let us love one another, for love comes from God.
> Everyone who loves has been born of God and knows God.
> 1 JOHN 4:7 NIV

> And pray in the Spirit on all occasions with all kinds of prayers and requests.
> With this in mind, be alert and always keep on praying for all the Lord's people.
> EPHESIANS 6:18 NIV

Real power is available when friends get together for fellowship and prayer, because Christ Himself is right there with them. Along with gaining another's insight and perspective, anytime we share a burden with a friend, our load instantly becomes lighter.

*Heavenly Father, thank You for faithful friends, and thank You for Jesus, the most faithful friend of all. Amen.*

# DAY 162 – *Spiritual Refreshment*

*Morning*  ———————————————————————

> *Though I walk in the midst of trouble, thou wilt revive me.*
> PSALM 138:7 KJV

> *You're my place of quiet retreat; I wait for your Word to renew me.*
> PSALM 119:114 MSG

There are many times when we find ourselves so starved spiritually that we take and take and take but give little back. God understands that, and He knows that by feeding us when we hunger, we are being strengthened to give to others later on.

> *Forgive me for the times when I take without offering anything in return. Amen.*

*Evening* ———————————————————————

> *They that dwell under his shadow shall return; they shall revive as*
> *the corn, and grow as the vine.*
> HOSEA 14:7 KJV

> *Anyone who renews others will be renewed.*
> PROVERBS 11:25 NIrV

God renews us and puts purpose into our being. We are spiritual batteries that constantly need recharged. We cannot be recharged apart from the power source: Jesus Christ.

> *Energize my life with the power of Your Holy Spirit, Lord.*
> *Grant that I might live life fully, not halfway. Amen.*

# DAY 163 – *Guidance*

*Let the wise hear and increase in learning, and the one who
understands obtain guidance.*
PROVERBS 1:5 ESV

*May the Lord direct your hearts into the love of God and into
the steadfastness of Christ.*
2 THESSALONIANS 3:5 NASB

Even before Jesus sent His Holy Spirit to dwell in believers, God used a
variety of means to guide His people. Praise be to God for giving us His
Spirit, who resides in us so that we need never lose our direction as we
navigate our way through life.

*Thank You, Jesus, for sending Your Holy Spirit
to lead me in the right direction. Amen.*

*The Spirit of the LORD will rest upon that king. The Spirit will give him
wisdom and understanding, guidance and power. The Spirit will teach
him to know and respect the LORD.*
ISAIAH 11:2 NCV

*"Woe to him who says to wood, 'Come to life!' Or to lifeless stone, 'Wake up!'
Can it give guidance? It is covered with gold and silver; there is no breath in it."*
HABAKKUK 2:19 NIV

Jesus, knowing that He needed guidance from His Father, constantly
sought His will by praying and asking for it. Instead of trying to find His own
way through the day, Jesus fully depended on directions from above and
actively pursued them.

*Jesus, please show me the way to go and lead me in it.
Help me seek Your guidance always. Amen.*

# DAY 164 - *Eternity*

*"My sheep hear My voice, and I know them, and they follow Me.
And I give them eternal life, and they shall never perish;
neither shall anyone snatch them out of My hand."*
JOHN 10:27–28 NKJV

*So just as sin ruled over all people and brought them to death, now God's wonderful
grace rules instead, giving us right standing with God and resulting
in eternal life through Jesus Christ our Lord.*
ROMANS 5:21 NLT

Jesus came to give us eternal life in heaven as well as abundant life
on earth. As we allow His Word to speak to our hearts, we grow in our
relationship with Him and assurance of eternal life to come.

*Dear Lord, help me pursue my relationship with You now. May I know You more
with each passing day so that I will be excited when we meet face-to-face. Amen.*

*"And everyone who has left houses or brothers or sisters or father or mother
or wife or children or lands, for My name's sake,
shall receive a hundredfold, and inherit eternal life."*
MATTHEW 19:29 NKJV

*For the wages of sin is death, but the gift of God is
eternal life in Christ Jesus our Lord.*
ROMANS 6:23 NKJV

Though God does not tell us all the details about eternity, He provides us
with the road map to get there. Though we have earned death through sin,
in Jesus we are brought to new, eternal life.

*God, thank You for the hope of eternity with You.
Thank You for providing a way to heaven. Amen.*

# DAY 165 - *Generosity*

*The generous soul will be made rich, and he who waters will also be watered himself.*
PROVERBS 11:25 NKJV

*The generous will themselves be blessed, for they share their food with the poor.*
PROVERBS 22:9 NIV

Christ asks each one of us where it is we keep our treasure. Is it on earth or is it in heaven? Surely, God wants every person to enjoy life and to share in good times, but He does not find joy in the celebration of a few when many suffer.

*O heavenly Father, open my eyes to the needs of those around me.*
*Help me share the blessings that I have been given. Amen.*

## *Evening*

*Each of you should give what you have decided in your heart to give,*
*not reluctantly or under compulsion, for God loves a cheerful giver.*
2 CORINTHIANS 9:7 NIV

*"Give, and it will be given to you. They will pour into your lap a good*
*measure—pressed down, shaken together, and running over. For by*
*your standard of measure it will be measured to you in return."*
LUKE 6:38 NASB

The Bible says that greed is keeping what we don't need. God rejoices in the life of a giver. With His help and guidance, we all can learn to be more giving.

*Lord, destroy the spirit of selfishness in my heart,*
*and teach me 7to give as You would give. Amen.*

# DAY 166 – *God's Will*

*And do not be conformed to this world, but be transformed by the renewing of your mind, so that you may prove what the will of God is, that which is good and acceptable and perfect.*
ROMANS 12:2 NASB

*I urge, then, first of all, that petitions, prayers, intercession and thanksgiving be made for all people—for kings and all those in authority, that we may live peaceful and quiet lives in all godliness and holiness. This is good, and pleases God our Savior, who wants all people to be saved and to come to a knowledge of the truth.*
1 TIMOTHY 2:1–4 NIV

Embracing God's love enables us to submit to His will. God not only loves us immensely, but He desires to bless us abundantly. However, from our human perspective, those spiritual blessings may be disguised. That is why we must cling to truth. We must believe that His will is perfect.

*Dear Lord, may I rest secure in Your unconditional love. Enable me to trust You more. May I desire that Your will be done in my life. Amen.*

*Be very careful, then, how you live—not as unwise but as wise, making the most of every opportunity, because the days are evil. Therefore do not be foolish, but understand what the Lord's will is.*
EPHESIANS 5:15–17 NIV

*For it is God's will that by doing good you should silence the ignorant talk of foolish people.*
1 PETER 2:15 NIV

Knowing God's will is not a matter of memorizing a few scripture verses, but of learning and living in His Word.

*Father, keep my life focused on You, that I may live by Your will. Amen.*

# DAY 167 – *Encouragement*

## *Morning*

May our Lord Jesus Christ himself and God our Father encourage you and
strengthen you in every good thing you do and say. God loved us, and through his
grace he gave us a good hope and encouragement that continues forever.
2 Thessalonians 2:16–17 ncv

And let us consider how we may spur one another on toward love and good deeds.
Hebrews 10:24 niv

We all need encouragement, but we all must learn to give encouragement
as well. We also must rely on our brothers and sisters; if we encourage
them, we believe that they, in turn, will encourage us.

*Lord, please help me encourage others toward love and good deeds. Please also
raise up brothers and sisters who will encourage me. Amen.*

## *Evening*

I am the Lord, the one who encourages you. Why are you afraid
of mere humans? They dry up and die like grass.
Isaiah 51:12 cev

You, Lord, hear the desire of the afflicted; you encourage them,
and you listen to their cry.
Psalm 10:17 niv

Encouragement is a wonderful gift. Simple gestures mean so much to those
around us. We don't have to make big, splashy scenes to give someone a
boost. Our smile can lift someone who is discouraged.

*Jesus, thank You for being an example of how to encourage and refresh others.
Help me see their need and be willing to reach out. Amen.*

# DAY 168 - *Comfort*

*Christ encourages you, and his love comforts you. God's Spirit unites you,*
*and you are concerned for others.*
PHILIPPIANS 2:1 CEV

*And God shall wipe away all tears from their eyes; and there shall be no more death,*
*neither sorrow, nor crying, neither shall there be any more pain:*
*for the former things are passed away.*
REVELATION 21:4 KJV

The Holy Spirit is often called the Comforter because He comes alongside
us and helps us live out our daily faith. But throughout scripture, God also
promises to comfort those who suffer affliction and hardship. We are not
alone in the tough moments of our lives!

*Lord, be with me this day. I need to feel You are near me, my Comforter. Amen.*

*Evening* ————————————————————

*I will not leave you comfortless: I will come to you.*
JOHN 14:18 KJV

*But the Comforter, which is the Holy Ghost, whom the Father will send in my name,*
*he shall teach you all things, and bring all things to your remembrance,*
*whatsoever I have said unto you.*
JOHN 14:26 KJV

There is a difference between receiving comfort and being comfortable.
God's comfort comes to those who suffer for their faith, not those who are
resting on their laurels.

*Father, never let me become too comfortable in my faith. Challenge me;*
*help me grow, I pray. Amen.*

# DAY 169 – *Spiritual Gifts*

## *Morning*

For as we have many members in one body, but all the members do not have
the same function, so we, being many, are one body in Christ, and individually
members of one another. Having then gifts differing according to the
grace that is given to us, let us use them.
ROMANS 12:4–6 NKJV

This is why I remind you to fan into flames the spiritual gift
God gave you when I laid my hands on you.
2 TIMOTHY 1:6 NLT

We need to awaken our latent gifts. Left unused, they cool down and lay
dormant and neglected. Prayerfully seek ways to share your talents with
those around you. Joy is yours when your gifts are used, and they are a
blessing for those you have given to.

*Father, show me creative ways to use my gifts. Help me be a good steward of the gifts
You have given me by using them for others, igniting them to live for You. Amen.*

## *Evening*

And God confirmed the message by giving signs and wonders and various
miracles and gifts of the Holy Spirit whenever he chose.
HEBREWS 2:4 NLT

Pursue love, and earnestly desire the spiritual gifts, especially that you may prophesy.
1 CORINTHIANS 14:1 ESV

Whether we are eight or eighty, it is never too late to surrender our gifts to
God. The wise trust that God will help them find the time and manner in
which to use their talents for His glory.

*Dear Lord, I surrender my gifts to You and pray for direction in when and how to use
those gifts to touch my world. Amen.*

# DAY 170 - *Harmony*

*Now make me completely happy! Live in harmony by showing love for each other.
Be united in what you think, as if you were only one person.*
PHILIPPIANS 2:2 CEV

*Live in harmony with one another. Do not be haughty, but associate with
the lowly. Never be wise in your own sight.*
ROMANS 12:16 ESV

Harmony with others isn't always easy. Differences can chafe at patience.
A willed choice of acting in love is needed instead of a rash response that
may feel good at the time but further divide. Only when peace is restored
can believers experience how good and pleasant it is to dwell in unity.

*Prince of Peace, help me make unity my focus. Enable me to make every
effort to preserve oneness with fellow believers. Then with one heart
and one mouth we can glorify You. Amen.*

*Evening* ———————————————————————

*How good and pleasant it is when God's people live together in unity!*
PSALM 133:1 NIV

*Harmony is as refreshing as the dew from Mount Hermon that falls on the mountains
of Zion. And there the LORD has pronounced his blessing, even life everlasting.*
PSALM 133:3 NLT

God loves harmony. Together, we can become a melody of beauty and
praise. We can become the rhythm of creation by affirming who God
created us to be.

*If there is any discordance in my life, Lord, remove it from me.
I want my life to be harmonious and beautiful. Amen.*

# DAY 171 - *Creation*

*Morning* ———————————————————————

*"I paid a huge price for you. . . That's how much you mean to me!*
*That's how much I love you! I'd sell off the whole world to get you back,*
*trade the creation just for you."*
ISAIAH 43:3–4 MSG

*Meanwhile, creation is confused, but not because it wants to be confused.*
*God made it this way in the hope that creation would be set free from decay*
*and would share in the glorious freedom of his children.*
ROMANS 8:20–21 CEV

We have been given life so that we may enjoy it. It is a gift from God. When
we pursue God, and a deeper knowledge of His will, we are seeking a
deeper understanding of all creation.

*Through Your wisdom, Lord, I can hope to come to know the fullness of life*
*and the beauty of Your creation. I praise You in Your greatness, O Father. Amen.*

*Evening* ———————————————————————

*The One who came down is the same as the One who went up higher*
*than all the heavens. He did it in order to fill all of creation.*
EPHESIANS 4:10 NIrV

*What a wildly wonderful world, GOD! You made it all, with Wisdom at your side,*
*made earth overflow with your wonderful creations.*
PSALM 104:24 MSG

There is nothing greater that anyone can desire than to see this world
of ours through the eyes of the Creator. In God's creation we can catch
glimpses of Him.

*O Lord, I want to learn to enjoy life as fully as I can. Open my eyes to see*
*anew with the eyes of Your divine love. Amen.*

# DAY 172 – *Worry*

## *Morning*

You will rest safe and secure, filled with hope and emptied of worry.
JOB 11:18 CEV

"And why do you worry about clothes? See how the flowers of the field grow.
They do not labor or spin. Yet I tell you that not even Solomon in all
his splendor was dressed like one of these."
MATTHEW 6:28–29 NIV

God knows that worries can easily overwhelm us. That's why He tells us not
to worry and encourages us to trust in Him. When our concerns are in His
hands, they are in the right place.

*Father, this life provides an endless source of worry. Thank You for being
the source of endless peace. I rest in Your care. Amen.*

## *Evening*

"Steep your life in God-reality, God-initiative, God-provisions. Don't worry about
missing out. You'll find all your everyday human concerns will be met."
MATTHEW 6:33 MSG

"But blessed is the man who trusts me, GOD, the woman who sticks with GOD.
They're like trees replanted in Eden, putting down roots near the rivers—never a
worry through the hottest of summers, never dropping a leaf, serene and calm through
droughts, bearing fresh fruit every season."
JEREMIAH 17:7–8 MSG

When we thrust ourselves into panic and fear, it is good to know that we
can turn to the Lord, and He will be faithful to comfort us. Open yourself to
His peace, and you will find new serenity.

*I let my mind get carried away sometimes, Lord. I need Your wisdom as an anchor
when I set myself adrift in worry and fear. Be my salvation, Father. Amen.*

# DAY 173 - *God's Protection*

*Morning* —————————————————————

*And I looked, and arose and said to the nobles, to the leaders, and to the rest of the
people, "Do not be afraid of them. Remember the Lord, great and awesome, and
fight for your brethren, your sons, your daughters, your wives, and your houses."*
NEHEMIAH 4:14 NKJV

*But Moses told the people, "Don't be afraid. Just stand still and watch the LORD
rescue you today. The Egyptians you see today will never be seen again.
The LORD himself will fight for you. Just stay calm."*
EXODUS 14:13–14 NLT

Rest easy in the knowledge that God guides your steps. He will protect
those who put their trust in Him.

*I need Your guiding love, almighty God. Thank You for Your
continual protection. Amen.*

*Evening* —————————————————————

*He saved me from my powerful enemies, from those who hated me,
because they were too strong for me.*
PSALM 18:17 NCV

*I will both lay me down in peace, and sleep: for thou, LORD,
only makest me dwell in safety.*
PSALM 4:8 KJV

The Lord is never far from us. Once we put our trust in Him, He is true to
protect and defend us. Though life may get stormy and rough, the Lord is
there to calm the waters and get us through safely.

*Dear Lord, be with me as I face the challenges of each new day.
Protect me from those things that can harm me. Stay close to me,
for I know of no greater strength than Yours. Amen.*

# DAY 174 – *Truth*

*Blessed is the man to whom the L*ORD *does not impute iniquity,*
*and in whose spirit there is no deceit.*
PSALM 32:2 NKJV

*God is not a man, that he should lie; neither the son of man, that he should repent:*
*hath he said, and shall he not do it? or hath he spoken, and shall he not make it good?*
NUMBERS 23:19 KJV

Unlike the words of human beings, God's words can be trusted. What a comfort to know He who has promised us salvation, strength for daily living, and a glorious future means what He says!

*Holy Lord, in a day when truth is hard to find, You won't change*
*Your mind about me. Thank You! Amen.*

*Honesty and fairness will be his royal robes.*
ISAIAH 11:5 CEV

*Yet you desired faithfulness even in the womb; you taught me*
*wisdom in that secret place.*
PSALM 51:6 NIV

Truth sets us free. New levels of communion with God are the result of an honest heart, deepening your walk with your Creator. Vibrancy and authentic joy bubble from within a heart that is clean, open, and entwined with God.

*Gracious Savior, strip me of any pretenses that hinder genuine communion*
*with You. Let my thoughts and prayers be truthful and real,*
*that we can walk in oneness. Amen.*

# DAY 175 – *God's Presence*

So now we have a high priest who perfectly fits our needs:
completely holy, uncompromised by sin, with authority extending as high
as God's presence in heaven itself.
HEBREWS 7:26 MSG

"I am with you and will watch over you wherever you go, and I will bring you back
to this land. I will not leave you until I have done what I have promised you."
GENESIS 28:15 NIV

Only when we realize that God is with us every moment of every day are we
compelled to live good and upright lives. We must admit our weakness and
that we need God to motivate us when we will not motivate ourselves to
right living.

*Guide my steps, O Lord, that I might always, in every way,
be found pleasing in Your sight. Amen.*

"The LORD our God be with us, as he was with our fathers.
May he not leave us or forsake us."
1 KINGS 8:57 ESV

God's bright presence will be evident in everything through Jesus, and he'll
get all the credit as the One mighty in everything—encores to the end of time.
1 PETER 4:11 MSG

All too often we miss God in our everyday lives. From the simple fact of our
existence, to the miracle of the life we have been given, to the talents we
each possess, we should always be aware of God's presence in our lives and
our world.

*Lord God, help me see You in the everyday. You are continually
at my side. Thank You! Amen.*

# DAY 176 – *Doubt*

*My friends, watch out! Don't let evil thoughts or doubts make
any of you turn from the living God.*
HEBREWS 3:12 CEV

*Jesus said unto him, If thou canst believe, all things are possible to him that believeth.*
MARK 9:23 KJV

Jesus Christ came that we might have a way to remove all doubt that God
works all things for good. Christ assured us that God indeed watches over
all people and that He reigns wisely and with justice.

*O Lord of creation and love, You hear even my most quiet cry.
Answer my every doubt with "I am." Amen.*

*Now when He rose early on the first day of the week, He appeared first to Mary
Magdalene, out of whom He had cast seven demons. She went and told those
who had been with Him, as they mourned and wept. And when they heard
that He was alive and had been seen by her, they did not believe.*
MARK 16:9–11 NKJV

*Later Jesus appeared to the Eleven as they were eating. He spoke firmly
to them because they had no faith. They would not believe those who
had seen him after he rose from the dead.*
MARK 16:14 NIrV

If we will only open our hearts to Christ, we will no more need to doubt and
question. We may rest in the knowledge that Christ is Lord and that God is
with us all the time.

*Almighty God, help me trust in Your truth and reality. You reign!
And I have no need to fear. Amen.*

## *Morning*

*"Do you understand how he moves the clouds with wonderful perfection and skill?"*
JOB 37:16 NLT

*Nothing is completely perfect, except your teachings. I deeply love your Law!*
*I think about it all day.*
PSALM 119:96–97 CEV

Perfection is not so perfect. Nothing is. We live in a flawed world no matter how much we work and strive. To love God's life-giving words is the closest we will ever come to achieving perfection here on earth.

*Dear Lord, nothing is as important as following You. Please remind me of that when my quest for perfection overwhelms me. Amen.*

## *Evening*

*This work must continue until we are all joined together in the same faith and in the same knowledge of the Son of God. We must become like a mature person, growing until we become like Christ and have his perfection.*
EPHESIANS 4:13 NCV

*Not that I have already obtained all this, or have already arrived at my goal, but I press on to take hold of that for which Christ Jesus took hold of me.*
PHILIPPIANS 3:12 NIV

Perfectionism. No matter how hard we work, we never feel successful. This type of thinking can be debilitating. And if we fail in one area, we're likely to consider ourselves dismal failures. That is an accurate picture of what life was like under Old Testament law. But grace frees us from the bondage of perfection.

*Father, thank You that I can be done with being a perfectionist since I am under grace. Amen.*

# DAY 178 - *Children*

*Morning*

> *Children's children are the crown of old men; and the glory*
> *of children are their fathers.*
> PROVERBS 17:6 KJV

> *For the grace of God that bringeth salvation hath appeared to all men,*
> *teaching us that, denying ungodliness and worldly lusts, we should*
> *live soberly, righteously, and godly, in this present world.*
> TITUS 2:11–12 KJV

Godliness comes from within, from a deep desire to please and obey our Lord. It is developed in children by careful, consistent training. Children must learn to obey parents, the first time, every time, so that their hearts are ready to obey Christ.

*Father, give me the strength to do the hard JOB of consistently training my children in obedience. Let me give them a pattern of obedience to follow. Amen.*

*Evening*

> *The just man walketh in his integrity: his children are blessed after him.*
> PROVERBS 20:7 KJV

> *For I know him, that he will command his children and his household after him,*
> *and they shall keep the way of the LORD, to do justice and judgment;*
> *that the LORD may bring upon Abraham that which he hath spoken of him.*
> GENESIS 18:19 KJV

We watch over the children in our lives. Two thousand years ago God watched over His Son, protected Him, and made His will plain. Today He also watches over His adopted children. He'll keep you—and your children—safe.

*Thank You, Lord, for watching over Your children—no matter what age. Amen.*

# DAY 179 – *Salvation*

*But I trust in your unfailing love; my heart rejoices in your salvation.*
PSALM 13:5 NIV

*For I am not ashamed of the gospel, for it is the power of God for salvation to everyone who believes, to the Jew first and also to the Greek.*
ROMANS 1:16 ESV

Like a lighthouse, true light sent out through the clouds and darkness, a voice speaking the truth of Christ can save lives.

*Lord, let me reflect Your divine light, clearing away the fog and helping others come into the safety of Your love. Amen.*

*Evening* —————————————————————

*And you also were included in Christ when you heard the message of truth, the gospel of your salvation. When you believed, you were marked in him with a seal, the promised Holy Spirit, who is a deposit guaranteeing our inheritance until the redemption of those who are God's possession—to the praise of his glory.*
EPHESIANS 1:13–14 NIV

*Jesus told him, "I am the way, the truth, and the life. No one can come to the Father except through me."*
JOHN 14:6 NLT

There's only one way to the Father—through Jesus Christ. Since the dawn of time, humans have sought eagerly after other paths to God, but His Word spells it out plainly: Jesus is the Way, the Truth, and the Life. He is our salvation.

*Father, forgive me for seeking You in ways other than through Jesus. Give me strength to share this fact with people who are looking for answers in the wrong places. Amen.*

# DAY 180 – *Stillness*

*Morning*

*Meditate in your heart upon your bed, and be still.*
PSALM 4:4 NASB

*He says, "Be still, and know that I am God; I will be exalted among the nations,
I will be exalted in the earth."*
PSALM 46:10 NIV

Stillness allows us to dwell on God's sovereignty, His goodness, and His deep
love for us. He wants us to remember that He is God and that He is in control,
regardless of our circumstances. Be still. . .and know that He is God.

*God, so often I do all the talking. Quiet me before You now.
Speak to my heart, I pray. Amen.*

*Evening*

*"The LORD will fight for you. Just be still."*
EXODUS 14:14 NIrV

*And He got up and rebuked the wind and said to the sea, "Hush, be still."
And the wind died down and it became perfectly calm.*
MARK 4:39 NASB

We have lost the art of being still. Everything is rush, rush, rush. Only
through the still times in our lives can we hope for God to break through to
help us make sense of our lives. Be still, and know that God is there.

*The day closes in on me, Lord, and I feel myself buried beneath a heavy layer of
noise and activity. Break me free of the bondage of commotion.
Bless me with quiet and rest. Amen.*

# DAY 181 – *Obedience*

*For as by the one man's disobedience the many were made sinners,*
*so by the one man's obedience the many will be made righteous.*
ROMANS 5:19 ESV

*But Samuel answered, "What pleases the LORD more: burnt offerings*
*and sacrifices or obedience to his voice? It is better to obey than to sacrifice.*
*It is better to listen to God than to offer the fat of sheep."*
1 SAMUEL 15:22 NCV

Obedience is a long walk in the same direction. Flirtation with sin is like
wandering in aimless circles. Each public or private action, no matter how
large or small, plays a key role in moving you either toward or away from
harmony in your relationship with God.

*O Lord, help me live a life of integrity and moral purity, a no-compromise*
*lifestyle in obedience to You. Amen.*

*Do you not know that when you present yourselves to someone as slaves for*
*obedience, you are slaves of the one whom you obey, either of sin resulting*
*in death, or of obedience resulting in righteousness?*
ROMANS 6:16 NASB

*The LORD came and stood there, calling as at the other times, "Samuel! Samuel!"*
*Then Samuel said, "Speak, for your servant is listening."*
1 SAMUEL 3:10 NIV

The Lord most often communicates to servant hearts that are ready to
listen—hearts committed to obedience. Servant hearts trust that God's
ways are best even when they might be difficult.

*Dear Lord, may I have a servant's heart that is committed to obedience.*
*Speak to my heart, Lord. Amen.*

# DAY 182 – *Trust*

*Morning*

*The instructions of the LORD are perfect, reviving the soul. The decrees of the LORD are trustworthy, making wise the simple.*
PSALM 19:7 NLT

*And we know that all things work together for good to them that love God, to them who are the called according to his purpose.*
ROMANS 8:28 KJV

God can and does use all things in our lives for His good purpose. It is easy to trust God when things are going well. And when we choose to trust Him in uncertain times, we receive a peace that gives us hope that sustains us. We are not disappointed, because God always keeps His promises. Our response is to trust Him.

*Lord, may I trust You to fulfill Your purpose in my life. Amen.*

*Evening*

*Even strong young lions sometimes go hungry, but those who trust in the LORD will lack no good thing.*
PSALM 34:10 NLT

*Then Christ will make his home in your hearts as you trust in him. Your roots will grow down into God's love and keep you strong.*
EPHESIANS 3:17 NLT

With God, the more we trust, the more we are convinced that our trust is well placed. The key to trust is to try. Try putting your faith in the Lord, and watch wonderful things happen.

*Lord, be with me as I step out in trust. Amen.*

# DAY 183 – *Listening*

## *Morning*

*I will listen to God the LORD. He has ordered peace for those who worship him.*
*Don't let them go back to foolishness.*
PSALM 85:8 NCV

*Don't fool yourself into thinking that you are a listener when you are anything but,*
*letting the Word go in one ear and out the other. Act on what you hear! Those who*
*hear and don't act are like those who glance in the mirror, walk away, and two*
*minutes later have no idea who they are, what they look like.*
JAMES 1:22–24 MSG

So often we find ourselves tuning out the minister on Sunday morning or thinking about other things as we read our Bibles or sing hymns of praise. Our minds must be disciplined to really listen to God's Word. Then we must do the more difficult thing—act on what we've finally heard.

*Dear Lord, please teach me to be attentive to Your Word. Help me act on the*
*things You teach me so that mine becomes a practical faith. Amen.*

## *Evening*

*Jesus called the crowd to him and said, "Listen and understand."*
MATTHEW 15:10 NIV

*"Incline your ear, and come to Me. Hear, and your soul shall live;*
*and I will make an everlasting covenant with you."*
ISAIAH 55:3 NKJV

Who do you listen to? The Lord calls us to listen only to Him. A relationship with Him—the Bread of Life—is what nourishes and sustains us, what fills the emptiness inside us.

*Lord Jesus, forgive me for following the world's voice instead of Yours.*
*Cause me to listen. Amen.*

God, who has ruled forever, will hear me and humble them.
For my enemies refuse to change their ways; they do not fear God.
PSALM 55:19 NLT

The LORD had said to Abram, "Leave your native country, your relatives, and your
father's family, and go to the land that I will show you. I will make you into a great
nation. I will bless you and make you famous, and you will be a blessing to others."
GENESIS 12:1–2 NLT

God wants us to be willing to embrace change that He brings into our lives.
Even unbidden change. You may feel as if you're out on a limb, but don't
forget that God is the tree trunk. He's not going to let you fall.

*Holy, loving Father, in every area of my life, teach me to trust
You more deeply. Amen.*

"I am the LORD, and I do not change."
MALACHI 3:6 NLT

Jesus Christ is the same yesterday, today, and forever.
HEBREWS 13:8 NLT

Change is everywhere, and although change can be good, not knowing
what the future holds can be unsettling. There is one thing, however, that is
unchangeable, and that is Jesus Christ. Changes will come, but Jesus will
be there through each one.

*Dear Jesus, I take comfort in knowing that You will remain the same,
always and forever. Amen.*

## *Morning*

*"It is also true that we must love God with all our heart, mind, and strength, and that we must love others as much as we love ourselves. These commandments are more important than all the sacrifices and offerings that we could possibly make."*
MARK 12:33 CEV

*May the Lord make your love grow more and multiply for each other and for all people so that you will love others as we love you.*
1 THESSALONIANS 3:12 NCV

We have been called by God to show love to everyone we come in contact with. We are even called to show love to those people that we will never meet. There are no shortcuts we can take. Love is a matter of giving everything we are, all the time.

*Father, grant me a deeper knowledge of who You are.*
*Fill me with an unselfish love. Amen.*

## *Evening*

*Above all things have intense and unfailing love for one another, for love covers a multitude of sins [forgives and disregards the offenses of others].*
1 PETER 4:8 AMP

*If I had such faith that I could move mountains, but didn't love others,*
*I would be nothing.*
1 CORINTHIANS 13:2 NLT

God can give us the love we do not possess on our own. He fills us with more than enough love, continually refilling us as we share what we have. Only fools will turn from the knowledge of God, which fills our hearts and enables us to love unselfishly.

*Some days it is hard to love, Lord. Fill my heart again,*
*so that I can share Your love. Amen.*

# DAY 186 - *Loss*

*But if the rest of the world's people were helped so much by Israel's
sin and loss, they will be helped even more by their full return.*
ROMANS 11:12 CEV

*Have mercy on me, my God, have mercy on me, for in you I take refuge.
I will take refuge in the shadow of your wings until the disaster has passed.*
PSALM 57:1 NIV

We find little good in the premature loss of things that harbor dear
memories for us. But God's Word is filled with promises of renewal and
restoration. We may not see it today or next month or even ten years from
now. Nevertheless, our Lord's name is Redeemer. He alone can and will
redeem the valuable, the precious, and the everlastingly worthwhile.

*Lord, when I'm overwhelmed by loss, draw me close to Your promises. Amen.*

*If any man's work is burned up, he will suffer loss; but he himself
will be saved, yet so as through fire.*
1 CORINTHIANS 3:15 NASB

*And many of the people had come to console Martha and Mary in their loss.*
JOHN 11:19 NLT

Christians will suffer as much grief as anyone else. Loss will hurt them just as
deeply. The difference is, a Christian's grief is always tempered by hope.

*Father, when loss comes to us, remind us of the joy found in You on earth
and the joy to come in heaven. Amen.*

# DAY 187 – *Prayer*

## *Morning*

*Now mine eyes shall be open, and mine ears attent
unto the prayer that is made in this place.*
2 CHRONICLES 7:15 KJV

*I will pray with the spirit, and I will also pray with the understanding.*
1 CORINTHIANS 14:15 NKJV

We need to see prayer as the greatest gift we can give, not as a last-ditch effort. Promising that you will keep others in your prayers means that you will continue to pray for them, without ceasing, until you hear of a resolution to their problem. "I'll pray for you" are words that offer hope and life to people who are hurting.

*Dear Jesus, please forgive me for all the times I promised prayer in vain. Call to mind
the people I need to bring before Your throne each day. Amen.*

## *Evening*

*Give ear to my words, O LORD, consider my meditation. Hearken unto
the voice of my cry, my King, and my God: for unto thee will I pray.
My voice shalt thou hear in the morning, O LORD; in the morning
will I direct my prayer unto thee, and will look up.*
PSALM 5:1–3 KJV

*Therefore confess your sins to each other and pray for each other so that you may
be healed. The prayer of a righteous person is powerful and effective.*
JAMES 5:16 NIV

Prayer is a powerful tool for communicating with God, an opportunity to commune with the Creator of the universe. But prayer isn't just a way to seek protection and guidance; it's how we develop a deeper relationship with our heavenly Father.

*Father, help me turn to You instantly, in need and in praise.
I desire to grow closer to You. Amen.*

## *Morning*

> LORD, *you are mine! I promise to obey your words!*
> *With all my heart I want your blessings.*
> PSALM 119:57–58 NLT

> *Every good and perfect gift is from above, coming down from the Father of the*
> *heavenly lights, who does not change like shifting shadows.*
> JAMES 1:17 NIV

God is a gift giver. He is, in fact, the Creator of all good gifts. He finds great joy in blessing you. The God who made you certainly knows your tastes and preferences. He even knows your favorites and your dreams. Most important, He knows your needs.

*God, calm my spirit and give me the patience to wait for Your perfect gifts. Amen.*

## *Evening*

> *Then Jesus turned to his disciples and said, "God blesses you who are poor, for*
> *the Kingdom of God is yours. God blesses you who are hungry now, for you will*
> *be satisfied. God blesses you who weep now, for in due time you will laugh. What*
> *blessings await you when people hate you and exclude you and mock you and curse*
> *you as evil because you follow the Son of Man. When that happens, be happy!*
> *Yes, leap for joy! For a great reward awaits you in heaven."*
> LUKE 6:20–23 NLT

> *For the LORD God is a sun and shield; the LORD will give grace and glory;*
> *no good thing will He withhold from those who walk uprightly.*
> PSALM 84:11 NKJV

Our heavenly Father wants to give us good things. Often His timing is different than ours, but His plan is always to bless and never to harm us.

*Father, give me patience, and help me see the good gifts from You each day. Amen.*

# DAY 189 - *Christian Life*

*It gave me great joy when some believers came and testified about
your faithfulness to the truth, telling how you continue to walk in it.*
3 JOHN 1:3 NIV

*My dear brothers and sisters, I love you and want to see you. You bring me joy
and make me proud of you, so stand strong in the Lord as I have told you.*
PHILIPPIANS 4:1 NCV

Being a Christian means so much more than just believing in the existence
of Christ. Many people believe in Christ, but they consciously remove Him
from their hearts and minds. As Christian people, we need to keep God
close by us.

*Be with me, O Lord. Plant Yourself firmly in my thoughts
and never let me turn from You. Amen.*

*You're not the only ones plunged into these hard times. It's the same with Christians
all over the world. So keep a firm grip on the faith. The suffering won't last forever.*
1 PETER 5:9–10 MSG

*Anyone who gets so progressive in his thinking that he walks out on
the teaching of Christ, walks out on God. But whoever stays with
the teaching, stays faithful to both the Father and the Son.*
2 JOHN 1:9 MSG

If we will take time to spend with Christ, through prayer, Bible reading, and
devotions, we will learn to follow the good paths that Jesus followed. This
is what it means to be a Christian. The key is in spending time with God.

*Remind me, heavenly Father, that I should spend time with You today and every day.
Make me a disciple of Yours, anxious to learn all that You would teach me. Amen.*

## *Morning*

*"You're blessed when your commitment to God provokes persecution.
The persecution drives you even deeper into God's kingdom."*
MATTHEW 5:10 MSG

*He who continually goes forth weeping, bearing seed for sowing, shall doubtless come
again with rejoicing, bringing his sheaves with him.*
PSALM 126:6 NKJV

With Jesus as our example, we can carry on, even when we're discouraged.
Being belittled for our faith is tough, but we have hope, knowing what is to
come. We can go out with seed for sowing, knowing there will come a time
of great rejoicing.

*Jesus, thank You for being the example I can follow. Help me to have the courage to
face each day, knowing my joy is in You and my hope is in heaven. Amen.*

## *Evening*

*Remember what you said to me, your servant—I hang on these words for dear life!
These words hold me up in bad times; yes, your promises rejuvenate me.
The insolent ridicule me without mercy, but I don't budge from your revelation.*
PSALM 119:49–51 MSG

*I was forty years old when Moses the servant of the LORD sent me from Kadesh
Barnea to spy out the land, and I brought back word to him as it was in my heart.*
JOSHUA 14:7 NKJV

If we are proud of our faith, we will find that God will give us special
strength to stand up in the face of ridicule. As scripture says, if we will be
proud of the Father, He will be proud of us.

*Heavenly Father, enable me to be everything You would have me to be. I desire to
reflect Your love even when it is hardest to do so. Amen.*

# DAY 191 – *Spiritual Gifts*

## *Morning*

*But the manifestation of the Spirit is given to each one for the profit of all: for to one is given the word of wisdom through the Spirit, to another the word of knowledge through the same Spirit, to another faith by the same Spirit, to another gifts of healings by the same Spirit, to another the working of miracles, to another prophecy, to another discerning of spirits, to another different kinds of tongues, to another the interpretation of tongues. But one and the same Spirit works all these things, distributing to each one individually as He wills.*
1 CORINTHIANS 12:7–11 NKJV

*God has given each of you a gift from his great variety of spiritual gifts.*
*Use them well to serve one another.*
1 PETER 4:10 NLT

God has given us many fine abilities, and it is important that we remember to use them for His service, not caring whether we receive praise.

*I want to serve You freely and without letting my ego get in the way.*
*Guide me in this pursuit. Amen.*

## *Evening*

*For I long to see you, that I may impart to you some spiritual gift to strengthen you.*
ROMANS 1:11 ESV

*Therefore you do not lack any spiritual gift as you eagerly wait*
*for our Lord Jesus Christ to be revealed.*
1 CORINTHIANS 1:7 NIV

God gives each of us strengths and talents. There is no reason for us to boast or brag. All that we are and all that we can do is a gift from God. Give Him thanks and praise for all you have.

*I can only marvel at the loving-kindness You have shown to me, O Lord.*
*I thank You for blessing me day by day. Amen.*

# DAY 192 - *Reflecting Christ*

*Morning*  ——————————————————

*Now when they saw the boldness of Peter and John, and perceived
that they were uneducated and untrained men, they marveled.
And they realized that they had been with Jesus.*
ACTS 4:13 NKJV

*What I'm getting at, friends, is that you should simply keep on doing what you've
done from the beginning. . . . Be energetic in your life of salvation, reverent and
sensitive before God. That energy is God's energy, an energy deep within you,
God himself willing and working at what will give him the most pleasure.*
PHILIPPIANS 2:12–13 MSG

When we meditate on scripture and seek the Lord in prayer regularly, we
naturally become a little more like Him. Just as slow Southern speech points
clearly to a particular region on the map, may our lives undeniably reflect
that we have been with the Son of God.

*Jesus, make me more like You today. Amen.*

*Evening* ——————————————————

*Then you will be the pure and innocent children of God. You live among people
who are crooked and evil, but you must not do anything that they can say is wrong.
Try to shine as lights among the people of this world.*
PHILIPPIANS 2:15 CEV

*"No one lights a lamp and puts it in a secret place or under a bowl,
but on a lampstand so the people who come in can see."*
LUKE 11:33 NCV

Being a light of the world is not about being a Bible thumper or bashing
others over the head with religion. It's about living out genuine faith that
allows Christ's light to break through our everyday lives.

*Jesus, I ask that You shine through me as I seek to follow after You. Amen.*

# DAY 193 – *Guidance*

## *Morning* ———————————————————

And God has placed in the church first of all apostles, second prophets,
third teachers, then miracles, then gifts of healing, of helping, of guidance,
and of different kinds of tongues.
1 CORINTHIANS 12:28 NIV

When people do not accept divine guidance, they run wild.
But whoever obeys the law is joyful.
PROVERBS 29:18 NLT

We would do best to become wise men and women, daily presenting
ourselves to Jesus, asking Him to lead us on the right path. By following
God's directions—in His Word, your quiet time, or conversations with
others—you will be sure to stay on the right path and arrive safely home.

*Jesus, I present myself to You. Show me the right path to walk with every step I take.
Keep me away from evil and lead me to Your door. Amen.*

## *Evening* ———————————————————

For I am giving you good guidance. Don't turn away from my instructions.
PROVERBS 4:2 NLT

"Call to me and I will answer you and tell you great and unsearchable
things you do not know."
JEREMIAH 33:3 NIV

God may not give you all the answers you are seeking at once. He knows
that some things you are not ready to know or able to comprehend.
Nonetheless, call on Him. Trust in Him. He will unfold the unknown to you
as He sees best.

*Thank You for being a Father who longs to reveal Himself to me.
Guide me always. Amen.*

# DAY 194 - *God's Presence*

*How we thank God for you! Because of you we have great joy*
*as we enter God's presence.*
1 THESSALONIANS 3:9 NLT

*Am I a God at hand, saith the LORD, and not a God afar off? Can any hide*
*himself in secret places that I shall not see him? saith the LORD. Do not I*
*fill heaven and earth? saith the LORD.*
JEREMIAH 23:23–24 KJV

If the "sky is falling" or the sun is shining, do you still recognize the One who orders all the planets and all your days? Whether we see Him or not, God tells us He is there. And He's here, too—in the good times and bad.

*Lord, empower me to trust You when it's hard to remember that You are near.*
*And help me live thankfully when times are good. Amen.*

*Evening* —————————————————————

*"No one will be able to defeat you all your life. Just as I was with Moses,*
*so I will be with you. I will not leave you or forget you."*
JOSHUA 1:5 NCV

*"Even then God did not leave you without something to see of Him. He did good.*
*He gave you rain from heaven and much food. He made you happy."*
ACTS 14:17 NLV

Omnipresent, always present everywhere. Our human minds cannot conceive of it, but it is true. Wherever you live or travel, whatever unfamiliar place you find yourself in, remember God is there with you to guide you and to hold you tight.

*Father, thank You that You are always with me to guide and protect me. Amen.*

# DAY 195 – *Heaven*

────────────────────────────────

"Even now I have one who speaks for me in heaven;
the one who is on my side is high above."
JOB 16:19 NCV

The LORD looks down from heaven on all mankind to see if there
are any who understand, any who seek God.
PSALM 14:2 NIV

We are each one precious in the Lord's sight, and He knows our individual stories by heart. We are His treasures, and He has set aside a special place for us.

*Thank You, Lord, that I am one of Your prized possessions.*
*Keep me ever in Your care. Amen.*

────────────────────────────────

Everything belongs to the LORD your God, not only the earth and everything on it,
but also the sky and the highest heavens.
DEUTERONOMY 10:14 CEV

"But will God indeed dwell on the earth? Behold, heaven and the highest heaven
cannot contain You, how much less this house which I have built!"
1 KINGS 8:27 NASB

The future glory that awaits all Christian believers in heaven is beyond our wildest imagination, and we can rest assured that it will far outshine anything we have yet experienced.

*I praise You for Your great love, Lord, and the promise of heaven. Amen.*

## *Morning*

*Therefore, dear brothers and sisters, you have no obligation to do what your sinful
nature urges you to do. For if you live by its dictates, you will die. But if through the
power of the Spirit you put to death the deeds of your sinful nature, you will live.*
ROMANS 8:12–13 NLT

*If we confess our sins, he is faithful and just to forgive us our sins,
and to cleanse us from all unrighteousness.*
1 JOHN 1:9 KJV

Ironically, blood is something that causes a stain that is hard to remove
from clothes. But the blood of Jesus eradicates all the dirt on human hearts,
removing every stain of sin. No matter how often we fail, we can return, and
a simple confession will wash away our sin.

*Thank You, Lord, for the cleansing power of Your blood. Amen.*

## *Evening*

*Therefore if any man be in Christ, he is a new creature:
old things are passed away; behold, all things are become new.*
2 CORINTHIANS 5:17 KJV

*Above all, love each other deeply, because love covers over a multitude of sins.*
1 PETER 4:8 NIV

In our effort to take sin seriously, we often make the mistake of condemning
the sinner with the sin. Jesus wants us to separate the person from his
actions. Sin He cannot tolerate, but people. . .He always loves them deeply.

*Jesus, be my model for loving others despite their sin. Amen.*

──────────────────────

*If you plan to do evil, you will be lost; if you plan to do good,*
*you will receive unfailing love and faithfulness.*
PROVERBS 14:22 NLT

*"For I know the plans I have for you," declares the LORD, "plans to prosper you and*
*not to harm you, plans to give you hope and a future."*
JEREMIAH 29:11 NIV

Looking at our aims or desires for life can give us a picture of what is most important to us individually. As we think of what the coming years will bring, we must remember that the things of earth are temporary. We need to make our plans with eternity in mind.

*Lord, with You I can have a future full of hope and promise.*
*May my plans be focused on You. Amen.*

──────────────────────

*Commit to the LORD whatever you do, and he will establish your plans.*
PROVERBS 16:3 NIV

*Why, you do not even know what will happen tomorrow. What is your life? You are*
*a mist that appears for a little while and then vanishes. Instead, you ought to say,*
*"If it is the Lord's will, we will live and do this or that."*
JAMES 4:14–15 NIV

The Bible warns us that we don't know how long this life will last. When we make our plans, we should remember that our sovereign God holds each day in His hands. Plan and pray within His will.

*Father, remind me that You are sovereign. Teach me to remember You*
*as I make plans. I want Your will above all else. Amen.*

*Morning* ────────────────────────────

> But they that wait upon the LORD shall renew their strength; they shall
> mount up with wings as eagles; they shall run, and not be weary;
> and they shall walk, and not faint.
> ISAIAH 40:31 KJV

> And he said unto me, My grace is sufficient for thee: for my strength
> is made perfect in weakness. Most gladly therefore will I rather glory
> in my infirmities, that the power of Christ may rest upon me.
> 2 CORINTHIANS 12:9 KJV

God wants us to prosper, and He loves for us to be in good health, even as
our souls prosper. If we really think about that, we have to conclude that the
health of our soul is even more important than our physical health. Spend
some time today giving your soul a workout.

*Lord, make me healthy. . .from the inside out. Amen.*

*Evening* ────────────────────────────

> Why art thou cast down, O my soul? and why art thou disquieted within me? hope thou
> in God: for I shall yet praise him, who is the health of my countenance, and my God.
> PSALM 42:11 KJV

> Don't you know that you yourselves are God's temple and that
> God's Spirit dwells in your midst?
> 1 CORINTHIANS 3:16 NIV

Our physical shells house the very Spirit of God, and God created our
bodies, so we are called to be good stewards of them. It's hard with our
modern, busy lifestyle to make health a priority, but we can ask God for
wisdom and discipline. He will equip us for the task.

*Lord, give me the discipline to make wise choices about what I drink and eat.*
*And help me make exercise a priority. Amen.*

# DAY 199 – *Desires*

*So I say, walk by the Spirit, and you will not gratify the desires of the flesh.*
GALATIANS 5:16 NIV

*As the deer pants for streams of water, so my soul pants for you, my God. My soul
thirsts for God, for the living God. When can I go and meet with God?*
PSALM 42:1–2 NIV

If we were completely honest with ourselves, we'd have to admit that
our earthly longings usually supersede our longing for God. Ask God to
give you His perspective on longing. He knows what it means to long for
someone, after all. His longing for you was so great that He gave His only
Son on the cross to be near you.

*Father, my earthly longings usually get in the way of my spiritual ones.*
*Reignite my longing for You. Amen.*

*Evening* _____

*What the wicked dread will overtake them; what the righteous desire will be granted.*
PROVERBS 10:24 NIV

*Take delight in the LORD, and he will give you the desires of your heart.*
PSALM 37:4 NIV

Delighting yourself in God should take precedence over anything or anyone
else. When you spend time with your heavenly Father, it brings joy to His
heart and to yours. You're also in the best possible place to receive the
secret desires of your heart. Only He can satisfy your longings.

*Lord, I come into Your presence, putting You first.*
*I find joy—my delight—in You. Amen.*

# DAY 200 - *Guilt*

## *Morning* ——————————————————————————

*Keep a clear conscience before God so that when people throw mud at you,
none of it will stick. They'll end up realizing that they're the ones who need a bath.*
1 PETER 3:16 MSG

*"If my people, who are called by my name, will humble themselves and pray
and seek my face and turn from their wicked ways, then I will hear from heaven,
and I will forgive their sin and will heal their land."*
2 CHRONICLES 7:14 NIV

When we accept Christ as our Lord and Savior, His life becomes ours. We
are no longer slaves to sin, but we own His righteousness. So we don't have
to go around thinking that we're scum.

*Father God, I praise You for Your forgiveness and healing.
Thank You that I am called by Your name. Amen.*

## *Evening* ——————————————————————————

*For God sent not his Son into the world to condemn the world;
but that the world through him might be saved.*
JOHN 3:17 KJV

*I, even I, am he that blotteth out thy transgressions for mine own sake,
and will not remember thy sins.*
ISAIAH 43:25 KJV

Who are we to hold on to past sins when our Lord has forgiven and
forgotten them? As long as we're human, we will have pasts filled with
sins abundant. To dwell on them is to make ourselves less than God wants
us to be.

*Teach me to let go of the things I have done wrong in the past,
Lord. Your forgiveness covers all! Amen.*

# DAY 201 - *Recognition*

## *Morning*

*"Take heed that you do not do your charitable deeds before men, to be seen by them.
Otherwise you have no reward from your Father in heaven."*
MATTHEW 6:1 NKJV

*Recognition comes from God, not legalistic critics.*
ROMANS 2:29 MSG

Often we feel as though our good acts are missed. What we need to remember is that none of our actions go unnoticed by God. He sees our every move, and He applauds us when we do good.

*Father, often I feel as though my good behavior is ignored or forgotten. Forgive me for being prideful, and help me know that You see me at both my best and worst, and love me all the time. Amen.*

## *Evening*

*The Lord rewards each of us according to what we do.*
PSALM 62:12 CEV

*For am I now seeking the approval of man, or of God? Or am I trying to please man?
If I were still trying to please man, I would not be a servant of Christ.*
GALATIANS 1:10 ESV

Our true rewards will never come from this life, but from the life that awaits us with our heavenly Father. His blessing is ever with us if we will only be patient and believe.

*Help me look forward to heavenly rewards, Lord. Your praise is worth more than all the praise this world can offer. Amen.*

## *Morning*

*So that we may boldly say, The Lord is my helper, and I will not fear
what man shall do unto me.*
HEBREWS 13:6 KJV

*The Spirit you received does not make you slaves, so that you live in fear again;
rather, the Spirit you received brought about your adoption to sonship.
And by him we cry, "Abba, Father."*
ROMANS 8:15 NIV

Do you struggle with fear? Do you feel it binding you with its invisible
chains? Today, acknowledge your fears to the Lord. He will loose your
chains and set you free.

*Lord, thank You that You are the great chain-breaker! I don't have to live in fear.
I am Your child, and You are my heavenly Father. Amen.*

## *Evening*

*"Fear nothing in the things you're about to suffer—but stay on guard!
Fear nothing! The Devil is about to throw you in jail for a time
of testing—ten days. It won't last forever."*
REVELATION 2:10 MSG

*And it shall come to pass in the day that the LORD shall give thee
rest from thy sorrow, and from thy fear, and from the hard bondage
wherein thou wast made to serve.*
ISAIAH 14:3 KJV

We serve an awesome and mighty God, One who longs to convince us He's
mighty enough to save us, even when the darkness seeps in around us. So
don't fear what you can't see. Or what you can see. Hand over that fear and
watch God-ordained faith rise up in its place.

*Father, thank You for replacing my fear with godly courage. Amen.*

# DAY 203 – *Spiritual Gifts*

## *Morning*

*So also you, since you are zealous of spiritual gifts, seek to abound*
*for the edification of the church.*
1 CORINTHIANS 14:12 NASB

*When they found Him, they said to Him, "Everyone is looking for You."*
*But He said to them, "Let us go into the next towns, that I may preach*
*there also, because for this purpose I have come forth."*
MARK 1:37–38 NKJV

God designed us for a special purpose. Using our gifts is what we're called
to do. When we step into a situation He didn't design for us, we're being
disobedient. Filling a position just because there is an opening is never a
good idea. We need to find our gifts and use them for God's glory.

*Lord, point me on the path You would have me follow.*
*Keep me from being distracted. Amen.*

## *Evening*

*The unspiritual self, just as it is by nature, can't receive the gifts of God's Spirit.*
*There's no capacity for them. They seem like so much silliness. Spirit can be known*
*only by spirit—God's Spirit and our spirits in open communion.*
1 CORINTHIANS 2:14 MSG

*There are different kinds of gifts, but the same Spirit distributes them.*
*There are different kinds of service, but the same Lord.*
1 CORINTHIANS 12:4–5 NIV

God has placed specific gifts within you, and you are needed in the body of
Christ. Although your gifts may be different than someone else's, they are all
from the same Spirit. Thank the Lord for entrusting you with spiritual gifts.

*Lord, thank You for the gifts You've placed within me. I want to reach others for You,*
*so place me in the very spot where I can be most effective. Amen.*

# DAY 204 - *Grace*

*That is the way we should live, because God's grace that can save everyone has come. It teaches us not to live against God nor to do the evil things the world wants to do. Instead, that grace teaches us to live in the present age in a wise and right way and in a way that shows we serve God.*
TITUS 2:11–12 NCV

*For by grace are ye saved through faith; and that not of yourselves: it is the gift of God.*
EPHESIANS 2:8 KJV

Before we come to know Jesus, our hearts are as cold and dead as winter, full of sin. We may do many good deeds. But no amount of good can bring a new creation to an unsaved soul. Only the grace of God has that kind of power.

*God, make a new creation in me. Save me that I might have an abundant life here on earth and eternal life in heaven. Thank You for grace! Amen.*

*Evening*

*And of His fullness we have all received, and grace for grace. For the law was given through Moses, but grace and truth came through Jesus Christ.*
JOHN 1:16–17 NKJV

*The Law came in so that the transgression would increase; but where sin increased, grace abounded all the more, so that, as sin reigned in death, even so grace would reign through righteousness to eternal life through Jesus Christ our Lord.*
ROMANS 5:20–21 NASB

God has given us His unmerited favor, or grace. As we recognize our need for grace and appreciate its work in us, God pours out His blessings in our lives.

*Lord, may I never forget Your sacrifice for my sake. Amen.*

# DAY 205 – *Confidence*

*"But blessed are those who trust in the L*ORD *and have made
the L*ORD *their hope and confidence."*
JEREMIAH 17:7 NLT

*For the L*ORD *will be your confidence, and will keep your foot from being caught.*
PROVERBS 3:26 NKJV

Sometimes we wish for more confidence. The next time you need a confidence boost, instead of worrying or trying to muster it up on your own, seek God. Remember that in your weakness, God shows up to be your strength. He will be your confidence.

*God, be my confidence when this world brings situations in which
I feel insecure or inadequate. Thank You. Amen.*

*Do not throw away your confidence; it will be richly rewarded.*
HEBREWS 10:35 NIV

*Let us then approach God's throne of grace with confidence, so that we
may receive mercy and find grace to help us in our time of need.*
HEBREWS 4:16 NIV

How can we cultivate confidence in a modern world? We can take our eyes off the world and focus on God. We can resolve to put our confidence in Christ, because He is trustworthy. We can approach His throne with confidence, finding all we'll ever need to live—and thrive.

*Lord, help me remember You when my confidence fails. Amen.*

# DAY 206 – *Appearance*

*On the contrary, we speak as those approved by God to be entrusted with the gospel.*
*We are not trying to please people but God, who tests our hearts.*
1 THESSALONIANS 2:4 NIV

*Do ye look on things after the outward appearance? if any man trust*
*to himself that he is Christ's, let him of himself think this again, that,*
*as he is Christ's, even so are we Christ's.*
2 CORINTHIANS 10:7 KJV

Much of what we say and do stems from our desire to be accepted by others. It is impossible to please both God and man. We must make a choice. Man looks at the outward appearance, but God looks at the heart. Align your heart with His. Receive God's unconditional love and enjoy the freedom to be yourself before Him.

*Dear Lord, help me transition from a people pleaser to a God pleaser. Amen.*

*Who is like the wise? Who knows the explanation of things? A person's wisdom*
*brightens their face and changes its hard appearance.*
ECCLESIASTES 8:1 NIV

*Charm is deceptive, and beauty is fleeting; but a woman who*
*fears the LORD is to be praised.*
PROVERBS 31:30 NIV

Look to the Word of God for the definition of true beauty. It comes from the innermost places and is developed by spending time in close relationship with the Lord. Even the plainest glow with the radiance of God after time spent with Him.

*Lord, I want to be attractive on the outside and on the inside. Amen.*

# DAY 207 – *Worship*

## *Morning*

"But an hour is coming, and now is, when the true worshipers will worship the Father
in spirit and truth; for such people the Father seeks to be His worshipers."
JOHN 4:23 NASB

Then the cloud covered the tabernacle of meeting, and the glory
of the LORD filled the tabernacle.
EXODUS 40:34 NKJV

God wants us to enter worship with a heart prepared to actually meet Him.
He longs for us to come in the frame of mind where we're not just singing
about Him, we're truly worshiping Him with every fiber of our being. He
wants wholehearted participants, not spectators.

*Lord, I don't want to go through the motions of worship. Today I offer myself to You,
not as a spectator, but as a participant in Your holy presence. Amen.*

## *Evening*

Therefore let us be grateful for receiving a kingdom that cannot be shaken,
and thus let us offer to God acceptable worship, with reverence and awe.
HEBREWS 12:28 ESV

Therefore, I urge you, brothers and sisters, in view of God's mercy,
to offer your bodies as a living sacrifice, holy and pleasing to God—
this is your true and proper worship.
ROMANS 12:1 NIV

Church worship gives us a glimpse of what heaven will be like—believers
of every nationality and background worshiping the Lord together. We will
acknowledge His holiness. We will bow before Him in adoration.

*Dear Lord, I need to worship You with other believers.
Help me be consistent in my church attendance. Amen.*

# DAY 208 – *Contentment*

## *Morning*

*For the despondent, every day brings trouble; for the happy heart,*
*life is a continual feast.*
PROVERBS 15:15 NLT

*"If they obey and serve him, they will spend the rest of their days*
*in prosperity and their years in contentment."*
JOB 36:11 NIV

Even the strongest Christian can struggle with discontentment. We're conditioned by the world to want more. Instead of focusing on all the things you don't have, spend some time praising God for the things you do have. Offer the Lord any discontentment, and watch Him give you a contented heart.

*Lord, I confess that I'm not always content. Take my discontentment and*
*replace it with genuine peace. Amen.*

## *Evening*

*"Because he knew no contentment in his belly, he will not let anything*
*in which he delights escape him."*
JOB 20:20 ESV

*Not that I was ever in need, for I have learned how to be*
*content with whatever I have.*
PHILIPPIANS 4:11 NLT

The grass isn't always greener on the other side. Learn contentment in all circumstances by taking your focus off yourself and putting it on the Lord. As you find contentment and satisfaction in Christ, He will meet your deepest needs.

*Dear Lord, teach me contentedness. May I find satisfaction in You. Amen.*

# DAY 209 - *Gratitude*

## *Morning*

*Thou hast turned for me my mourning into dancing: thou hast put off my sackcloth,
and girded me with gladness; to the end that my glory may sing praise to thee,
and not be silent. O LORD my God, I will give thanks unto thee for ever.*
PSALM 30:11–12 KJV

*Not that we are competent in ourselves to claim anything for ourselves,
but our competence comes from God.*
2 CORINTHIANS 3:5 NIV

In times of trouble or weakness, when circumstances seem beyond our
control, we pray. But when everything is moving along smoothly and we
have a handle on life, it is easy to forget who God is and who we are.
Acknowledge the giver behind every good thing you have received.

*Heavenly Father, I have been blind to the goodness that dwells in You.
Thank You for all Your gifts to me. Amen.*

## *Evening*

*O give thanks unto the LORD; for he is good: for his mercy endureth for ever.*
PSALM 136:1 KJV

*It is a good thing to give thanks unto the LORD, and to sing praises unto thy name,
O Most High: to shew forth thy lovingkindness in the morning,
and thy faithfulness every night.*
PSALM 92:1–2 KJV

Taking God's gifts for granted is easy to do. Remember that even the
most basic of our needs is met by the loving grace of God. Thank Him for
everything He has given You.

*For the air that I breathe, the warmth of the springtime sun, the food that nourishes
me, and for so much more, I lift my voice in thanks and praise to You, Lord. Amen.*

# DAY 210 – *Hope*

*Why, my soul, are you downcast? Why so disturbed within me? Put your hope in
God, for I will yet praise him, my Savior and my God.*
PSALM 42:11 NIV

*For God alone, O my soul, wait in silence, for my hope is from him.*
PSALM 62:5 ESV

Hope is like a little green shoot poking up through hard, cracked ground.
When you're depressed, do what David and Jeremiah did—pour out your
heart to God. Seek help from a trusted friend or godly counselor. Look for
hope. It's all around you, and it's yours for the taking.

*Father, even when I am depressed, You are still God. Help me find a ray of hope
in the midst of dark circumstances. Amen.*

*Hopes placed in mortals die with them; all the promise of
their power comes to nothing.*
PROVERBS 11:7 NIV

*Be joyful in hope, patient in affliction, faithful in prayer.*
ROMANS 12:12 NIV

Are you hoping for something? Remember, your hope is found in Jesus.
He's your hope for a life full of happiness and love. He's your hope for a
victorious life and, most important, your hope for an eternal future.

*Dear God, my hope lies in You. Remind me when I am hopeless. Amen.*

# DAY 211 – *Grief*

*Morning* ——————————————

The LORD is near to the brokenhearted and saves those who are crushed in spirit.
PSALM 34:18 NASB

God is our refuge and strength, an ever-present help in trouble. Therefore we will not
fear, though the earth give way and the mountains fall into the heart of the sea.
PSALM 46:1–2 NIV

If you are in a place of sadness, trust in this. There will come a day, an hour,
a moment when God will transform gloom into joy. Your feet will be planted
on a mountain, where once you fought to climb out of a valley. Suffering is
but for a time, and God's mercies are new every day.

*Father, when You find me in the pit, put a new song of praise in my heart
that I might live again a life of abundance and joy. Amen.*

*Evening* ——————————————

"You're blessed when you feel you've lost what is most dear to you.
Only then can you be embraced by the One most dear to you."
MATTHEW 5:4 MSG

Yea, though I walk through the valley of the shadow of death, I will fear no evil:
for thou art with me; thy rod and thy staff they comfort me.
PSALM 23:4 KJV

If you're going through a grieving season, look for God to surprise you with
rays of sunshine that break through your dark days. If you will open your
heart to the possibilities, He will send comfort to mend your brokenness.

*Lord, sometimes I feel like the valley I'm in will never end.
Today I choose to look up to see those rays of sunshine above. Amen.*

# DAY 212 – *God's Love*

*But God demonstrates his own love for us in this:*
*While we were still sinners, Christ died for us.*
ROMANS 5:8 NIV

*"For the mountains may depart and the hills be removed, but my steadfast love shall*
*not depart from you, and my covenant of peace shall not be removed,"*
*says the LORD, who has compassion on you.*
ISAIAH 54:10 ESV

Mountains will move before God's love will leave us. In the sacrifice of Christ on the cross, He demonstrated His amazing love for us. Regardless of what we have done or will do, God's love is set upon us. By faith, we have only to believe what Jesus has done for us.

*Father, I thank You for Your unmovable love. Amen.*

*Evening* ────────────────────────

*Therefore be imitators of God as dear children. And walk in love, as Christ*
*also has loved us and given Himself for us, an offering and a sacrifice*
*to God for a sweet-smelling aroma.*
EPHESIANS 5:1–2 NKJV

*Behold what manner of love the Father has bestowed on us, that we should be called*
*children of God! Therefore the world does not know us, because it did not know Him.*
1 JOHN 3:1 NKJV

God is a big God. Unfathomable. And He made you. You were knit together by a one-of-a-kind, amazing God who is absolutely, undeniably, head-over-heels crazy in love with you. Try to wrap your brain around that.

*Heavenly Father, thank You for Your amazing love.*
*Help me use my life as a gift of praise to You. Amen.*

## *Morning*

*And God shall wipe away all tears from their eyes; and there shall be
no more death, neither sorrow, nor crying, neither shall there
be any more pain: for the former things are passed away.*
REVELATION 21:4 KJV

*My flesh and my heart faileth: but God is the strength of my heart,
and my portion for ever.*
PSALM 73:26 KJV

There are very few things that can be counted on to last forever. Souls are eternal; they remain even when our earthly bodies decay. We need to see beyond the physical by focusing on the spiritual. There is life beyond what we are experiencing in this moment.

*Dear Lord, help us keep an eternal focus when we struggle with the physical
limitations of our bodies here on earth. Amen.*

## *Evening*

*But he was wounded for our transgressions, he was bruised for our iniquities:
the chastisement of our peace was upon him; and with his stripes we are healed.*
ISAIAH 53:5 KJV

*And ye shall serve the LORD your God, and he shall bless thy bread,
and thy water; and I will take sickness away from the midst of thee.*
EXODUS 23:25 KJV

Our bodies belong to God. They are a reflection of Him to others. Taking care of ourselves shows others that we honor God enough to respect and use wisely what He has given us.

*Lord, thank You for letting me belong to You. May my body
be a comfortable place for You. Amen.*

# DAY 214 – *Family*

*Wives, submit to your own husbands, as to the Lord. For the husband is head of the wife, as also Christ is head of the church; and He is the Savior of the body. Therefore, just as the church is subject to Christ, so let the wives be to their own husbands in everything. Husbands, love your wives, just as Christ also loved the church and gave Himself for her.*
EPHESIANS 5:22–25 NKJV

*Consequently, you are no longer foreigners and strangers, but fellow citizens with God's people and also members of his household.*
EPHESIANS 2:19 NIV

How wonderful to know God has made you part of His household! You're not an outcast. You're not a stranger on the street, one who doesn't belong. You not only belong—you're priceless to Him. He loves you more deeply than you can fathom as a child of God.

*Father, thank You for inviting me into Your wonderful family. I praise You for loving me as if I were an only child. Amen.*

*Children are a gift from the LORD; they are a reward from him.*
PSALM 127:3 NLT

*God sets the lonely in families.*
PSALM 68:6 NIV

Sometimes God provides a family that comes in a different form. As a Christian, you are part of God's family. There will always remain in this world a remnant of God's people; therefore, there will always be a family available for any believer.

*Lord, thank You for the family You have given me. Help me surround myself with other believers in the family of God as well. Amen.*

# DAY 215 – *Patience*

*Then he passed in front of Moses and called out, "I am the Lord God. I am
merciful and very patient with my people. I show great love, and I can be trusted."*
EXODUS 34:6 CEV

*The Lord is merciful! He is kind and patient, and his love never fails.*
PSALM 103:8 CEV

We humans are impatient and want what we want right now. But our Father
in heaven knows better. He has created a world that unfolds according to
His timetable. Wait for God to reveal His perfect plan. He's in control.

*Dear Lord, You know my heart's desires. Help me wait upon Your
answer for my life. Amen.*

*Or do you think lightly of the riches of His kindness and tolerance and patience,
not knowing that the kindness of God leads you to repentance?*
ROMANS 2:4 NASB

*"This vision is for a future time. It describes the end, and it will be fulfilled.
If it seems slow in coming, wait patiently, for it will surely take place.
It will not be delayed."*
HABAKKUK 2:3 NLT

Patience. It's the stuff frustration is made of. And yet it's a virtue the Lord
expects His people to have plenty of. God's plans may come slowly, but
they come steadily, surely. God is going to do what He says He'll do. We
don't know when, but we can be found faithful while we're waiting.

*Give me patience, Lord, and remind me daily that Your timetable
is the only one that matters. Amen.*

# DAY 216 – *Sharing the Gospel*

## *Morning*

*Therefore do not be ashamed of the testimony about our Lord.*
2 TIMOTHY 1:8 ESV

*Jesus said, "I tell you the truth, all those who have left houses,
brothers, sisters, mother, father, children, or farms for me
and for the Good News will get more than they left."*
MARK 10:29–30 NCV

The lives of those people who are touched by the love of Christ are like
guiding lights to others who have yet to find Christ. They can provide
guidance and help, and they shine forth as bright examples of how good
life can be.

*Father, please make me a light for my world. Let me shine forth with Your
goodness, care, and love. Amen.*

## *Evening*

*But I do not consider my life of any account as dear to myself,
so that I may finish my course and the ministry which I received from the Lord Jesus,
to testify solemnly of the gospel of the grace of God.*
ACTS 20:24 NASB

*For if I preach the gospel, I have nothing to boast of, for I am under compulsion;
for woe is me if I do not preach the gospel.*
1 CORINTHIANS 9:16 NASB

God's light can shine through us if we will only let it. We have the
opportunity to show others the difference that Christ can make. When we
live life empowered by the light of God, we live as He wishes we would.

*Lord, let all who look to me see Your grace. Help me magnify the saving light of
Christ that You have lovingly given me. Amen.*

## *Morning*

*For the love of money is a root of all kinds of evil. Some people, eager for money,
have wandered from the faith and pierced themselves with many griefs.*
1 TIMOTHY 6:10 NIV

*"No one can serve two masters. Either you will hate the one and love
the other, or you will be devoted to the one and despise the other.
You cannot serve both God and money."*
MATTHEW 6:24 NIV

As you feel yourself start to worry about money, stop and change your focus
from wealth to God. Thank Him for what He has provided for you and then
humbly ask Him to give you wisdom about your financial situation.

*Dear God, help me remember that I can absolutely trust You
to provide for me and to sustain me. Amen.*

## *Evening*

*The rich ruleth over the poor, and the borrower is servant to the lender.*
PROVERBS 22:7 KJV

*And it is a good thing to receive wealth from God and the good health to enjoy it.
To enjoy your work and accept your lot in life—this is indeed a gift from God.*
ECCLESIASTES 5:19 NLT

Financial troubles are a reality for many. You may lose money on the stock
market or find yourself the victim of identity theft. When you face such
trials, recall God's promises. His deposit is His Spirit. And He is preparing a
place for you even now in heaven.

*Father, we face times of economic uncertainty. Thank You that Your deposit
of the Holy Spirit in my heart is secure. Amen.*

## *Morning*

"Take heed to yourselves. If your brother sins against you, rebuke him; and if he repents, forgive him. And if he sins against you seven times in a day, and seven times in a day returns to you, saying, 'I repent,' you shall forgive him."
LUKE 17:3–4 NKJV

Bear with each other and forgive one another if any of you has a grievance against someone. Forgive as the Lord forgave you.
COLOSSIANS 3:13 NIV

People—even loved ones—sometimes say and do hurtful things. Instead of holding a grudge against these people, Jesus has another answer: hand the hurt over to Him and forgive. Forgiveness is a process that is successful only with God's help. After all, He's the perfect example of forgiveness, forgiving us again and again. . .and again.

*Jesus, give me strength to let go of bad feelings and forgive. Amen.*

## *Evening*

When people sin, you should forgive and comfort them, so they won't give up in despair. You should make them sure of your love for them.
2 CORINTHIANS 2:7–8 CEV

But I say unto you, That ye resist not evil: but whosoever shall smite thee on thy right cheek, turn to him the other also. And if any man will sue thee at the law, and take away thy coat, let him have thy cloak also. And whosoever shall compel thee to go a mile, go with him twain.
MATTHEW 5:39–41 KJV

It is not enough that we try to put on a good front when we are around people we don't like. We need to search our hearts for reconciliation and forgiveness. Tap into the saving love of Christ, which heals all hurts.

*Creator God, search my heart, and transform it. Let love reign. Amen.*

# DAY 219 - *Laughter*

*Morning* ─────────────────────────────

*Laughter can conceal a heavy heart, but when the laughter ends, the grief remains.*
PROVERBS 14:13 NLT

*A cheerful disposition is good for your health; gloom and doom leave you bone-tired.*
PROVERBS 17:22 MSG

It's a scientifically proven fact that laughter lowers blood pressure and strengthens the immune system. In short, laughter is good medicine. Imagine the effect we could have on our world today if our countenances reflected the joy of the Lord. Maybe it's time we looked for something to laugh about.

*Lord, help me find happiness in this day. Let me laugh and give praises to the King. Amen.*

*Evening* ─────────────────────────────

*A time to weep and a time to laugh,*
*a time to mourn and a time to dance.*
ECCLESIASTES 3:4 NIV

*"Blessed are you who weep now,*
*for you will laugh."*
LUKE 6:21 NIV

Being a Christian is the most joy-filled and lively experience we can have. Others need to see that. Live the happiness, laughter, and singing of being a Christian, so the whole world might know.

*Turn my tears to laughter, Lord.*
*Let me spread my delight to everyone. Amen.*

DAY 220 – *Trust*

*Morning* ——————————————————————

> *Many are the woes of the wicked, but the LORD's unfailing love*
> *surrounds the one who trusts in him.*
> PSALM 32:10 NIV

> *Trust in the LORD with all thine heart; and lean not unto thine own understanding.*
> *In all thy ways acknowledge him, and he shall direct thy paths.*
> PROVERBS 3:5–6 KJV

Try trusting the Lord with all your heart. Not just a little piece of your heart, but all of it. Remember, it's really pretty simple: you either trust Him or you don't.

> *Dear Lord, I trust You with all my heart and all my being.*
> *I acknowledge You as Lord of my life. Amen.*

*Evening* ——————————————————————

> *Commit your way to the LORD, trust also in Him, and He shall bring it to pass.*
> PSALM 37:5 NKJV

> *"The eternal God is your refuge, and underneath are the everlasting arms."*
> DEUTERONOMY 33:27 NIV

As Christians, we trust in a God who is able to do all things. We trust in a God who cares. We trust in a God with whom we may have a personal relationship. The Bible tells us so.

> *Dear Lord, I admit that I don't always trust You like I should.*
> *Help me realize You are ever present and will care for me. Amen.*

# DAY 221 – *Jealousy*

## *Morning*

*Anger is cruel, and wrath is like a flood, but jealousy is even more dangerous.*
PROVERBS 27:4 NLT

*A peaceful heart leads to a healthy body; jealousy is like cancer in the bones.*
PROVERBS 14:30 NLT

When we compare ourselves to others we become jealous, and this jealousy has a way of growing like cancer—quickly and out of control. It can wreak havoc with our inner lives because we are never satisfied, never at peace. For true satisfaction, we must look to God and God alone.

*Heavenly Father, guard my heart against comparing myself to others.*
*Help me be at peace. Amen.*

## *Evening*

*Let us not be desirous of vain glory, provoking one another, envying one another.*
GALATIANS 5:26 KJV

*" 'My son,' the father said, 'you are always with me,*
*and everything I have is yours.' "*
LUKE 15:31 NIV

Have you ever experienced jealousy over blessings that you see in the life of a new Christian? Take comfort in knowing you have been with Him since you accepted His gift of grace, and His blessings are now and forever yours in abundance.

*Father, I rejoice in knowing You love each of Your children with an everlasting love.*
*Help me be thankful, not envious, when others receive Your blessings. Amen.*

## *Morning*

*Now if Christ is preached that He has been raised from the dead, how do some among you say that there is no resurrection of the dead? But if there is no resurrection of the dead, then Christ is not risen. And if Christ is not risen, then our preaching is empty and your faith is also empty.*
1 CORINTHIANS 15:12–14 NKJV

*"False messiahs and false prophets will rise up and perform signs and wonders so as to deceive, if possible, even God's chosen ones. Watch out! I have warned you about this ahead of time!"*
MARK 13:22–23 NLT

Only God can give us the help and support we need to deal with the regular pressures of life. There is no other way, for it is only with God that all things are possible.

*There is no answer apart from You, almighty God! In every situation, both good and bad, You are the strength and the hope. Amen.*

## *Evening*

*"I know your deeds and your toil and perseverance, and that you cannot tolerate evil men, and you put to the test those who call themselves apostles, and they are not, and you found them to be false."*
REVELATION 2:2 NASB

*Christ gave you a special gift that is still in you, so you do not need any other teacher. His gift teaches you about everything, and it is true, not false.*
1 JOHN 2:27 NCV

Thousands of people turn to cults and sects, hoping to find something Christianity can't give them. But Jesus is the only true answer to a life that is empty and void.

*Lord, do not let me be swayed by false teachings that sound so appealing. Protect me with Your love. Amen.*

# DAY 223 – *Joy*

*You will show me the way of life, granting me the joy of your presence
and the pleasures of living with you forever.*
PSALM 16:11 NLT

*You make known to me the path of life; you will fill me with joy in your presence,
with eternal pleasures at your right hand.*
PSALM 16:11 NIV

Our Creator God is a joy giver, and He pours it out when you need it most.
At your very lowest point, He's there, ready to fill you with that bubbling-
over kind of joy. And how wonderful to know that in His right hand there is
happiness forever.

*O Lord, I need joy today. Thank You for the reminder that You are a joy giver and
that You want me to be happy. Pour out Your joy, Father! Amen.*

*You have turned my sorrow into joyful dancing. No longer am I sad
and wearing sackcloth. I thank you from my heart, and I will never stop
singing your praises, my LORD and my God.*
PSALM 30:11–12 CEV

*Satisfy us in the morning with your unfailing love, that we may sing
for joy and be glad all our days.*
PSALM 90:14 NIV

God's goodness isn't just for when we get to heaven. God wants us to enjoy
ourselves and Him along the journey. Look for the good that He is doing
in your life and find joy in knowing that your Friend on the journey deeply
cares for you.

*Dear Lord, thank You for allowing me to see Your goodness each day.
Help me enjoy the life You have given me. Amen.*

# DAY 224 – *Worry*

 *Morning* —————————————————————

*"And you? Go about your business without fretting or worrying. Relax.
When it's all over, you will be on your feet to receive your reward."*
DANIEL 12:13 MSG

*"So don't worry about tomorrow, for tomorrow will bring its own worries.
Today's trouble is enough for today."*
MATTHEW 6:34 NLT

If we're honest with ourselves, we admit we sometimes hold on our worries, thinking that keeping them close somehow keeps us in control of the situation. In reality, most of our worries concern things completely out of our hands. Instead, Jesus offers us freedom from our chains of worry.

*Jesus, You know the toll worries take on my heart and mind. Help me place my concerns in Your capable hands so that I can be free to praise You. Amen.*

*Evening* —————————————————————

*Worry is a heavy burden, but a kind word always brings cheer.*
PROVERBS 12:25 CEV

*Then Jesus said to his disciples: "Therefore I tell you, do not worry about your life."*
LUKE 12:22 NIV

Jesus told the disciples not to let their hearts be troubled. Sometimes we feel as if we can't control feeling troubled. But when we focus on the Lord and meditate upon His promises, we can gain control of our worries and replace them with trust.

*Father, please replace trouble with trust in this heart of mine. Amen.*

# DAY 225 – *Coveting*

Then He said to them, "Beware, and be on your guard against every form of greed;
for not even when one has an abundance does his life consist of his possessions."
LUKE 12:15 NASB

"You shall not covet your neighbor's house; you shall not covet
your neighbor's wife, nor his male servant, nor his female servant, nor his ox,
nor his donkey, nor anything that is your neighbor's."
EXODUS 20:17 NKJV

To covet means to feel unreasonable desire for something that belongs to
another. The Lord knows we have wishes and dreams, but He wants us to
have the right perspective on them and not let them control our lives. Wish
for anything you want; covet nothing.

*Lord, help me keep my desires under control. Help me live in contentment with the
many things You've blessed me with. Amen.*

Set your affection on things above, not on things on the earth.
COLOSSIANS 3:2 KJV

We didn't bring anything into this world, and we won't take
anything with us when we leave.
1 TIMOTHY 6:7 CEV

It is okay to want something. The danger comes when we want what
someone else has. When God tells us that we "shall not," we must pay
attention. His commandments are for our good. Catch yourself when you
sense a desire for that which is not yours.

*God, You have poured out so many blessings on me. Protect my heart
from desiring that which belongs to others. Amen.*

*Morning*

---

*In peace I will lie down and sleep, for you alone,*
*O LORD, will keep me safe.*
PSALM 4:8 NLT

*The LORD gives perfect peace to those whose faith is firm.*
ISAIAH 26:3 CEV

In every age, in every place, there are people who live by the rule of violence. How much better it is to live a life of peace and love.

*Rule in my heart with peace and love, Lord. Amen.*

*Evening*

---

*Blessed are the peacemakers:*
*for they shall be called the children of God.*
MATTHEW 5:9 KJV

*"Peace I leave with you, My peace I give to you;*
*not as the world gives do I give to you.*
*Let not your heart be troubled, neither let it be afraid."*
JOHN 14:27 NKJV

Peacemakers—they are blessed in the sight of the Lord. It may seem that the instigators of violence rule this world, but it is the rule of Christ which is the real power, and it reigns in the hearts of all who believe in Him.

*Almighty God, grant that I might be protected from*
*the people who would do me harm, yet let me always face*
*others with forgiveness. Amen.*

# DAY 227 – *Belonging*

—————————————————————

*Then I heard a voice from heaven, saying, "Write these words: 'From now
on those who are dead who died belonging to the Lord will be happy.' "*
REVELATION 14:13 NLV

*"For truly, I say to you, whoever gives you a cup of water to drink
because you belong to Christ will by no means lose his reward."*
MARK 9:41 ESV

When the Lord said He has engraved us on the palms of His hands, He was
telling us that He remembers us. All day, every day, He remembers us. We
are of utmost importance to Him. We cannot be forgotten.

*Father, thank You that through Christ You have brought me to Yourself, You reign
over my life, and You always remember me. Amen.*

*Evening* —————————————————————

*He who comes from above is above all. He who is of the earth belongs to the earth
and speaks in an earthly way. He who comes from heaven is above all.*
JOHN 3:31 ESV

*Be content with what you have, because God has said,
"Never will I leave you; never will I forsake you."*
HEBREWS 13:5 NIV

We all experience rejection from friends, family, coworkers, or members of
the opposite sex. However, God will never decide He's had enough of us. In
fact, He longs to spend time with us, and the more time, the better.

*Lord, the pain of rejection is tough. Help me tear down the wall I've
built in my heart and receive Your unfailing love. Amen.*

# DAY 228 – *Obedience*

*Blessed are all who fear the LORD, who walk in obedience to him.*
PSALM 128:1 NIV

*But if we walk in the light as He is in the light, we have fellowship with one another,
and the blood of Jesus Christ His Son cleanses us from all sin.*
1 JOHN 1:7 NKJV

How do we remain in the light? We ask the Holy Spirit to guide us, and
when we get an uneasy feeling regarding a choice, we pay attention to it. It
may be hard to say no, but the payoff for obedience will be great.

*Father of light, help me be sensitive to Your Holy Spirit.
Shine Your light into my life. Amen.*

*Evening* ——————————————————————————

*For your obedience is known to all, so that I rejoice over you,
but I want you to be wise as to what is good and innocent as to what is evil.*
ROMANS 16:19 ESV

*"And I will give them singleness of heart and put a new spirit within them.
I will take away their stony, stubborn heart and give them a tender,
responsive heart, so they will obey my decrees and regulations.
Then they will truly be my people, and I will be their God."*
EZEKIEL 11:19–20 NLT

God wants us to obey Him not because we're afraid He'll punish us if we
don't, but because we love Him. If you obey out of a sense of obligation,
ask God to change your heart. When you meditate on His character and are
convinced of His love for you, obedience will become not a duty but a delight.

*Lord God, I praise You for the love that left heaven behind.
Help me obey out of love. Amen.*

## *Morning*

*O LORD, who shall sojourn in your tent? Who shall dwell on your holy hill?*
*He who walks blamelessly and does what is right and speaks truth in his heart.*
PSALM 15:1–2 ESV

*The LORD is near to all who call on him, to all who call on him in truth.*
PSALM 145:18 ESV

Honesty is a valuable virtue. We have the power to change lives when we speak the truth. If we tell people fables, we lose credibility and weaken our power to help them.

*Father, let me be honest and open so that I might have the opportunity*
*to make a difference in lives. Amen.*

## *Evening*

*Then your light will shine like the dawning sun, and you will quickly be healed.*
*Your honesty will protect you as you advance, and the glory*
*of the LORD will defend you from behind.*
ISAIAH 58:8 CEV

*Do not let kindness and truth leave you; bind them around your neck,*
*write them on the tablet of your heart.*
PROVERBS 3:3 NASB

God loves those who will be honest and trustworthy. Lying is abominable in the sight of God, and no one who lives by deception will have any place in His kingdom.

*Purify my thoughts and my words, Lord, that they may reflect*
*Your grace and love. Amen.*

# DAY 230 – *Pride*

*Mockers are proud and haughty; they act with boundless arrogance.*
PROVERBS 21:24 NLT

*Pride ends in humiliation, while humility brings honor.*
PROVERBS 29:23 NLT

It's hard to remember that everything is a gift from God—even our accomplishments. If we're not careful, we can begin to think we've brought about those things ourselves. Nothing could be further from the truth. Every detail of our lives is orchestrated by God.

*Remind me daily, Father, that every good and perfect gift comes not from my hard work, but from You. Amen.*

*Your herds and flocks increase their numbers. You also get more and more silver and gold. And everything you have multiplies. Then your hearts will become proud. And you will forget the LORD your God.*
DEUTERONOMY 8:13–14 NIrV

*My soul makes its boast in the LORD; let the humble hear and be glad.*
*Oh, magnify the LORD with me, and let us exalt his name together!*
PSALM 34:2–3 ESV

It is the humble soul that desires that God be glorified instead of self. Try as we might, we can't produce this humility in ourselves. It is our natural tendency to be self-promoters. We need the help of the Spirit to remind us that God has favored each of us with His presence.

*Christ Jesus, help me remember what You have done for me. Amen.*

# DAY 231 - *Praise*

*Others have praised God for what he has done, so join with them.*
JOB 36:24 CEV

*Through Jesus, therefore, let us continually offer to God a sacrifice
of praise—the fruit of lips that openly profess his name.*
HEBREWS 13:15 NIV

Jesus was willing to live among us, suffer, and die on the cross for us. How
do we respond? With a sacrifice of praise. God desires to hear us praise
Jesus. God is pleased with our faith in Jesus and our sacrifice of praise.

*Father, I praise You for clothing me in the righteousness of Christ.
May my life reflect His transforming grace. Amen.*

*For they loved the praise of men more than the praise of God.*
JOHN 12:43 NKJV

*I bless GOD every chance I get; my lungs expand with his praise.*
PSALM 34:1 MSG

If we try to place praise high on our list of priorities, it's often difficult to
follow through; praise isn't something that comes naturally to most of us.
Start developing a spirit of praise every day: pray, find new reasons to offer
thanks, and spread the joy of your salvation with others.

*God, I praise You because of the wonderful things You do in my life every day.
Let everything within me praise the Lord! Amen.*

# DAY 232 – *Fear*

*The fear of man bringeth a snare: but whoso*
*putteth his trust in the L*ord *shall be safe.*
Proverbs 29:25 kjv

*For I, the L*ord *your God, hold your right hand; it is I who say to you,*
*"Fear not, I am the one who helps you."*
Isaiah 41:13 esv

God holds your hand. He protects you. He is with you in your darkest
moments. With the clasp of His hand comes courage for any situation. He
tells you not to fear, for He is your ever-present help in times of trouble.

*Almighty God, forgive me for the times I let fear reign in my life. Grant me the*
*courage that comes from knowing You are my helper. Amen.*

*Be not afraid of sudden fear, neither of the desolation of the wicked, when it cometh.*
*For the L*ord *shall be thy confidence, and shall keep thy foot from being taken.*
Proverbs 3:25–26 kjv

*"So do not fear, for I am with you; do not be dismayed, for I am your God. I will*
*strengthen you and help you; I will uphold you with my righteous right hand."*
Isaiah 41:10 niv

Fear reigns when faith is not exercised. Because you are God's precious
child, He who watches over you will not slumber nor sleep. He will protect
you as a shepherd protects his sheep. So do not fear.

*Dear Lord, may I experience Your presence. Grant me*
*peaceful sleep as I trust You. Amen.*

## *Morning*

*Let your light so shine before men, that they may see your good works,
and glorify your Father which is in heaven.*
MATTHEW 5:16 KJV

*For if anyone is a hearer of the word and not a doer, he is like a man
who looks intently at his natural face in a mirror. For he looks at himself
and goes away and at once forgets what he was like.*
JAMES 1:23–24 ESV

Loving the unlovable, giving to the needy, forgiving the unforgivable, being honest, and striving to be Christlike are all perfect ways to share the light of Jesus. Let your life be a beacon of light and hope to all you meet.

*Dear Lord, thank You for bringing light to my darkness. Help me to spread
the light of Jesus to those who don't know You. Amen.*

## *Evening*

*In their case the god of this world has blinded the minds of the unbelievers,
to keep them from seeing the light of the gospel of the glory
of Christ, who is the image of God.*
2 CORINTHIANS 4:4 ESV

*Let me [as God's representative] sing of and for my greatly Beloved [God, the Son]
a tender song of my Beloved concerning His vineyard [His chosen people].
My greatly Beloved had a vineyard on a very fruitful hill.*
ISAIAH 5:1 AMP

When we call ourselves Christians, we are claiming to be mirror images of Christ for all the world to see. We are presenting ourselves as examples of what God had in mind when He put men and women on this earth.

*Lord, be with me to shine Your light through my life that
others may see Your greatness. Amen.*

## *Morning*

*Saying with a loud voice, Fear God, and give glory to him; for the hour of his judgment is come: and worship him that made heaven, and earth, and the sea, and the fountains of waters.*
REVELATION 14:7 KJV

*Only fear the LORD, and serve him in truth with all your heart: for consider how great things he hath done for you.*
1 SAMUEL 12:24 KJV

We stand in awe before God, wisely cautious in the face of His power, and yet we long to know Him, to be united with Him. The wise pursue Him with all their heart, while the foolish ignore Him or reject Him through their fear.

*O Lord, help me know fear in a positive way. Allow me to feel healthy fear, but never let that fear separate me from You. Amen.*

## *Evening*

*Wherefore we receiving a kingdom which cannot be moved, let us have grace, whereby we may serve God acceptably with reverence and godly fear: For our God is a consuming fire.*
HEBREWS 12:28–29 KJV

*He will fulfil the desire of them that fear him: he also will hear their cry, and will save them.*
PSALM 145:19 KJV

Fear of the Lord should not drive us from Him; it should help us understand Him and deal with Him reverently and respectfully. When we encounter our Lord with both joy and trembling, we know Him in a special and meaningful way.

*Lord, help me never forget Your awesome power, as well as Your awesome love. Amen.*

## *Morning*

*From his abundance we have all received one gracious blessing after another.*
*For the law was given through Moses, but God's unfailing love*
*and faithfulness came through Jesus Christ.*
JOHN 1:16–17 NLT

*LORD, you alone are my inheritance, my cup of blessing. You guard all that is mine.*
PSALM 16:5 NLT

Why do we not recognize all our blessings? Because it's human nature to zero in on what's wrong and miss what's very right. We need to open our arms and become thankful recipients for all He's given.

*Lord, You have given me so much, and I am thankful.*
*Let me give thanks for Your gifts. Amen.*

## *Evening*

*Through Christ Jesus, God has blessed the Gentiles with the same blessing*
*he promised to Abraham, so that we who are believers might receive*
*the promised Holy Spirit through faith.*
GALATIANS 3:14 NLT

*The LORD had said to Abram, "Leave your native country, your relatives, and your*
*father's family, and go to the land that I will show you. I will make you into a great*
*nation. I will bless you and make you famous, and you will be a blessing to others.*
*I will bless those who bless you and curse those who treat you with contempt.*
*All the families on earth will be blessed through you."*
GENESIS 12:1–3 NLT

The Lord sees all that we do, and His pleasure is ever with us. His abundant blessings come to all who truly love Him and pursue Him with all their hearts, minds, and souls.

*God, thank You for blessing me, despite my many failures. Amen.*

But now that you have been set free from sin and have become slaves of God, the fruit you get leads to sanctification and its end, eternal life. For the wages of sin is death, but the free gift of God is eternal life in Christ Jesus our Lord.
ROMANS 6:22–23 ESV

"Yet they say to each other, 'Don't come too close or you will defile me! I am holier than you!' These people are a stench in my nostrils, an acrid smell that never goes away."
ISAIAH 65:5 NLT

There is no good end that can come from a life of sin. Ultimately, we must answer for our actions before God. If we do not repent of our misdeeds, we find ourselves hopelessly separated from God. But with God's help, we will never be ensnared.

*Forgive my sins, almighty God, and help me live the life You desire— free from sin and devoted to You. Amen.*

And if Christ is in you, the body is dead because of sin, but the Spirit is life because of righteousness.
ROMANS 8:10 NKJV

For as in Adam all die, so in Christ all will be made alive.
1 CORINTHIANS 15:22 TNIV

For some people, sin isn't something they are attracted to, it is something they are addicted to. Just like drugs, though, if it isn't cleaned out of the system, it can kill.

*Almighty God, sin so readily takes control of my heart and mind. Be my strength to overcome, I pray. Amen.*

*Morning* ─────────────────────────────────

*Daniel said, I saw in my vision by night, and behold, the four winds*
*of the heavens [political and social agitations] were stirring up*
*the great sea [the nations of the world].*
DANIEL 7:2 AMP

*"Step out of the traffic! Take a long, loving look at me, your High God,*
*above politics, above everything."*
PSALM 46:10 MSG

It's our duty and privilege as citizens to vote. But whether we line up
with the conservative or liberal side of politics, we must not trust in
government—or any politician—to save us. Jesus Christ is the only Savior.
And He never breaks any of His promises.

*Lord, thank You that You promise to take care of us. Help us to not put*
*too much trust in men or agencies. Amen.*

*Evening* ─────────────────────────────────

*Moderation is better than muscle, self-control better than political power.*
PROVERBS 16:32 MSG

*You, O God, are my king from ages past, bringing salvation to the earth.*
PSALM 74:12 NLT

Every election cycle we see politicians come and go. It's different in God's
kingdom. We can rely—absolutely depend on—His unchanging nature.
Take comfort in the stability of the King—He's our leader now and forever!

*Almighty King, You are my anchor and my center of balance.*
*Thank You for never changing. Amen.*

## *Morning*

*Give me a sign of your goodness, that my enemies may see it and be put to shame,*
*for you, LORD, have helped me and comforted me.*
PSALM 86:17 NIV

*All praise to God, the Father of our Lord Jesus Christ. God is our merciful*
*Father and the source of all comfort. He comforts us in all our troubles so*
*that we can comfort others. When they are troubled, we will be able to*
*give them the same comfort God has given us.*
2 CORINTHIANS 1:3–4 NLT

As God comforts us, we can comfort others. Is there someone in your life
who could use some comfort? Offer it in any small way that you are able.
The God of comfort has comforted you. So comfort others in His name.

*Merciful Father, comfort me in my times of need and show me*
*those that I might comfort. Amen.*

## *Evening*

*He will swallow up death in victory; and the Lord GOD will wipe away tears*
*from off all faces; and the rebuke of his people shall he take away from off*
*all the earth: for the LORD hath spoken it.*
ISAIAH 25:8 KJV

*Finally, brethren, farewell. Become complete. Be of good comfort, be of one mind,*
*live in peace; and the God of love and peace will be with you.*
2 CORINTHIANS 13:11 NKJV

God promises to uphold you when your soul clings to Him. In order to cling
to Him, you must first release other things that you are holding on to for
your comfort. Then you will know the peace of being upheld by the right
hand of Immanuel—God with Us.

*Jesus, Immanuel, my Comforter, will You hold me? I feel secure in You. Amen.*

# DAY 239 – *Argument*

*Let all bitterness, and wrath, and anger, and clamour, and evil speaking,*
*be put away from you, with all malice.*
EPHESIANS 4:31 KJV

*Don't make friends with quick-tempered people or spend time with those who have*
*bad tempers. If you do, you will be like them. Then you will be in real danger.*
PROVERBS 22:24–25 NCV

Following the Golden Rule—doing unto others as you would have them
do unto you—and loving others as you love yourself is tough to do when
you're arguing. But just how important is it to prove your point—in the
grand scheme of things?

*Lord, show me what to say and what not to say to avoid strife.*
*Give me Your heart toward others. Amen.*

*Better to dwell in the wilderness, than with a contentious and angry woman.*
PROVERBS 21:19 NKJV

*Better a dry crust with peace and quiet than a house full of feasting, with strife.*
PROVERBS 17:1 NIV

Senseless argument and criticism is destructive. It divides people so that
they cannot communicate with each other. There is never anything to be
gained by causing tension with other people without cause.

*O Lord, guide me as I try to live a good and righteous life. I want so much*
*to do what I should. With Your help I will. Amen.*

# DAY 240 – *Encouragement*

## *Morning*

*I am acting with great boldness toward you; I have great pride in you;
I am filled with comfort. In all our affliction, I am overflowing with joy.*
2 CORINTHIANS 7:4 ESV

*So if there is any encouragement in Christ, any comfort from love,
any participation in the Spirit, any affection and sympathy.*
PHILIPPIANS 2:1 ESV

Let's encourage one another to take steps of faith—to get out of our
comfortable boats. Through our own example, we can inspire others to
desire to follow Jesus. As we experience life together, let's spur one another
on toward love and good deeds!

*Dear Lord, help me look for ways to encourage others in their Christian walk.
May my words and life inspire them to follow Jesus. Amen.*

## *Evening*

*But God, Who comforts and encourages and refreshes and cheers the depressed
and the sinking, comforted and encouraged and refreshed
and cheered us by the arrival of Titus.*
2 CORINTHIANS 7:6 AMP

*He restoreth my soul: he leadeth me in the paths of righteousness for his name's sake.*
PSALM 23:3 KJV

Sometimes we become discouraged with the direction of our lives. Be
encouraged. The Lord has promised He hears our pleas and knows our
situations. Our God is not a God of negativity, but of possibility. He will
guide us through our difficulties and beyond them.

*Father, You are my unending source of encouragement.
Gather me in Your arms for always. Amen.*

# DAY 241 – *Patience*

*Be still before the LORD and wait patiently for him.*
PSALM 37:7 NIV

*LORD, I wait for you; you will answer, Lord my God.*
PSALM 38:15 NIV

Waiting on God is hard. But God's Word tells us to wait patiently—with peace. Rather than sighing with impatience, try praying, reading scripture, and making your waiting time productive and meaningful. Wait patiently and with confidence. God will come through.

*Heavenly Father, when the waiting seems unbearable, remind me that*
*Your timing is always perfect. Amen.*

*For whatever things were written before were written for our learning,*
*that we through the patience and comfort of the Scriptures might have hope.*
ROMANS 15:4 NKJV

*The LORD is good to those whose hope is in him, to the one who seeks him;*
*it is good to wait quietly for the salvation of the LORD.*
LAMENTATIONS 3:25–26 NIV

Patience is more than a virtue in today's world—it is an essential survival tool for a happy life. God's hand is at work in our lives when we are totally surrendered to His clock. He longs for His children to quit fretting and just wait patiently.

*Dear Father, I'm not good at waiting patiently.*
*Help me learn to lean on You. Amen.*

# DAY 242 – *Eternity*

*"I'll give authority over the nations to all who overcome*
*and who carry out my plans to the end."*
REVELATION 2:26 NIrV

*But as it is written, Eye hath not seen, nor ear heard, neither have entered into the*
*heart of man, the things which God hath prepared for them that love him.*
1 CORINTHIANS 2:9 KJV

God doesn't want any of us to suffer, especially eternally. In His infinite love, God provided us with another way. He gave us a new Tree of Life, His Son, Jesus Christ.

*Thank You, O Lord, for giving me the chance to have eternal life.*
*Through Your love, I have come to know Your glory. Amen.*

*For we know that if our earthly house of this tabernacle were dissolved, we have a*
*building of God, an house not made with hands, eternal in the heavens.*
2 CORINTHIANS 5:1 KJV

*Behold, I shew you a mystery; We shall not all sleep, but we shall all be changed,*
*In a moment, in the twinkling of an eye, at the last trump: for the trumpet shall*
*sound, and the dead shall be raised incorruptible, and we shall be changed. For this*
*corruptible must put on incorruption, and this mortal must put on immortality.*
1 CORINTHIANS 15:51–53 KJV

Christ died to undo the harm done by Adam and Eve's disobedience. Once He reconciled us to God, God invited us to once more share in the fruit of the Tree of Life. Through Christ, we have the promise of eternity in God's heavenly home.

*Jesus, thank You for not leaving us to live forever in a fallen state.*
*Your life, death, and resurrection has brought me new life. Amen.*

*Morning* ───────────────────────────────

And Isaac spake unto Abraham his father, and said, My father: and he said,
Here am I, my son. And he said, Behold the fire and the wood: but where
is the lamb for a burnt offering? And Abraham said, My son, God will provide
himself a lamb for a burnt offering: so they went both of them together.
GENESIS 22:7–8 KJV

Hitherto have ye asked nothing in my name: ask, and ye shall receive,
that your joy may be full.
JOHN 16:24 KJV

Often we ask God for more than our daily needs. We look into the future,
and with fearful hearts we plead with God concerning our needs. We don't
give God the chance to show us that He will provide day by day. In the
coming days, try to rely on God for daily provision without asking for more.

God, give me this day my daily bread. Let me trust You for this day,
believing You are a God who knows my needs. Amen.

*Evening* ───────────────────────────────

But seek ye first the kingdom of God, and his righteousness;
and all these things shall be added unto you.
MATTHEW 6:33 KJV

And I say unto you, Ask, and it shall be given you; seek, and ye shall find;
knock, and it shall be opened unto you.
LUKE 11:9 KJV

We may need forgiveness, wisdom, courage, endurance, patience, health,
protection, or even love. God promises to come to our aid when He sees us
with a hand up, reaching for His assistance.

Father, thank You for caring about the needs of Your children.
Help me remember to always seek You first. Amen.

## *Morning*

*Therefore, my beloved, as you have always obeyed, not as in my presence only,
but now much more in my absence, work out your own salvation with fear
and trembling; for it is God who works in you both
to will and to do for His good pleasure.*
PHILIPPIANS 2:12–13 NKJV

*Like newborn babies, crave pure spiritual milk, so that by it you may grow up
in your salvation, now that you have tasted that the Lord is good.*
1 PETER 2:2–3 NIV

Christ is the Living Water, continually refreshing and nourishing us, giving
life to our bodies and souls. Daily we need to go to the well of our
salvation, remembering our need for Jesus and drawing out the living water
with joy.

*Lord, thank You for saving me. Cause me to remember that
my life is hidden in Yours. Amen.*

## *Evening*

*"The earth will wear out like a garment and its inhabitants will die
in like manner; but My salvation will be forever."*
ISAIAH 51:6 NASB

*And inasmuch as it is appointed for men to die once and after this comes judgment,
so Christ also, having been offered once to bear the sins of many, will appear a
second time for salvation without reference to sin, to those who eagerly await Him.*
HEBREWS 9:27–28 NASB

Live your life—your whole life—by seeking daily joy in the Savior of your
soul, Jesus Christ. He's already done the rescuing by dying on the cross for
our sins! He's the true white knight who secured your eternity in heaven.

*Jesus, thank You for my salvation. Amen.*

# DAY 245 – *Following Jesus*

## *Morning*

*Then Jesus spoke to them again, saying, "I am the light of the world.*
*He who follows Me shall not walk in darkness, but have the light of life."*
JOHN 8:12 NKJV

*And now, Israel, what does the LORD your God ask of you but to fear the LORD your*
*God, to walk in obedience to him, to love him, to serve the LORD your God with all*
*your heart and with all your soul, and to observe the LORD's commands*
*and decrees that I am giving you today for your own good?*
DEUTERONOMY 10:12–13 NIV

The pursuit of God is one of the few life choices we can make that has no
strings attached. We give very little and receive so much.

*Lord, the gift of knowing You is given freely. When life distracts me,*
*help me seek You with all my heart. Amen.*

## *Evening*

*"You shall follow the LORD your God and fear Him; and you shall keep*
*His commandments, listen to His voice, serve Him, and cling to Him."*
DEUTERONOMY 13:4 NASB

*So I say, walk by the Spirit, and you will not gratify the desires of the flesh.*
GALATIANS 5:16 NIV

When we pursue the things of this life, we gain temporary benefits that fade
away, leaving us feeling empty, lost, and alone. Give your life to God and
walk in the ways that He chooses, and you will find that He will bless you
continually.

*Turn me from the things that cannot offer me lasting satisfaction.*
*Turn me instead, Lord, to the things that are eternal and holy. Amen.*

DAY 246 – *Family*

*Morning* —————————————————————————

My son, keep your father's command, and do not forsake the law of your mother.
PROVERBS 6:20 NKJV

So in Christ Jesus you are all children of God through faith.
GALATIANS 3:26 NIV

Whether your childhood reflected love or abandonment, there is good
news! As a Christian, you are a child of the King of kings, the Lord of lords,
the sovereign God. You are not just God's friend or distant relative. You are
His child!

*Thank You, Father, for adopting me through Christ. Teach me to live
as a reflection of my Father's love. Amen.*

*Evening* —————————————————————————

But if anyone does not provide for his relatives, and especially for members of his
household, he has denied the faith and is worse than an unbeliever.
1 TIMOTHY 5:8 ESV

"Bless my family; keep your eye on them always. You've already as much as said that
you would, Master GOD! Oh, may your blessing be on my family permanently!"
2 SAMUEL 7:29 MSG

Did you know that you can trust God with both your own life and the lives
of your family members? You can trust the Lord with their dreams, their
attitudes, their problems. God's got it covered. It's in His master plan to
bless your family. . .permanently!

*God, thank You for the reminder that You have great plans, not just for me,
but for my family, too. Amen.*

# DAY 247 – *Repentance*

*"Repent, then, and turn to God, so that your sins may be wiped out,
that times of refreshing may come from the Lord."*
ACTS 3:19 NIV

*And he said, "Who told you that you were naked? Have you eaten from the tree
that I commanded you not to eat from?" The man said, "The woman you put
here with me—she gave me some fruit from the tree, and I ate it."*
GENESIS 3:11–12 NIV

If you long to be like Christ, determine today not to play the "blame game"
anymore. When confronted with sin, ask God for His mercy and accept His
forgiveness.

*Lord, give me the strength of character to admit when I'm wrong
and turn from my sin. Amen.*

*Evening* ——————————————————————

*So they went out and proclaimed that people should repent.*
MARK 6:12 ESV

*"Produce fruit in keeping with repentance."*
MATTHEW 3:8 NIV

To reconcile with God, we must make the first move. We must acknowledge
our wrongdoing and ask forgiveness for it. God will be faithful to answer,
but it is so much easier to rely on His power to strengthen us in times of
temptation.

*Forgive me, Lord, for the times I stray from Your commands.
Keep my eyes centered on You. Amen.*

# DAY 248 – *Loneliness*

## *Morning* ———————————————

*The time will come and is already here when all of you will be scattered.*
*Each of you will go back home and leave me by myself. But the Father*
*will be with me, and I won't be alone.*
JOHN 16:32 CEV

*For I am persuaded, that neither death, nor life, nor angels, nor principalities,*
*nor powers, nor things present, nor things to come, nor height, nor depth,*
*nor any other creature, shall be able to separate us from the love*
*of God, which is in Christ Jesus our Lord.*
ROMANS 8:38–39 KJV

Everyone experiences loneliness sometimes. We can feel cast off, rejected
by life's circumstances. God promises that He will never leave you or forsake
you. You can have full confidence in knowing that with God's love, you'll
never, ever be alone.

*Dear God, according to Your Word, if I dwell in love, I dwell with You. Remind me*
*that nothing can separate me from You, not even feelings of loneliness. Amen.*

## *Evening* ———————————————

*Be satisfied with what you have. For God has said, "I will never fail you.*
*I will never abandon you."*
HEBREWS 13:5 NLT

*The LORD is near to all who call on him.*
PSALM 145:18 NIV

The next time you find yourself in a lonely spot, call on God. He does not
require fancy words or prayers of great faith. Just talk to Him. Just tell Him
that you need Him to put His arms around you and fill the empty places in
your heart.

*Father, help me remember Your promises when I feel alone. Amen.*

## *Morning*

*Blessed is the man that endureth temptation: for when he is tried, he shall receive the crown of life, which the Lord hath promised to them that love him.*
JAMES 1:12 KJV

*Because thou hast kept the word of my patience, I also will keep thee from the hour of temptation, which shall come upon all the world, to try them that dwell upon the earth.*
REVELATION 3:10 KJV

Evil abounds in our fallen world, and there are temptations around every corner. The devil never takes a day off. Be wary. We need to turn away from the lure of evil and place our lives in the center of God's will.

*Lord, help me keep my armor and obey Your Word so that ultimate victory will be Yours. Amen.*

## *Evening*

*"Woe to the world for temptations to sin! For it is necessary that temptations come, but woe to the one by whom the temptation comes!"*
MATTHEW 18:7 ESV

*The highway of the upright is to depart from evil; he who keeps his way preserves his soul.*
PROVERBS 16:17 NKJV

Life is a journey. There is a road that will take us where we want to go, but there are also many opportunities to take detours—sin that distracts us from the path God has laid out for us. When tempted to stray, ask God to direct your steps.

*Father, show me the boundaries I need for my life so I may resist temptation. Amen.*

# DAY 250 – *Spiritual Refreshment*

*Morning* ————————————————————

*Let's do our best to know the LORD. His coming is as certain as the morning sun;
he will refresh us like rain renewing the earth in the springtime.*
HOSEA 6:3 CEV

*Take My yoke upon you and learn of Me, for I am gentle (meek) and humble
(lowly) in heart, and you will find rest (relief and ease and refreshment and
recreation and blessed quiet) for your souls.*
MATTHEW 11:29 AMP

The Bible, the church, fellowship with other believers, prayer; these and
many other activities draw us close to God and therefore energize our
spiritual lives.

*Lord, draw me close to You. I need a spiritual boost today. Amen.*

*Evening* ————————————————————

*So we do not lose heart. Though our outer self is wasting away,
our inner self is being renewed day by day.*
2 CORINTHIANS 4:16 ESV

*God washed us by the power of the Holy Spirit.
He gave us new birth and a fresh beginning.*
TITUS 3:5 CEV

Many of us have experienced spiritual droughts. God's loving touch is so
necessary in our lives in these times. His living water quenches our spiritual
thirst and brings our drought to an end. Ask God for the living water. He will
issue forth a flood to wash you and refresh you.

*I am waiting, Lord, for Your Spirit to rain down upon me and soak me with Your
loving-kindness. Drench me in the waters of love and life. Amen.*

# DAY 251 – *Strength*

## *Morning*

*The LORD is constantly watching everyone, and he*
*to those who faithfully obey him.*
2 CHRONICLES 16:9 CEV

*He gives strength to the weary and increases the power of the weak.*
ISAIAH 40:29 NIV

A strong spiritual core will help ensure that you remain stable and secure in a changing world. That you are able to keep from falling. As you exercise your physical body, also make a commitment to regularly exercise your spiritual core as well.

*Father, help me return again and again to the core foundations*
*of my spiritual health. Amen.*

## *Evening*

*O my strength, I will sing praises to You; for God is my stronghold,*
*the God who shows me lovingkindness.*
PSALM 59:17 NASB

*Splendor and majesty are before him; strength and joy are in his place.*
1 CHRONICLES 16:27 ESV

The very God of the UNIVERSE strengthens us with His might, not ours. If it were up to us, we'd make a mess of things. We might muster up a little strength on good days, but what about the bad ones? Begin to memorize scripture on a daily basis and watch His strength within you begin to grow!

*Lord, in myself I am weak. In Your mighty power, I am strong! Amen.*

DAY 252 – *Evil*

*orning* _____

> Turn your back on evil, work for the good and don't quit.
> GOD loves this kind of thing.
> PSALM 37:27–28 MSG

> Do not be overcome by evil, but overcome evil with good.
> ROMANS 12:21 NASB

You are placed at this point in history for a reason. God has a job—a specific purpose—for you. You are a believer in Jesus Christ in a world that is increasingly hostile to Him in order that you might shine the light of His love.

> *Lord, I know You want me to overcome evil with good.*
> *Give me the courage to do just that. Amen.*

*Evening* _____

> Do not fret because of those who are evil or be envious of those who do wrong;
> for like the grass they will soon wither, like green plants they will soon die away.
> PSALM 37:1–2 NIV

> Even though I walk through the darkest valley, I will fear no evil.
> PSALM 23:4 NIV

We have felt the reality of evil in our own lives and seen it in others', too. In His Word, our holy God clearly outlines the reality of evil and shows us how to avoid the danger it presents.

> *Lord, search out the depths of my heart and remove any evil*
> *that You might find within me. Amen.*

# DAY 253 – *Ridicule*

## *Morning*

> LORD, *see how my enemies persecute me! Have mercy and lift me up*
> *from the gates of death.*
> PSALM 9:13 NIV

> *Persecuted, but not forsaken; cast down, but not destroyed.*
> 2 CORINTHIANS 4:9 KJV

God promises that even though we may be persecuted at times, He will never forsake us. That means He's right there, walking us through the pain. And even when we're cast down, we will never be destroyed. If we stick close to Jesus, we are buoyed by His faithfulness.

> *Father, when I go through seasons of persecution,*
> *I know You will walk with me. Amen!*

## *Evening*

> *The stupid ridicule right and wrong, but a moral life is a favored life.*
> PROVERBS 14:9 MSG

> *"But I say to you, Love your enemies and pray for those who persecute you."*
> MATTHEW 5:44 ESV

There are so many people in this world who will not understand our faith in the Lord Jesus Christ. They will ridicule us, persecute us, and turn us aside. That does not justify us hiding our faith. We are to shine as a light in this world.

> *Lord, You are the brightest light shining in my life. Help me reflect*
> *Your light in all that I do and say. Amen.*

# DAY 254 – *God's Glory*

*Thine, O LORD is the greatness, and the power, and the glory, and the victory, and the majesty: for all that is in the heaven and in the earth is thine; thine is the kingdom, O LORD, and thou art exalted as head above all.*
1 CHRONICLES 29:11 KJV

*So shall they fear the name of the LORD from the west, and His glory from the rising of the sun; when the enemy comes in like a flood, the Spirit of the LORD will lift up a standard against him.*
ISAIAH 59:19 NKJV

Knowing the power of the name and glory of the Lord is essential to our Christian lives. His name is above every other name; none has more authority than the One who spoke the world into being. His glory fills the whole earth.

*Lord, forgive me for forgetting how powerful You are and that Your glory is displayed throughout the whole earth. Help me remember who my God is. Amen.*

*And, lo, the angel of the Lord came upon them, and the glory of the Lord shone round about them.*
LUKE 2:9 KJV

*Now to him who is able to do immeasurably more than all we ask or imagine, according to his power that is at work within us, to him be glory in the church and in Christ Jesus throughout all generations, for ever and ever! Amen.*
EPHESIANS 3:20–21 NIV

It's amazing to think that God, in His infinite power, can do immeasurably more than all we could ask or imagine. His power in us gets the job done. . .and more.

*Heavenly Father, I praise You for being a God who goes above and beyond. Amen.*

DAY 255 – *Actions*

*Morning* ———————————————

> "Boast no more so very proudly, do not let arrogance come out of your mouth;
> for the LORD is a God of knowledge, and with Him actions are weighed."
> 1 SAMUEL 2:3 NASB

> Make the most of every opportunity in these evil days. Don't act thoughtlessly,
> but understand what the Lord wants you to do.
> EPHESIANS 5:16–17 NLT

Are you an actor or a reactor? The Lord longs for us to think before we act—to act on His behalf. To react takes little or no thought, but to live a life that reflects the image of Christ takes lots of work!

*God, today I give You my knee-jerking tendencies. Guard my actions. Amen.*

*Evening* ———————————————

> What you believe about these things should be kept between you and God.
> You are fortunate, if your actions don't make you have doubts.
> ROMANS 14:22 CEV

> Then Jesus said to them, "I ask you, which is lawful on the Sabbath:
> to do good or to do evil, to save life or to destroy it?"
> LUKE 6:9 NIV

Jesus is more concerned about the heart than with outward actions. In Jesus' mind, if you were going to do the right thing with the wrong heart, you might as well not even bother. In Jesus' book, a clean heart is far more important than clean hands.

*Father, help me focus on the condition of my heart, just as You do. Amen.*

## *Morning*

*Not only so, but we also glory in our sufferings, because we know that suffering produces perseverance; perseverance, character; and character, hope.*
ROMANS 5:3–4 NIV

*With your help I can advance against a troop; with my God I can scale a wall.*
PSALM 18:29 NIV

We often become discouraged when we face a mountain-size task. Tasks like these are best faced one step at a time. Chipping away instead of moving the whole mountain at once. With perseverance, and God's help, your goals may be more attainable than you think.

*Dear Father, when tasks seem impossible, remind me to seek You.*
*With Your help each step of the way, I will succeed. Amen.*

## *Evening*

*Let us strip off every weight that slows us down, especially the sin that so easily trips us up. And let us run with endurance the race God has set before us. We do this by keeping our eyes on Jesus, the champion who initiates and perfects our faith. Because of the joy awaiting him, he endured the cross.*
HEBREWS 12:1–2 NLT

*When your faith is tested, your endurance has a chance to grow. So let it grow, for when your endurance is fully developed, you will be perfect and complete, needing nothing.*
JAMES 1:3–4 NLT

Continually strive toward the completion of your godly goals with faith and perseverance, and one day you'll reach your goals, and your eternal prize will be one of heaven's greatest rewards.

*Dear God, help me to continuously aim for the goals*
*that You've placed in my heart. Amen.*

# DAY 257 – *Trust*

## *Morning*

*For I will not trust in my bow, nor will my sword save me. But You have saved us from our adversaries, and You have put to shame those who hate us.*
PSALM 44:6–7 NASB

*He was oppressed, and he was afflicted, yet he opened not his mouth; like a lamb that is led to the slaughter, and like a sheep that before its shearers is silent, so he opened not his mouth.*
ISAIAH 53:7 ESV

Jesus' silence can teach us important lessons. Underneath His silence was an implicit trust in His Father and His purposes. Christ knew who He was and what He had come to do. Trust is built in silence, and confidence strengthens in silence.

*Lord Jesus, help me learn from Your silence. Help me trust You more so that I don't feel the need to explain myself. Amen.*

## *Evening*

*Bad news won't bother them; they have decided to trust the LORD.*
PSALM 112:7 CEV

*I will say of the LORD, "He is my refuge and my fortress, my God, in whom I trust."*
PSALM 91:2 NIV

Trust is key to any relationship—between parent and child, between friends, certainly between a husband and wife. And trust is the cornerstone of our relationship with God as well. Over and over, the Bible tells us to "trust in the Lord." If we can't trust Him, who can we trust?

*Father, sometimes it's hard to trust something I can't see. But I know You are there—always! I trust in You! Amen.*

## *Morning*

Now listen, you who say, "Today or tomorrow we will go to this or that city, spend a year there, carry on business and make money." Why, you do not evenknow what will happen tomorrow. What is your life? You are a mist that appears for a little while and then vanishes. Instead, you ought to say, "If it is the Lord's will, we will live and do this or that."
JAMES 4:13–15 NIV

For where you have envy and selfish ambition,
there you find disorder and every evil practice.
JAMES 3:16 NIV

It is easy to fall into a trap of trying to live up to society's standards. This is sad, because who we should really be trying to please is God. He has created each of us with special gifts and talents, and it is His will that we do nothing more than live up to the potential He created for us.

*Lord, help me realize my potential. Make me less a person pleaser,
and more a God pleaser. Amen.*

## *Evening*

He who tills his land will have plenty of bread, but he who follows
frivolity will have poverty enough!
PROVERBS 28:19 NKJV

People who want to be rich fall into all sorts of temptations and traps. They are
caught by foolish and harmful desires that drag them down and destroy them.
1 TIMOTHY 6:9 CEV

The top of the corporate ladder is far short of the top of the spiritual ladder that God has set before us. What does it profit a man to save his life if he forfeits his soul?

*Lord, set my sights on treasures that never fade away. Amen.*

# DAY 259 – *Obedience*

"May he turn our hearts to him, to walk in obedience to him and keep
the commands, decrees and laws he gave our ancestors."
1 KINGS 8:58 NIV

"Do not add to or subtract from these commands I am giving you. Just obey the
commands of the LORD your God that I am giving you."
DEUTERONOMY 4:2 NLT

Following the unknown path that God has prepared leads us to a greater
obedience, obedience that helps us to learn more of Him. This newfound
knowledge will ultimately lead to happiness and contentment.

*Father, guide me on Your path. Help me learn of You and use what You
teach me for Your glory. Amen.*

*Evening* —————————————

Suffering made Jesus perfect, and now he can save forever all who obey him.
HEBREWS 5:9 CEV

Obey my commands and live! Guard my instructions as you guard your own eyes.
PROVERBS 7:2 NLT

Every rule God gives is given out of perfect love for us. We can truly enjoy
our lives the way God intends us to by obeying.

*Dear God, help me be obedient to Your will.
Please help me to not question Your wisdom,
but to always trust You. Amen.*

# DAY 260 – *Following Jesus*

## *Morning*

*And walk in love, as Christ also hath loved us, and hath given himself
for us an offering and a sacrifice to God for a sweetsmelling savour.*
EPHESIANS 5:2 KJV

*For we are his workmanship, created in Christ Jesus unto good works,
which God hath before ordained that we should walk in them.*
EPHESIANS 2:10 KJV

Jesus asked His disciples to follow Him, and He asks us to do the same.
It sounds simple, but following Jesus can be a challenge. Sometimes we
become impatient, not wanting to wait upon the Lord. Or perhaps we aren't
diligent to keep in step with Him. Following Jesus requires staying right on
His heels.

*Jesus, grant me the desire to follow You. Help me to not run ahead or lag behind. Amen.*

## *Evening*

*And thou shalt love the Lord thy God with all thy heart, and with all thy soul, and
with all thy mind, and with all thy strength: this is the first commandment.*
MARK 12:30 KJV

*"Follow me and I'll show you how. Self-help is no help at all. Self-sacrifice is the
way, my way, to finding yourself, your true self. What kind of deal is it to get
everything you want but lose yourself?"*
MATTHEW 16:24–26 MSG

The Holy Spirit's presence in our lives gives us comfort, guidance, and
the strength to follow Jesus. As we surrender ourselves to Him, He will
empower us to embrace self-sacrifice.

*Lord, help me learn and follow Your way. Amen.*

DAY 261 – *Idols*

*Morning* ─────────────────────────────

*Put to death therefore what is earthly in you: sexual immorality, impurity,
passion, evil desire, and covetousness, which is idolatry.*
COLOSSIANS 3:5 ESV

*The idols of the nations are silver and gold, the work of men's hands. They have
mouths, but they do not speak; eyes they have, but they do not see; they have ears,
but they do not hear; nor is there any breath in their mouths. Those who make them
are like them; so is everyone who trusts in them.*
PSALM 135:15–18 NKJV

Idols can be made from good things like relationships, families, religion, or
work. Anything we love and desire more than Christ becomes an idol. But
idols are powerless compared to our God. Spend time in prayer and ask
God to reveal any powerless idols you serve.

*Great Savior, who died to set me free, please show me the things
I love more than You. Amen.*

*Evening* ─────────────────────────────

*"Don't go back to worshiping worthless idols that cannot help
or rescue you—they are totally useless!"*
1 SAMUEL 12:21 NLT

*I hate those who cling to worthless idols; as for me, I trust in the LORD.*
PSALM 31:6 NIV

Although it may be unintentional, we can allow many other gods to take
Christ's place: friends, work, money, power, or even ourselves. The Lord
knows that when we put Him first, our lives will be fruitful and fulfilling.
Worshiping anything else eventually leaves us empty.

*Dear Lord, You alone are God. May my allegiance be to You and You alone. Amen.*

## *Morning*

First, God chose some people to be apostles and prophets and teachers
for the church. But he also chose some to work miracles or heal the sick
or help others or be leaders or speak different kinds of languages.
1 CORINTHIANS 12:28 CEV

"Give, and it will be given to you. A good measure, pressed down,
shaken together and running over, will be poured into your lap.
For with the measure you use, it will be measured to you."
LUKE 6:38 NIV

The Bible tells us to help carry each other's loads. There's someone out
there who needs your help. Ask God to show you that person and what you
can do to help meet his or her needs. Giving to others will always bring an
abundance of blessings back to you.

*Dear God, show me ways to help others so I bring glory
and honor to Your name. Amen.*

## *Evening*

Christian brother, you were chosen to be free. Be careful that you
do not please your old selves by sinning because you are free.
Live this free life by loving and helping others.
GALATIANS 5:13 NLV

Children, you show love for others by truly helping them,
and not merely by talking about it.
1 JOHN 3:18 CEV

Helping others is not an option for Christians, but a basic mandate upon
which our faith is built. We are the hands, the feet, and the voice of our
Lord. Let us serve Him well.

*O Lord, make me an instrument of Thy glory and will. Amen.*

# DAY 263 – *Holy Spirit*

*Do you not know that your bodies are temples of the Holy Spirit, who is in you,
whom you have received from God? You are not your own; you were
bought at a price. Therefore honor God with your bodies.*
1 CORINTHIANS 6:19–20 NIV

*O LORD, I know that the way of man is not in himself: it is not in man
that walketh to direct his steps. O LORD, correct me, but with judgment;
not in thine anger, lest thou bring me to nothing.*
JEREMIAH 10:23–24 KJV

Our hearts are wicked, and we can't understand our own feelings and
actions. Thankfully, God has given us the gift of the Holy Spirit to help us on
our journey. If we ask, the Lord is faithful to His Word and He will reveal our
motivations to us.

*Thank You, Father, that You are the discerner of hearts, that You have given
me Your Holy Spirit to help me. Amen.*

*Behold, I will pour out my spirit unto you, I will make known my words unto you.*
PROVERBS 1:23 KJV

*And the Holy Spirit helps us in our weakness. For example, we don't know
what God wants us to pray for. But the Holy Spirit prays for us with
groanings that cannot be expressed in words.*
ROMANS 8:26 NLT

The Lord has given every believer the gift of the Holy Spirit as a guide,
counselor, and prayer warrior. The Holy Spirit intercedes for us in accordance
with God's will, even when we're at a loss for words in our prayers.

*Dear Lord, thank You for providing the Holy Spirit to intercede for me
when I have no idea how to pray. Amen.*

# DAY 264 – *God's Word*

*He who keeps God's Word keeps his soul, but he who is
not careful of his ways will die.*
PROVERBS 19:16 NLV

*"The Spirit gives life; the flesh counts for nothing. The words I have
spoken to you—they are full of the Spirit and life."*
JOHN 6:63 NIV

How God works through His Word is a mystery, but He does. When we hear
it, meditate on it, pray it, memorize it, and ask for faith to believe it, He
comes to us in it and transforms our lives through it.

*Thank You, Jesus, the Living Word, who changes my heart and my mind
through the power of Your Word. Amen.*

*Everything that was written in the Holy Writings long ago was written to teach us.
By not giving up, God's Word gives us strength and hope.*
ROMANS 15:4 NLV

*"Heaven and earth will pass away, but My words will by no means pass away."*
LUKE 21:33 NKJV

When God's Word is planted in our lives it can transform us. Because Jesus
lives, every word spoken by Him has power today. By the Holy Spirit, God's
words can accomplish His will in our lives.

*Lord Jesus, I have forgotten the power of Your Word. Give me the desire
to read and obey Your voice. Amen.*

# DAY 265 – *Serving God*

How much more is done by the blood of Christ. He offered himself through the eternal Spirit as a perfect sacrifice to God. His blood will make our consciences pure from useless acts so we may serve the living God.

HEBREWS 9:14 NCV

"But if serving the LORD seems undesirable to you, then choose for yourselves this day whom you will serve, whether the gods your ancestors served beyond the Euphrates, or the gods of the Amorites, in whose land you are living. But as for me and my household, we will serve the LORD."

JOSHUA 24:15 NIV

The truth is, we all serve something. We may serve careers, money, appearance, or even relationships. Although we may not admit it, we become slaves to whatever we choose to serve. Choose to serve the Lord!

*Dear Lord, forgive me for choosing to serve anything other than You. Help me to faithfully love You. Amen.*

Dear friends, God is good. So I beg you to offer your bodies to him as a living sacrifice, pure and pleasing. That's the most sensible way to serve God.

ROMANS 12:1 CEV

Serve wholeheartedly, as if you were serving the Lord, not people, because you know that the Lord will reward each one for whatever good they do, whether they are slave or free.

EPHESIANS 6:7–8 NIV

In ROMANS, the apostle Paul exhorts believers to be fervent in spirit, serving the Lord. Fervent means bubbling or boiling, zealous. We can become zealous in our service if we allow the Holy Spirit to guide and direct us.

*Lord, when my energy to serve You runs low, push me one more degree. Amen.*

DAY 266 – *Priorities*

## *Morning*

*"You blind men, which is more important, the offering,
or the altar that sanctifies the offering?"*
MATTHEW 23:19 NASB

*Before daybreak the next morning, Jesus got up
and went out to an isolated place to pray.*
MARK 1:35 NLT

Jesus' days were packed with urgency. And yet He never seemed to be in a hurry and always accomplished everything that needed to be done. His secret? Jesus' priorities were clearly in order. He did the important things—like spending time with His Father—first.

*Father, order my priorities; help me put You first and trust You
to help me do the rest. Amen.*

## *Evening*

*"To love him with all your heart, with all your understanding and with all
your strength, and to love your neighbor as yourself is more important
than all burnt offerings and sacrifices."*
MARK 12:33 NIV

*"For because you did not do it the first time, the LORD our God broke out against us,
because we did not consult Him about the proper order."*
1 CHRONICLES 15:13 NKJV

Until the first crop was planted, early settlers didn't waste time building a real house but instead lived in sod homes. We still need to prioritize today. Anytime you see your desires rushing ahead of your means, think of those pioneers.

*Father, set our priorities in order for us, and give us the patience we need to
realize our goals come one step at a time. Amen.*

# DAY 267 – *Acceptance*

"Cease striving and know that I am God; I will be exalted among the nations,
I will be exalted in the earth."
PSALM 46:10 NASB

Then David got up from the ground. After he had washed, put on lotions and
changed his clothes, he went into the house of the LORD and worshiped. Then he went
to his own house, and at his request they served him food, and he ate.
2 SAMUEL 12:20 NIV

Acceptance of difficult situations isn't denial, and it isn't acting as if nothing
has happened. It is a quiet surrender, opening ourselves to the Lord's work
in our hearts.

*Heavenly Father, help me accept what You offer me—the good and the bad.
Help me worship You in my pain. Amen.*

Tremble, and do not sin; meditate in your heart upon your bed, and be still.
PSALM 4:4 NASB

"It may be that the LORD will look upon my misery and restore to me
his covenant blessing instead of his curse today."
2 SAMUEL 16:12 NIV

Some days it's hard to accept that God made us just the way He wanted us.
God doesn't have bad days or lapses in judgment. We have to assume we
are exactly what we were meant to be and go on from there. The one thing
we can always do is accept God's blessing, just as we are.

*Father, we can't always understand why we are what we are,
but we know You have a plan for our lives. Amen.*

# DAY 268 – *Encouragement*

## *Morning* ———————————————

*As soon as I pray, you answer me; you encourage me by giving me strength.*
PSALM 138:3 NLT

*But do not forget this one thing, dear friends: With the Lord a day is like a thousand years, and a thousand years are like a day.*
2 PETER 3:8 NIV

If you are feeling discouraged, take a step back and look at the big picture. Ask God to give you some of His perspective. Maintaining a biblical perspective on our circumstances can mean the difference between peace and anxiety, between joy and sorrow.

*Father, I admit that I often become discouraged. Please give me a fresh perspective to see life through Your eyes. Amen.*

## *Evening* ———————————————

*"I could encourage you with my mouth, and the solace of my lips would assuage your pain."*
JOB 16:5 NRSV

*But encourage one another daily, as long as it is called "Today," so that none of you may be hardened by sin's deceitfulness.*
HEBREWS 3:13 NIV

How can we make this world a better place? Begin by encouraging at least one person every day. Praise a loved one. Do something special for an absolute stranger. Stretch out a helping hand to someone in need. Make this a better world by being an encouragement to those around you.

*Father God, I want to make this world a better place. Show me whom You want me to bless today. Allow me to be Your conduit of love. And I'll praise You for it! Amen.*

# DAY 269 – *Strength*

*In a loud voice they were saying: "Worthy is the Lamb, who was slain, to receive power and wealth and wisdom and strength and honor and glory and praise!"*
REVELATION 5:12 NIV

*I can do all things through Christ who strengthens me.*
PHILIPPIANS 4:13 NKJV

It's human nature to try to handle things on our own. But the same God who created the heavens and the earth stands ready to work through you. Talk about power! It's above and beyond anything we could ever ask or think.

*God, today I lean on Your strength. Remind me daily that I can do all things through You. Amen.*

*Evening* ——————————————

*The Sovereign LORD is my strength! He makes me as surefooted as a deer, able to tread upon the heights.*
HABAKKUK 3:19 NLT

*My flesh and my heart may fail, but God is the strength of my heart and my portion forever.*
PSALM 73:26 NIV

In your weakness, God's strength shines through. His strength spoke the heavens and the earth into existence. And it's the same strength that made the journey up the hill to the cross. Acknowledge your weakness; then allow God's strong arms to encompass you.

*Lord, invigorate me with Your strength today. Amen.*

## *Morning*

*Jesus said, "No procrastination. No backward looks. You can't put
God's kingdom off till tomorrow. Seize the day."*
LUKE 9:62 MSG

*Farmers who wait for perfect weather never plant. If they watch
every cloud, they never harvest.*
ECCLESIASTES 11:4 NLT

Make a list of the things you've been putting off. . .then begin today to
work through the list. With each item crossed off, you'll find it becomes
easier to tackle the next.

*Father, I'm avoiding some things in my life. Help me take the first step. Amen.*

## *Evening*

*Yes, remember your Creator now while you are young, before the silver cord of life
snaps and the golden bowl is broken. Don't wait until the water jar is smashed at the
spring and the pulley is broken at the well.*
ECCLESIASTES 12:6 NLT

*Don't procrastinate—there's no time to lose. Run like a deer from the hunter,
fly like a bird from the trapper!*
PROVERBS 6:4–5 MSG

Sometimes it's hard to know when to move forward and when to sit still.
But if the Lord has called you to a particular task, you can't let lack of
understanding of the details keep you from doing what He's called you
to do. Hesitation and procrastination tend to keep us from achieving our
goals.

*Lord, sometimes I procrastinate. Help me get back on track.
Remove my hesitation and propel me forward. Amen.*

*I said to myself, "Relax, because the LORD takes care of you."*
PSALM 116:7 NCV

*And He said to them, "Come aside by yourselves to a deserted place
and rest a while." For there were many coming and going,
and they did not even have time to eat.*
MARK 6:31 NKJV

In our hurry-scurry world, a seaside vacation might be nice, but it's not always practical. Short periods of time garnered throughout a week might suffice. The front seat of your car, your bedroom, a park bench. All places where conversation with God can restore your soul.

*Dear Lord, grant me rest during hectic times. Amen.*

*One hand full of rest is better than two hands full of work
and trying to catch the wind.*
ECCLESIASTES 4:6 NLV

*And so my heart is glad. My soul is full of joy. My body also will rest without fear.*
PSALM 16:9 NLV

Give yourself permission to rest. Put it on your calendar. Your Father longs to see you relax, enjoy a hobby, nurture relationships, and draw close to Him through prayer and the reading of His Word.

*Lord, please increase my strength and guide me as I seek to find rest. Amen.*

## *Morning*

*Night is coming for them, and nightmares, for God takes the side of victims.*
*Do you think you can mess with the dreams of the poor? You can't,*
*for God makes their dreams come true.*
PSALM 14:5–6 MSG

*Those who work their land will have plenty of food, but the one who*
*chases empty dreams is not wise.*
PROVERBS 12:11 NCV

When our dreams are dashed, we have a choice. We can wallow in disappointment and cling to lost dreams, or we can look forward to the bright future that God has promised to every believer. It is a choice, and that choice is always ours.

*Lord, even when plans don't go my way, help me trust in the future*
*that You have planned for me. Amen.*

## *Evening*

*For in many dreams and in many words there is emptiness. Rather, fear God.*
ECCLESIASTES 5:7 NASB

*Foolish dreamers live in a world of illusion; wise realists plant*
*their feet on the ground.*
PROVERBS 14:18 MSG

Some people will go to extremes to achieve their dreams. But as children of God, we are to trust in God's timing and His plan. We might plan and take steps to achieve our goals, but we shouldn't run ahead of God's leadership.

*Lord, help me want You more than anything else. And teach me never to trade my*
*soul for something temporary. Amen.*

## *Morning*

> *I will declare that your love stands firm forever,*
> *that you have established your faithfulness*
> *in heaven itself.*
> PSALM 89:2 NIV

> *The LORD has established his throne in heaven,*
> *and his kingdom rules over all.*
> PSALM 103:19 NIV

God gives us glimpses of heaven here on earth so that we might long for such a place from the deepest reaches of our hearts.

*Father, when I see the beauty of Your creation, it reminds me of the beauty of heaven that awaits. Thank You for the promise of heaven. Amen.*

## *Evening*

> *"This is none other than the house of God,*
> *and this is the gate of heaven."*
> GENESIS 28:17 ESV

> *"In My Father's house are many mansions; if it were not so,*
> *I would have told you. I go to prepare a place for you."*
> JOHN 14:2 NKJV

Christ makes us strangers to the earth. His home is in heaven, and when He dwells within us, He prepares us for our true, eternal home.

*Sometimes I forget that this life is only temporary, Father. Remind me that my forever home awaits in heaven, where I will live forever with You. Amen.*

# DAY 274 – *Patience*

*Be completely humble and gentle; be patient, bearing with one another in love.*
EPHESIANS 4:2 NIV

*Wait on the LORD; be of good courage, and He shall strengthen your heart;*
*wait, I say, on the LORD!*
PSALM 27:14 NKJV

God's patience is without question. Sometimes He finds Himself having to repeat something. When our heavenly Father takes the time to repeat Himself, it must be important. He longs to strengthen your heart. How does He do that? He asks you to wait—and wait again.

*Father, sometimes I don't think I can keep up my courage. Today I recommit myself*
*to trusting You with all the things I'm waiting for. Amen.*

*I pray that the Lord will guide you to be as loving as God and as patient as Christ.*
2 THESSALONIANS 3:5 CEV

*For God is pleased when, conscious of his will, you patiently endure unjust*
*treatment. Of course, you get no credit for being patient if you are beaten*
*for doing wrong. But if you suffer for doing good and endure it patiently,*
*God is pleased with you.*
1 PETER 2:19–20 NLT

Patience is one of those Christian virtues we'd quite honestly like to avoid. As we rush about, trying to complete as many tasks as possible, patience gets shoved off to one side, until God forces it on us. But we'd be pretty terrible Christians if God never taught us to wait patiently for His will.

*Father, remind me of the importance of patience. As I rush to fulfill my goals,*
*slow me down so I might see Your will for my life. Amen.*

# DAY 275 – *Desires*

## *Morning*

*Those who live according to the flesh have their minds set on what the flesh desires; but those who live in accordance with the Spirit have their minds set on what the Spirit desires.*
ROMANS 8:5 NIV

*The eyes of all look expectantly to You, and You give them their food in due season. You open Your hand and satisfy the desire of every living thing.*
PSALM 145:15–16 NKJV

We can give God every desire of our heart. He can satisfy them. Prayer is the link. As you commune with Him, you will find your desires are either fulfilled or they begin to change to the blessings He wants to give you.

*Lord, help me be open and honest before You with all my yearnings. Enable me to trust You to fulfill or change the desires of my heart. Amen.*

## *Evening*

*Now those who belong to Christ Jesus have crucified the flesh with its passions and desires.*
GALATIANS 5:24 NASB

*"Just as the living Father sent me and I live because of the Father, so the one who feeds on me will live because of me."*
JOHN 6:57 NIV

Jesus said He is the Living Water and the Bread of Life. Water and food satisfy basic appetites. Jesus alone satisfies our deepest desires and needs.

*Christ Jesus, give me a desire for You. Help me examine my soul hunger and turn to You to fill it. Amen.*

## *Morning*

*A quick-tempered person does foolish things, and the one
who devises evil schemes is hated.*
PROVERBS 14:17 NIV

*For wrath killeth the foolish man, and envy slayeth the silly one.*
JOB 5:2 KJV

When we pause to meditate, to go to a quiet place to get alone with God
and be still, we are choosing to let Him have control in a situation. In going
to God about our anger, we open the door for Him to calm us. In handing
over our feelings of anger, we make room for peace.

*Lord, enable me to trust You wholly with my anger and keep me from sin. Amen.*

## *Evening*

*Stop being angry! Turn from your rage! Do not lose your
temper—it only leads to harm.*
PSALM 37:8 NLT

*The beginning of strife is like letting out water, so quit before the quarrel breaks out.*
PROVERBS 17:14 ESV

There is no end to the destruction that can occur when anger runs
rampant. Whether an explosive tantrum or seething resentment, anger is
as destructive to our relationships as floods are to the earth. Realize your
triggers, and ask the Father to help you stop anger when you feel it welling
up inside.

*Lord, I cannot control my anger without Your help. Soften my heart. Amen.*

DAY 277 - *God's Love*

*Morning* ─────────────────────────────

*No one has seen God at any time; if we love one another, God abides in us,*
*and His love is perfected in us.*
1 JOHN 4:12 NASB

*When I consider your heavens, the work of your fingers, the moon and the stars,*
*which you have set in place, what is mankind that you are mindful of them,*
*human beings that you care for them?*
PSALM 8:3-4 NIV

You are important to your heavenly Father, more important than the sun, the moon, and the stars. In fact, He cares so much that He sent His Son, Jesus, to offer His life as a sacrifice for your sins. Now that's love!

*Father, who am I that You would think twice about me? And yet You love me,*
*and for that I am eternally grateful. Amen.*

*Evening* ─────────────────────────────

*We have come to know and have believed the love which God has for us. God is love,*
*and the one who abides in love abides in God, and God abides in him.*
1 JOHN 4:16 NASB

*In this was manifested the love of God toward us, because that God sent his only*
*begotten Son into the world, that we might live through him.*
1 JOHN 4:9 KJV

Children don't always deserve the love their parents have for them, but love, true love, cannot be earned. Love is a gift, and God freely gives His love to each and every child who will accept it.

*Gracious and giving God, I cannot give You great enough thanks for all*
*You offer me, a humble child. Amen.*

# DAY 278 - *Refuge*

## *Morning*

"This God—his way is perfect; the word of the LORD proves true; he is a shield
for all those who take refuge in him."
2 SAMUEL 22:31 ESV

You are my hiding place; you will protect me from trouble and surround
me with songs of deliverance.
PSALM 32:7 NIV

Jesus is your hiding place, a haven, a quietness. Give the Lord your worries,
your troubles, and your questions. Give Him your praise and thanksgiving,
too. He promises to sing songs of deliverance over you.

*Jesus, be my Refuge. Lift my burdens. Sing songs of
deliverance over me, I ask. Amen.*

## *Evening*

O my Strength, to you I sing praises, for you, O God, are my refuge,
the God who shows me unfailing love.
PSALM 59:17 NLT

The name of the LORD is a strong tower; the righteous runs into it and is safe.
PROVERBS 18:10 NASB

The name of the Lord is a haven, a strong tower into which we can run.
But how do we do this? We claim His promises, read His Word, and pray.
Sometimes, when we are too weak even to do these things, we simply
speak His name.

*Lord, show Yourself to me. Grant me wisdom to call upon Your name
when I need a place of refuge. Amen.*

## *Morning*

*Make it your ambition to lead a quiet life: You should mind your own business and work with your hands, just as we told you, so that your daily life may win the respect of outsiders and so that you will not be dependent on anybody.*
1 Thessalonians 4:11–12 niv

*Now when the Sabbath was past, Mary Magdalene, Mary the mother of James, and Salome bought spices, that they might come and anoint Him.*
Mark 16:1 nkjv

There is spiritual value in the monotonous tasks essential to our lives. Often it's in these times that we are surprised by the Lord. As we engage our bodies in work, our minds are free to feel His presence and sense His leading.

*Lord, help me look and listen for You during the ordinary moments of my daily work. Amen.*

## *Evening*

*Whatsoever thy hand findeth to do, do it with thy might.*
Ecclesiastes 9:10 kjv

*What do workers gain from their toil? I have seen the burden God has laid on the human race. He has made everything beautiful in its time. He has also set eternity in the human heart; yet no one can fathom what God has done from beginning to end.*
Ecclesiastes 3:9–11 niv

Work is a necessity, but it doesn't have to consume you. Be on the lookout for telltale signs that you're working too hard. If your prayer time is suffering or you don't feel as close to the Lord, it might be time to reorganize your schedule.

*Father, I sometimes think my life is out of balance. Hard work is good—but even more so is spending time with You. Amen.*

## *Morning*

*Listen to advice and accept instruction, that you may gain wisdom in the future.*
PROVERBS 19:20 ESV

*The heartfelt counsel of a friend is as sweet as perfume and incense.*
PROVERBS 27:9 NLT

How encouraging to know that God longs to counsel us—to advise. And He's fully aware that nighttime is hard. Instead of fretting when you climb into bed, use the nighttime as your special time with God. Meet with Him and expect to receive His counsel.

*When the cares of the day overwhelm me, Father, I turn to Your counsel. Instruct my heart. Amen.*

## *Evening*

*If you have good sense, instruction will help you to have even better sense. And if you live right, education will help you to know even more.*
PROVERBS 9:9 CEV

*The king answered the people harshly, for he forsook the advice of the elders which they had given him.*
1 KINGS 12:13 NASB

It is rarely easy to accept advice and correction, and yet it is important that we heed the words of those wiser than ourselves. Often the words may seem harsh, but if they are offered out of love, then they may turn into the sweetest sounds we ever hear.

*Lord, tell me what I must do to grow, and give me the acceptance to deal with those things I would rather avoid. Amen.*

# DAY 281 – *Righteousness*

*For the LORD is righteous, He loves righteousness; the upright will behold His face.*
PSALM 11:7 NASB

*"If only there were someone to mediate between us, someone to bring us together,
someone to remove God's rod from me, so that his terror
would frighten me no more."*
JOB 9:33–34 NIV

God knew of our need for someone to bridge the gap between us and
our perfect heavenly Father. So He sent Jesus to be our arbitrator and the
perfect sacrifice for our sins. Because of His death, we don't have to fear
God's wrath.

*Lord, thank You for sending Jesus to be the bridge between us.
Thank You that Christ's righteousness, not mine, saves me. Amen.*

*"And the LORD has rewarded me according to my righteousness,
according to my cleanness in his sight."*
2 SAMUEL 22:25 ESV

*In the way of righteousness there is life; along that path is immortality.*
PROVERBS 12:28 NIV

If we are honest with ourselves, we have to admit that it's a scary thought
that God should judge us according to our measure of righteousness. But
by the forgiveness of sin offered through the cross, we are made clean and
able to pass the scrutinous eye of God.

*Thank You for the cross, Lord Jesus! Create in me a new and clean heart. Make me
like You. In the ways that I am lacking, remake me in the image of Christ. Amen.*

# DAY 282 - *Trials*

*For you know that the testing of your faith produces steadfastness.*
JAMES 1:3 ESV

*The spider taketh hold with her hands, and is in kings' palaces.*
PROVERBS 30:28 KJV

Life might have knocked us down, but it hasn't knocked us out if we summon what God has put within. With the power of prayer, we can stand on God's Word and draw forth what we need to rise again.

*Father, please allow the Holy Spirit to work in my life.*
*I need Your help through this trial. Amen.*

*"The third that is left I will test with fire, purifying them like silver, testing them like gold. Then they will call on me, and I will answer them. I will say, 'You are my people,' and they will say, 'The LORD is our God.' "*
ZECHARIAH 13:9 NCV

*And the Lord said, I have surely seen the affliction of My people who are in Egypt, and have heard their cry because of their taskmasters and oppressors; for I know their sorrows and sufferings and trials.*
EXODUS 3:7 AMP

In daily struggles, it is vital that we remember we have an ally who is greater than anyone who might oppose us or wish to make us unhappy. Jesus Christ became victor over everything this world could throw at Him—even death itself. If we give Him control of our hearts, He will be true to us.

*Father, You have made me a conqueror through Your Son, Jesus Christ. Help me to live as a victor and not as one defeated. Lift me up to be a sign to the world that in Christ we need never be afraid. Amen.*

# DAY 283 - *Anxiety*

*As pressure and stress bear down on me, I find joy in your commands.*
PSALM 119:143 NLT

*Do not be anxious about anything, but in every situation, by prayer and petition, with thanksgiving, present your requests to God.*
PHILIPPIANS 4:6 NIV

When was the last time you did an anxiety check? After all, we're instructed not to be anxious about anything. Instead, we're to turn to God in prayer so that He can take our burdens. Once they're lifted, it's bye-bye anxiety!

*Lord, I don't always remember to check my stress levels.*
*Today I hand my anxieties to You. Amen.*

*We are hard pressed on every side, but not crushed; perplexed, but not in despair; persecuted, but not abandoned; struck down, but not destroyed.*
2 CORINTHIANS 4:8–9 NIV

*But more than anything else, put God's work first and do what he wants. Then the other things will be yours as well.*
MATTHEW 6:33 CEV

Our bodies were designed to cope with anxiety in short bursts, but not day after day. Fix your eyes on Jesus during stress. It's not about burying your head in the sand; it's about knowing how the story ends. Jesus said the world would bring trouble, but He promises peace.

*Jesus, thank You for offering an eternal solution to my stress. With the hope of heaven, nothing will consume me on earth. Amen.*

# DAY 284 – *Salvation*

*If you declare with your mouth, "Jesus is Lord," and believe in your heart that God raised him from the dead, you will be saved. For it is with your heart that you believe and are justified, and it is with your mouth that you profess your faith and are saved.*
ROMANS 10:9–10 TNIV

*For by grace you have been saved through faith. And this is not your own doing; it is the gift of God, not a result of works, so that no one may boast.*
EPHESIANS 2:8–9 ESV

When we know the truth of salvation in Jesus, the burdens of the world that used to be overwhelming are lifted from our shoulders. Real freedom is simply this: God has everything under control, including our salvation.

*Jesus, show me how to take hold of my salvation, that I may experience total freedom in You. Amen.*

*For this is good and acceptable in the sight of God our Saviour; Who will have all men to be saved, and to come unto the knowledge of the truth.*
1 TIMOTHY 2:3–4 KJV

*Therefore, there is now no condemnation for those who are in Christ Jesus.*
ROMANS 8:1 NIV

By accepting God's gift of eternal life, we will never be condemned. Our security is rooted in Christ's unconditional love for us. That is the hope and assurance that we can stake our lives on.

*Jesus, thank You for salvation. My security comes in knowing You. Amen.*

# DAY 285 - *Generosity*

*Anyone who has been stealing must steal no longer, but must work, doing something useful with their own hands, that they may have something to share with those in need.*
EPHESIANS 4:28 NIV

*If I give all I possess to the poor and give over my body to hardship that I may boast, but do not have love, I gain nothing.*
1 CORINTHIANS 13:3 NIV

Jesus told the people that whenever they came to the aid of another person in need, they were aiding Him. Without God we would not possess the things we do. All things come to us from God, and true prosperity comes when we learn to give to others as freely as God gives to us.

*O Father, soften my heart to those who are less fortunate than I am. Help me appreciate the blessings I have been given and share from my abundance. Amen.*

*Evening*

*Give generously to them and do so without a grudging heart; then because of this the LORD your God will bless you in all your work and in everything you put your hand to.*
DEUTERONOMY 15:10 NIV

*"O our God, we thank you and praise your glorious name! But who am I, and who are my people, that we could give anything to you? Everything we have has come from you, and we give you only what you first gave us!"*
1 CHRONICLES 29:13–14 NLT

Christians should be sensitive to the need that exists in our world. It should be impossible for the Christian to selfishly hoard possessions when God calls on us to share from our abundance.

*Lord, let me share what I have and avoid the things I really don't need. Amen.*

# DAY 286 – *God's Protection*

*And they shall no more be a prey to the heathen, neither shall the beast of the land devour them; but they shall dwell safely, and none shall make them afraid.*
EZEKIEL 34:28 KJV

*Though I walk in the midst of trouble, thou wilt revive me: thou shalt stretch forth thine hand against the wrath of mine enemies, and thy right hand shall save me.*
PSALM 138:7 KJV

Our health, our safety, our ability to move, to think, and to play, all comes from God's power. He is protecting our minds and hearts from evil. He surrounds us with the Holy Spirit. God is aware of every detail of our lives and is carefully tending us.

*Thank You, God, for preserving me. Help me remember that I am valuable to You and You are concerned with every detail of my life. Amen.*

*Evening* —————————————————————————

*And of Benjamin he said, The beloved of the LORD shall dwell in safety by him; and the Lord shall cover him all the day long, and he shall dwell between his shoulders.*
DEUTERONOMY 33:12 KJV

*And who is he that will harm you, if ye be followers of that which is good?*
1 PETER 3:13 KJV

No matter how careful we try to be, we need someone to catch us when we stumble. God is that Someone. He waits with open arms to catch His children when they fall.

*Without You, I am sure to fall, Lord. Thank You for being with me, picking me up when I fall. Amen.*

# DAY 287 – *Words*

*Israel, I will teach you. My words will be like gentle rain on
tender young plants, or like dew on the grass.*
DEUTERONOMY 32:2 CEV

*Gracious words are a honeycomb, sweet to the soul and healing to the bones.*
PROVERBS 16:24 NIV

Our words should reflect the presence of God in our hearts. Only the most
excellent and right things should spring forth from our mouths.

*Let me build up, rather than tear down. May my speech reflect
my great love for You, Lord. Amen.*

*The words of the mouth are deep waters,
but the fountain of wisdom is a rushing stream.*
PROVERBS 18:4 NIV

*The unfolding of your words gives light; it gives understanding to the simple.*
PSALM 119:130 NIV

We are called to be Christians in our thoughts, deeds, and words. What we
say matters a great deal, and God will judge us based on our words and
thoughts, as well as on our actions.

*Lord, keep me from hurting others with my words. Never let me forget
that to grow, I must continually examine myself. Amen.*

# DAY 288 – *Health*

## *Morning*

LORD, make me to know mine end, and the measure of my days,
what it is: that I may know how frail I am.
PSALM 39:4 KJV

Is any sick among you? let him call for the elders of the church; and let them pray
over him, anointing him with oil in the name of the Lord: And the prayer of faith shall
save the sick, and the Lord shall raise him up.
JAMES 5:14–15 KJV

Investment in exercising, getting enough sleep, and eating properly reaps
countless benefits in helping us be more productive, clearheaded, and
energetic. God created our bodies as temples, and we only get one.

*Father, thank You for my temple. Help me care for it to the best of my ability
and honor You with healthy habits. Amen.*

## *Evening*

Ye shall walk in all the ways which the LORD your God hath commanded you,
that ye may live, and that it may be well with you, and that ye may prolong
your days in the land which ye shall possess.
DEUTERONOMY 5:33 KJV

And when he was come into the house, the blind men came to him: and Jesus saith
unto them, Believe ye that I am able to do this? They said unto him, Yea, Lord.
Then touched he their eyes, saying, According to your faith be it unto you.
MATTHEW 9:28–30 KJV

We need discipline in our spiritual (and physical) diet, but we can't do it on
our own. We need God's power to help us crave those things that are the
healthiest.

*Lord, help me to feed my body and soul the things that will keep me
most healthy and useful to You. Amen.*

# DAY 289 – *Commitment*

*But You, O Lord, know and understand me and my devotion to You; You see me and try my heart toward You. [O Lord] pull [these rebellious ones] out like sheep for the slaughter and devote and prepare them for the day of slaughter.*
JEREMIAH 12:3 AMP

*Therefore, my dear brothers and sisters, stand firm. Let nothing move you. Always give yourselves fully to the work of the Lord, because you know that your labor in the Lord is not in vain.*
1 CORINTHIANS 15:58 NIV

It's not only possible to stand firm during tough times, it's what God expects. He doesn't want anything to move us. Today, if you're faced with challenges, resolve to stand firm—no matter what. Remain committed to the faith.

*Lord, give me the spiritual backbone to stand firm, to remain committed to You. . . no matter what. Amen.*

*"So commit yourselves wholeheartedly to these words of mine. Tie them to your hands and wear them on your forehead as reminders."*
DEUTERONOMY 11:18 NLT

*He who tills his land will have plenty of bread, but he who follows frivolity will have poverty enough!*
PROVERBS 28:19 NKJV

Diligence to work yields positive results. The principle of sowing and reaping also is true in our spiritual lives. Diligent prayer and self-examination lead to repentance. The harvest is the life of Christ that grows in us.

*Gracious God, give me the desire to sow the things of the Spirit. Produce Your life in me. Amen.*

DAY 290 – *Perseverance*

*Morning* ─────────────────────────────────

As you know, we count as blessed those who have persevered. You have heard of job's
perseverance and have seen what the Lord finally brought about.
The Lord is full of compassion and mercy.
JAMES 5:11 NIV

You need to persevere so that when you have done the will of God,
you will receive what he has promised.
HEBREWS 10:36 TNIV

Our world is upside down. To be good is foreign or alien to the majority.
The key is not to give up. The Lord will reward those who persevere in the
face of frustration. God loves the pure in heart, and it is well worth it to hold
on for His sake.

*Be with me, Lord, to strengthen me and to help me deal with people who think wrong
is right. I want to be Your child, not a child of the world. Amen.*

*Evening* ─────────────────────────────────

Though he fall, he shall not be utterly cast down: for the LORD
upholdeth him with his hand.
PSALM 37:24 KJV

But the path of the just is as the shining light, that shineth more and
more unto the perfect day.
PROVERBS 4:18 KJV

No one ever rises completely above sin. God wants people who will try and
who will strive to do better, even when they know they can't be perfect.
God will judge us on the intentions of our hearts to be reconciled to Him.
He loves us that much.

*Lord, fill me with strength and continually remind me of Your great mercy. Though I
am not worthy, I am loved. Help me persevere even when I fail. Amen.*

*The LORD is truthful; he can be trusted.*
PSALM 33:4 CEV

*Send out your light and your truth; let them lead me; let them bring me*
*to your holy hill and to your dwelling!*
PSALM 43:3 ESV

The world is full of darkness and confusion. God's enemies would have us believe there is no such thing as absolute truth, no difference between right and wrong. But God's Word tells us otherwise. God's truth brings freedom to our lives that in turn produces joy.

*Jesus, cause me to remember that all truth and all light come from You. Amen.*

*But whoever lives by the truth comes into the light, so that it may be seen plainly that*
*what they have done has been done in the sight of God.*
JOHN 3:21 NIV

*Invest in truth and wisdom, discipline and good sense, and don't part with them.*
PROVERBS 23:23 CEV

Jesus said that He was the Truth. If we want to get close to Christ, we must put lies and deceitfulness out of our hearts. Our words must be kind and reflect the concern and care of Jesus Christ Himself.

*My desire is to be close to You, Lord. Help me live a life of*
*honesty and integrity. Amen.*

## *Morning*

*Therefore I say unto you, Take no thought for your life, what ye shall eat, or what ye shall drink; nor yet for your body, what ye shall put on. Is not the life more than meat, and the body than raiment? Behold the fowls of the air: for they sow not, neither do they reap, nor gather into barns; yet your heavenly Father feedeth them. Are ye not much better than they? . . . And why take ye thought for raiment? Consider the lilies of the field, how they grow; they toil not, neither do they spin: And yet I say unto you, That even Solomon in all his glory was not arrayed like one of these.*
MATTHEW 6:25–26, 28–29 KJV

*For all the animals of the forest are mine, and I own the cattle on a thousand hills.*
PSALM 50:10 NLT

God's resources are vast and He has promised to meet all our needs. Regardless of the circumstances, we can depend on Him to provide for us. You do not have a need that God cannot meet. Rest in the knowledge that God will take care of you.

*Heavenly Father, thank You for being my Provider. Amen.*

## *Evening*

*If then God so clothe the grass, which is to day in the field, and to morrow is cast into the oven; how much more will he clothe you, O ye of little faith?*
LUKE 12:28 KJV

*And my God will meet all your needs according to the riches of his glory in Christ Jesus.*
PHILIPPIANS 4:19 NIV

As a child of God, it's important to remember that He will supply all your needs. He is your source of all things—financial, physical, mental, and spiritual.

*Dear God, You know my needs before I even ask. Thank You. Amen.*

DAY 293 – *Spiritual Growth*

*Morning* ───────────────────────────────

> Like newborn infants, long for the pure spiritual milk,
> that by it you may grow up into salvation.
> 1 PETER 2:2 ESV

> Therefore, my dear friends, as you have always obeyed—not only in my presence,
> but now much more in my absence—continue to work out your salvation
> with fear and trembling, for it is God who works in you to will
> and to act in order to fulfill his good purpose.
> PHILIPPIANS 2:12–13 NIV

Spiritual growth doesn't just happen—it takes a lot of discipline. Reading God's Word is a great start, but we need to transfer our head knowledge to the heart by applying God's truth in everyday life.

> *Dear Lord, remind me of the importance of spiritual growth—*
> *in this life and eternity to come. Amen.*

*Evening* ───────────────────────────────

> What a person plants, he will harvest. The person who plants selfishness, ignoring the
> needs of others—ignoring God!—harvests a crop of weeds. All he'll have to show for
> his life is weeds! But the one who plants in response to God, letting God's Spirit do
> the growth work in him, harvests a crop of real life, eternal life.
> GALATIANS 6:7–8 MSG

> Dear brothers and sisters, I close my letter with these last words: Be joyful. Grow to
> maturity. Encourage each other. Live in harmony and peace.
> 2 CORINTHIANS 13:11 NLT

As you focus on getting to know the person of Christ, your sanctification will take place. As you look to Jesus, His glory will transform you, one degree at a time; and slowly but surely you will begin to look like Him.

> *Lord Jesus, help me become more like You. Amen.*

# DAY 294 – *Rebellion*

## *Morning*

*He turned the sea into dry land; they passed through the river on foot. There did we rejoice in him, who rules by his might forever, whose eyes keep watch on the nations—let not the rebellious exalt themselves.*
PSALM 66:6-7 ESV

*Where there is no revelation, the people cast off restraint;
but happy is he who keeps the law.*
PROVERBS 29:18 NKJV

The law was given for our good, to lead us to Christ and to instruct us in how to live. When we do not focus on Christ, we will cast off all restraint, rebelling against the very things that are good for us.

*Father, keep my eyes focused on You. Enable me by Your Spirit to love and keep Your law. Amen.*

## *Evening*

*The Sovereign LORD has opened my ears; I have not been rebellious,
I have not turned away.*
ISAIAH 50:5 NIV

*At one time you all had your backs turned to God, thinking rebellious thoughts of him, giving him trouble every chance you got. But now, by giving himself completely at the Cross, actually dying for you, Christ brought you over to God's side and put your lives together, whole and holy in his presence.
You don't walk away from a gift like that!*
COLOSSIANS 1:21-23 MSG

We all need to feel free to voice our feelings. But always remember that our heavenly Father has the final word. But be careful that freedom doesn't turn to rebellion.

*Lord, thank You for hearing my words. May I always follow Your ways. Amen.*

DAY 295 – *Repentance*

## *Morning*

*"But if a wicked person turns away from all the sins they have committed
and keeps all my decrees and does what is just and right,
that person will surely live; they will not die."*
EZEKIEL 18:21 NIV

*"Come, let us return to the LORD. He has torn us to pieces; now he will heal us.
He has injured us; now he will bandage our wounds."*
HOSEA 6:1 NLT

When we sin, it is a private matter between God and ourselves. Take your sins before God, repent for each one, and glory in the grace of God, by which we receive full pardon for all we do wrong.

*Forgive me, Lord. Make a new creation out of this old soul. Prepare me for the kingdom to come each day of my life. Amen.*

## *Evening*

*"I tell you that in the same way there will be more rejoicing in heaven over one sinner
who repents than over ninety-nine righteous persons who do not need to repent."*
LUKE 15:7 NIV

*Do you despise the riches of his kindness and forbearance and patience?
Do you not realize that God's kindness is meant to lead you to repentance?*
ROMANS 2:4 NRSV

The word *repent* means to turn away from. God wants us to turn from the things that are wrong in our lives and to turn toward Him. If we will always try to do just that, the Lord's face will shine upon us, and we shall be saved.

*Be patient with me, Lord. I run off in so many wrong directions, but I want always to come back to You. Thank You for not giving up on me. Amen.*

# DAY 296 – *Appearance*

*And being found in appearance as a man, he humbled himself by becoming obedient to death—even death on a cross!*
PHILIPPIANS 2:8 NIV

*But the LORD said to Samuel, "Don't judge by his appearance or height, for I have rejected him. The LORD doesn't see things the way you see them. People judge by outward appearance, but the LORD looks at the heart."*
1 SAMUEL 16:7 NLT

Where we humans make snap judgments about others by their appearance, God looks deep into our hearts. Make it a priority to value others—and yourself—for the appearance of the heart.

*Dear Father, thank You for being a God who values me for far more than my physical appearance. Help me always look at others with the same depth. Amen.*

*Evening*

*"There is far more to your life than the food you put in your stomach, more to your outer appearance than the clothes you hang on your body."*
MATTHEW 6:25 MSG

*What matters is not your outer appearance—the styling of your hair, the jewelry you wear, the cut of your clothes—but your inner disposition.*
1 PETER 3:3-4 MSG

You don't admire Christians because of their physical beauty. You admire them because the beauty of God shines from within them, and such beauty is irresistible.

*Lord, when we begin to worry too much about outward appearance, remind us that others see You in us. Amen.*

# DAY 297 – *Temptation*

## *Morning*

*The Lord knoweth how to deliver the godly out of temptations.*
2 PETER 2:9 KJV

*How long must I wrestle with my thoughts and day after day have sorrow in my heart? How long will my enemy triumph over me?*
PSALM 13:2 NIV

Every day we struggle with thoughts that may not be pleasing to God. Your mind is a battlefield. Instead of wrestling with your thoughts, make a conscious effort to give your thought life to the One capable of handling it.

*Father, sometimes I don't like the thoughts flitting through my mind. Today I give my thoughts to You. Amen.*

## *Evening*

*"Those on the rocky soil are those who, when they hear, receive the word with joy; and these have no firm root; they believe for a while, and in time of temptation fall away."*
LUKE 8:13 NASB

*Now the serpent was more cunning than any beast of the field which the LORD God had made. And he said to the woman, "Has God indeed said, 'You shall not eat of every tree of the garden'?"*
GENESIS 3:1 NKJV

Sometimes it's very difficult to say no to evil. It can be lonely, when so many people love to do what they know is wrong. It is a rare individual who will say no even when it means being rejected. But have faith! Call on the Lord, and He will give you strength and conviction.

*All around me I see people doing things that are not pleasing to You. I want to live a good life, Father. Fill me with Your Spirit, that I might follow Your ways. Amen.*

## *Morning*

> *You are my God. I worship you. In my heart, I long for you,*
> *as I would long for a stream in a scorching desert.*
> PSALM 63:1 CEV

> *Worship the LORD in the splendor of his holiness; tremble before him, all the earth.*
> PSALM 96:9 NIV

There's great joy in lifting up praises to God. And He loves it when you come into His presence with singing. If you're not convinced, read the book of PSALMS!

> *O Father, You've been so good to me! Today the song in my heart erupts.*
> *I'll make a joyful noise because of Your goodness.*

## *Evening*

> *Our God, you are the one who rides on the clouds, and we praise you.*
> *Your name is the LORD, and we celebrate as we worship you.*
> PSALM 68:4 CEV

> *"God is spirit, and those who worship Him must worship in spirit and truth."*
> JOHN 4:24 NASB

God wants to hear music from our hearts, not arias with perfect notes. So we lift up our voices and join in the worship of our Creator and Lord. Harmonious, harsh, or hoarse, He's filtering our melodies with His love.

> *Dear heavenly Father, I worship You.*
> *Thank You for Your goodness and mercy. Amen.*

# DAY 299 – *Time*

*No one knows the day or hour. The angels in heaven don't know,
and the Son himself doesn't know. Only the Father knows.*
MATTHEW 24:36 CEV

*And God said, "Let there be lights in the expanse of the heavens to separate the day
from the night. And let them be for signs and for seasons, and for days and years."*
GENESIS 1:14 ESV

We may dwell too much in the past or worry too much about our future.
Think about God's hands that hold our time. Our moments to our years
are in the hands of the Creator, Healer, Sustainer, Provider, Redeemer, and
Lover of our souls.

*Gracious God who rules and reigns over all my days, cause me to remember that I
am held by Your loving hands—always. Amen.*

*Surely your goodness and love will follow me all the days of my life,
and I will dwell in the house of the LORD forever.*
PSALM 23:6 NIV

*He has made everything beautiful in its time. He has also set eternity in the human
heart; yet no one can fathom what God has done from beginning to end.*
ECCLESIASTES 3:11 NIV

When it comes to the length of your life, you don't get "extra" days. God
already has in mind how many years you'll have and how many days will be
in each one. You can't change that. What you can change is how wisely you
use your time.

*Help us use each day wisely, Lord, to serve You and others. Amen.*

# DAY 300 – *Idols*

*What is an idol worth? It's merely a false god. Why trust a speechless image made from wood or metal by human hands?*
HABAKKUK 2:18 CEV

*Do any of the worthless idols of the nations bring rain? Do the skies themselves send down showers? No, it is you, LORD our God. Therefore our hope is in you, for you are the one who does all this.*
JEREMIAH 14:22 NIV

Compared to God, the wood and stone idols in the Bible are useless. Similarly, when we trust someone or something other than God, then we trust something as useless as wood and stone idols.

*Lord, help me rely on You—and not things that cannot provide the comfort, protection, and salvation I need. Amen.*

*Because the LORD is great; he should be praised at all times. He should be honored more than all the gods, because all the gods of the nations are only idols, but the LORD made the heavens.*
PSALM 96:4–5 NCV

*You can be sure that using people or religion or things just for what you can get out of them—the usual variations on idolatry—will get you nowhere, and certainly nowhere near the kingdom of Christ, the kingdom of God.*
EPHESIANS 5:5 MSG

Although we don't set up figurines in our homes and bow down to them, we may become idol worshipers in more sophisticated ways. We accept non-Christian practices without batting an eye.

*Lord, we don't want to live in unfaithfulness. Make our hearts and lips devoted to You. Amen.*

*Morning*

---

*The man knew what each servant could do. So he handed five thousand coins to the first servant, two thousand to the second, and one thousand to the third. Then he left the country. As soon as the man had gone, the servant with the five thousand coins used them to earn five thousand more.*
MATTHEW 25:15–16 CEV

*Whoever loves pleasure will become poor; whoever loves wine and olive oil will never be rich.*
PROVERBS 21:17 NIV

Most of us can relate to the temptation to spend more than we have. It takes wisdom and discipline to be able to say no. But wise spending decisions bring peace and security, especially during tough economic times.

*Father, help me spend my money wisely. Amen.*

*Evening*

---

*You people who don't want to work, think about the ant! Consider its ways and be wise! It has no commander. It has no leader or ruler. But it stores up its food in summer. It gathers its food at harvest time.*
PROVERBS 6:6–8 NIrV

*By wisdom a house is built, and by understanding it is established; and by knowledge the rooms are filled with all precious and pleasant riches.*
PROVERBS 24:3–4 NASB

It is never wise to live beyond our means. In all ways, we should try to work with what God has given to us, waiting on the time when we may attain good things without going into debt.

*Lord, thank You for the many blessings in my life. Help me be content with what I have and not strive for what I cannot afford. Amen.*

## *Morning*

*Surely our griefs He Himself bore, and our sorrows He carried.*
ISAIAH 53:4 NASB

*For his anger lasts only a moment, but his favor lasts a lifetime; weeping may stay for the night, but rejoicing comes in the morning.*
PSALM 30:5 NIV

Times of true mourning don't last forever. They may feel like it, but they eventually pass. Hang tight to the One who can best minister to your broken heart. He wants you to know that your pain and your tears will only last for a season. Joy is coming.

*God, thank You for Your healing balm. I'm so grateful that my tears are only temporary. Amen.*

## *Evening*

*"Truly, truly, I say to you, that you will weep and lament, but the world will rejoice; you will grieve, but your grief will be turned into joy."*
JOHN 16:20 NASB

*Brothers and sisters, we do not want you to be uninformed about those who sleep in death, so that you do not grieve like the rest of mankind, who have no hope.*
1 THESSALONIANS 4:13 NIV

Sometimes as Christians we are given the impression that grieving somehow implies that we don't trust God. We are to grieve, but not without hope. Jesus feels your pain and your tears are precious to Him. But when you grieve, be sure to grieve with hope in the coming of our Lord.

*Jesus, thank You for loving me and feeling my pain. Help me grieve with hope. Amen.*

# DAY 303 – *Anger*

## *Morning*

> *It's smart to be patient, but it's stupid to lose your temper.*
> PROVERBS 14:29 CEV

> *Whoever is slow to anger is better than the mighty,*
> *and he who rules his spirit than he who takes a city.*
> PROVERBS 16:32 ESV

Rather than letting the fire in your heart spew from your tongue, take your hurt to the Lord before you speak. Ask Him to help you forgive. Forgiveness squelches anger like cold water thrown on a fire, and through forgiveness, God is glorified in your life.

*Dear Lord, help me deal with anger when it first arises in my heart. Amen.*

## *Evening*

> *"But I say, if you are even angry with someone, you are subject to judgment!*
> *If you call someone an idiot, you are in danger of being brought before the court.*
> *And if you curse someone, you are in danger of the fires of hell."*
> MATTHEW 5:22 NLT

> *Wherefore, my beloved brethren, let every man be swift to hear, slow to speak,*
> *slow to wrath: For the wrath of man worketh not the righteousness of God.*
> JAMES 1:19–20 KJV

Jesus saved His anger for things like oppression. Injustice. Unfairness. Not for when His rights were violated, but when others' rights were—for when the powerful took advantage of the powerless. Anger is a potent emotion. Save it for issues that really matter.

*Jesus, help me be more like You, to be angry about the right things and to use my anger in a way that honors You. Amen.*

# DAY 304 – *Joy*

*When anxiety was great within me, your consolation brought me joy.*
PSALM 94:19 NIV

*I'm thanking you, GOD, from a full heart, I'm writing the book on your wonders.*
*I'm whistling, laughing, and jumping for joy; I'm singing your song, High God.*
PSALM 9:1–2 MSG

Have you ever experienced joy that couldn't be contained? Such joy rises from a heart filled with hope. You feel like telling everyone just what God has done for you. Celebrate the victories you've experienced, large or small. Jump for joy!

*Lord, my heart is overwhelmed with joy. You've done so much for me,*
*and I don't deserve it. Thank You! Amen.*

*The hope of the righteous brings joy, but the expectation of the wicked will perish.*
PROVERBS 10:28 ESV

*"If you keep my commands, you will remain in my love, just as I have kept my*
*Father's commands and remain in his love. I have told you this so that my joy*
*may be in you and that your joy may be complete."*
JOHN 15:10–11 NIV

Joy is a key part of the Christian life, because knowing God brings security and delight in the Savior. No one experiences such joy without an intimate relationship with Him.

*Father, when I struggle to find joy in my life, draw my attention back to You.*
*You are my joy. Amen.*

# DAY 305 – *Abiding*

*"Abide in Me, and I in you. As the branch cannot bear fruit of itself, unless it abides in the vine, neither can you, unless you abide in Me. I am the vine, you are the branches. He who abides in Me, and I in him, bears much fruit; for without Me you can do nothing."*
JOHN 15:4–5 NKJV

*Now he who keeps His commandments abides in Him, and He in him. And by this we know that He abides in us, by the Spirit whom He has given us.*
1 JOHN 3:24 NKJV

Abiding in God means we trust in Him and live with our entire lives centered on our Lord. This is more than lip-service "faith"; it means putting our money where our mouths are when we face everyday difficulties.

*May my life be more than surface-level faith to You, Lord. Be my focus. Amen.*

*Evening* ───────────────────────────

*He who dwells in the shelter of the Most High will abide in the shadow of the Almighty.*
PSALM 91:1 NASB

*And now, little children, abide in him; that, when he shall appear, we may have confidence, and not be ashamed before him at his coming.*
1 JOHN 2:28 KJV

God fills us with His Spirit so we can abide in Him. When life doesn't seem to be going in the right direction, abiding can be a real challenge. But we abide either in Christ or in something else. And how we're living tells us and others where our lives are focused.

*Search my life, Lord. I want my life to be centered on You, that others might see You through my life. Amen.*

DAY 306 – *Angels*

*Morning*

*The angel of the Lord encampeth round about them
that fear him, and delivereth them.*
PSALM 34:7 KJV

*For he shall give his angels charge over thee, to keep thee in all thy ways.
They shall bear thee up in their hands, lest thou dash they foot against a stone.*
PSALM 91:11–12 KJV

Who's to say where God's angels are? Perhaps we each have an angel who watches us and guides us. God, in His love for us, has set the angels over us. Rest secure. The angels are watching.

*Help me believe in the angels that You send, Lord. I need watching over.
I need You to be with me. Amen.*

*Evening*

*"Likewise, I say to you, there is joy in the presence of the angels of God
over one sinner who repents."*
LUKE 15:10 NKJV

*Don't forget to show hospitality to strangers, for some who have done this have
entertained angels without realizing it!*
HEBREWS 13:2 NLT

Though angels have been shoved aside to the category of myth by many, we know that there is another realm where everything doesn't always make sense to us. Angels are God's ambassadors of goodwill in this world.

*May I be like Your angels, Father, and be an ambassador of goodwill.
Thank You for Your marvelous creation. Amen.*

# DAY 307 - *Trust*

*Ah Lord GOD! behold, thou hast made the heaven and the earth by thy great power
and stretched out arm, and there is nothing too hard for thee.*
JEREMIAH 32:17 KJV

*But it is good for me to draw near to God: I have put my trust in the Lord GOD,
that I may declare all thy works.*
PSALM 73:28 KJV

Trust is a tricky thing. It is difficult to put our trust in others, because we
can't be sure whether they will value it. That fear should not apply when it
comes to putting our trust in God. He will follow us to the ends of the earth
to make sure we know of His great love.

*Wherever I go, Lord, I need to know that You are with me. I will put my trust in
You, knowing that You will always do what is best for me. Help me
trust You more each day. Amen.*

*"Such is the destiny of all who forget God; so perishes the hope of the godless.
What they trust in is fragile; what they rely on is a spider's web. They lean on the
web, but it gives way; they cling to it, but it does not hold."*
JOB 8:13–15 NIV

*Some trust in chariots and some in horses, but we trust in the
name of the LORD our God.*
PSALM 20:7 NIV

Trust takes time. We need to practice putting our trust in the Lord, but
when we do, we find a new confidence that He will be faithful to us.

*Assist me as I try to let go of my doubt and fear and put my trust in You. I sometimes
become my own worst enemy, Father. Save me from myself. Amen.*

*Morning* ───────────────────────────

> Jesus answered them, "Truly, truly, I say to you, everyone who
> commits sin is the slave of sin."
> JOHN 8:34 NASB

> When you follow the desires of your sinful nature, the results are very clear: sexual
> immorality, impurity, lustful pleasures, idolatry, sorcery, hostility, quarreling,
> jealousy, outbursts of anger, selfish ambition, dissension, division, envy,
> drunkenness, wild parties, and other sins like these. Let me tell you again, as I have
> before, that anyone living that sort of life will not inherit the Kingdom of God.
> GALATIANS 5:19–21 NLT

Scripture does not mention many specific addictions, like gambling or
drugs, but it clearly sets forth principles that make it clear that believers
should not engage in an addictive lifestyle.

> Lord, help me avoid addiction in my life, I pray. And should I find myself straying
> from Your commands, lead me back to Your love. Amen.

*Evening* ───────────────────────────

> If the Son gives you freedom, you are free!
> JOHN 8:36 CEV

> Therefore, dear brothers and sisters, you have no obligation to do what your sinful
> nature urges you to do. For if you live by its dictates, you will die. But if through the
> power of the Spirit you put to death the deeds of your sinful nature, you will live.
> For all who are led by the Spirit of God are children of God.
> ROMANS 8:12–14 NLT

Letting go of the things we're addicted to is a struggle. . .and can leave us
feeling empty. Turn to your heavenly Father. Only He can fill the deepest
parts of you.

> Father, fill me with Your love. Be my source of joy. Amen.

# DAY 309 – *Advice*

## *Morning*

*Where there is no guidance the people fall, but in abundance
of counselors there is victory.*
PROVERBS 11:14 NASB

*The wise also will hear and increase in learning, and the person of
understanding will acquire skill and attain to sound counsel [so that he
may be able to steer his course rightly].*
PROVERBS 1:5 AMP

Wisdom comes from God, not people. But those who walk closely with Him
can be good advisers when we need help. No one should avoid getting
good advice when it's needed, and going first to God, then to godly
humans, will lead us into wise decisions.

*Lord, help me seek godly advice. Amen.*

## *Evening*

*I will open my mouth with a parable; I will utter hidden things, things from of old—
things we have heard and known, things our ancestors have told us.*
PSALM 78:2–3 NIV

*"He captures the wise by their own shrewdness, and the advice
of the cunning is quickly thwarted."*
JOB 5:13 NASB

When our egos get in the way of clear thinking, we are on a pathway that
leads away from God. God glories in the person who will listen to good
advice and do what is right.

*Destroy my foolish pride and lead me to paths of good sense
and smart choices. Amen.*

*But now you must stop doing such things. You must quit being angry, hateful, and evil. You must no longer say insulting or cruel things about others.*
COLOSSIANS 3:8 CEV

*Good sense makes one slow to anger, and it is his glory to overlook an offense.*
PROVERBS 19:11 ESV

There is enough argument and strife in the world without Christians adding to it senselessly. It is not enough that Christians try to do good. It is also vital that they always strive to do no harm.

*Lord God, help me do good to those around me so that I do no harm. Amen.*

*As surely as rain blows in from the north, anger is caused by cruel words.*
PROVERBS 25:23 CEV

*Wherefore, my beloved brethren, let every man be swift to hear, slow to speak, slow to wrath: For the wrath of man worketh not the righteousness of God.*
JAMES 1:19–20 KJV

Wouldn't the world be a wonderful place if people spent as much time trying to make peace as they did trying to tear each other apart? A few choice words can turn an entire community away, but likewise, just a few words can pave a smooth road.

*May the words of my mouth always sound sweet and loving.*
*I want to spread peace, not discord. Amen.*

# DAY 311 – *Backsliding*

*Morning* ───────────────────────────

*For, as I have often told you before and now tell you again even with tears, many live as enemies of the cross of Christ. Their destiny is destruction, their god is their stomach, and their glory is in their shame. Their mind is set on earthly things.*
PHILIPPIANS 3:18–19 NIV

*For if after they have escaped the pollutions of the world through the knowledge of the Lord and Saviour Jesus Christ, they are again entangled therein, and overcome, the latter end is worse with them than the beginning.*
2 PETER 2:20 KJV

All other paths lead to destruction and pain. How wonderful it is to know that the road to God is never blocked. We cannot do anything to make God stop loving us.

*I never want to be without You in my life, Lord. Thank You for remaining even as I stray. Amen.*

*Evening* ───────────────────────────

*Watch out that you do not lose what we have worked for, but that you may be rewarded fully.*
2 JOHN 1:8 NIV

*Rend your heart and not your garments. Return to the LORD your God, for he is gracious and compassionate, slow to anger and abounding in love, and he relents from sending calamity.*
JOEL 2:13 NIV

If you've spent time away from prayer and Bible study, or if you've wandered into sin, you may feel God is angry with you. God despises sin, but He always loves you. Don't believe the lie that He doesn't want you back.

*Lord, thank You for being slow to anger and abounding in love. Amen.*

## *Morning*

*I thank you from my heart, and I will never stop singing your praises,
my LORD and my God.*
PSALM 30:12 CEV

*But you are a chosen generation, a royal priesthood, a holy nation,
His own special people, that you may proclaim the praises of Him who called
you out of darkness into His marvelous light.*
1 PETER 2:9 NKJV

As Christians, we are people of praise. Every prayer we offer unto God should acknowledge the many wonderful things that He has done for us. God gives good things to His children, and we should be thankful for all that we have.

*Lord, I cannot believe how much I have been given. Help open my eyes to the many blessings that have been bestowed upon me. Make me thankful, Lord. Amen.*

## *Evening*

*For great is the LORD and most worthy of praise; he is to be feared above all gods.*
PSALM 96:4 NIV

*Why, my soul, are you downcast? Why so disturbed within me? Put your hope in God, for I will yet praise him, my Savior and my God.*
PSALM 42:11 NIV

Celebrating God's wonders is a snap when we're on a spiritual high. But every Christian has times when it's hard to praise God. Remember: God does not change. He always deserves our praise.

*No matter what challenges we face, Jesus, You are still the mighty Lord, worthy of our praise. Amen.*

# DAY 313 – *Blessings*

*I will bless the LORD at all times; His praise shall continually be in my mouth.*
*My soul will make its boast in the LORD; the humble will hear it and rejoice.*
PSALM 34:1–2 NASB

*The godly always give generous loans to others, and their children are a blessing.*
PSALM 37:26 NLT

If our only blessings were possessions, in heaven we would be the poorest of souls. But because God made Himself our best blessing, we are rich both here and for eternity.

*Father, when I forget the wonderful blessings You bestow, remind me of the*
*greatest blessing—Your Son, Jesus Christ.*

*Sing to the LORD, bless His name; proclaim good tidings of His*
*salvation from day to day.*
PSALM 96:2 NASB

*But Mary treasured all these things, pondering them in her heart.*
LUKE 2:19 NASB

Take a few moments to ponder the blessings God has given you. You may be in the midst of a mountaintop experience in your life, or you may find yourself in a deep valley of turmoil. Wherever you are, remember this: God sent His one and only Son to die for you. The greatest blessing of all.

*Father, when I am tempted to dwell on the troubles in my heart,*
*help me instead focus on the blessings. Amen.*

# DAY 314 – *Church*

*God has put all things under the authority of Christ and has made*
*him head over all things for the benefit of the church.*
EPHESIANS 1:22 NLT

*We will speak the truth in love, growing in every way*
*more and more like Christ, who is the head of his body,*
*the church. He makes the whole body fit together perfectly.*
EPHESIANS 4:15–16 NLT

Because He dwells in them and works out His plan through them, God's
people are His church. Wherever people who love Him are gathered
together, God is there.

*Father, as I gather together with other believers in communion,*
*I pray we are a reflection of Your church. Amen.*

*Now these are the gifts Christ gave to the church: the apostles, the prophets, the*
*evangelists, and the pastors and teachers. Their responsibility is to equip God's people*
*to do his work and build up the church, the body of Christ.*
EPHESIANS 4:11–12 NLT

*So I will call you* PETER, *which means "a rock." On this rock I will build my church,*
*and death itself will not have any power over it.*
MATTHEW 16:18 CEV

The church should be a place where people find hope and safety. If it does
not provide these things, it is not really the church. We need to reach out
to those who reach out to us. Only by doing so can we stand proud, calling
Jesus Christ our Lord and Savior.

*Let the feelings of my heart be made real through my actions, Lord. Let the church be*
*a safe haven for hurting hearts, just as we find rest in Your love. Amen.*

# DAY 315 – *Christian Life*

*Work for the things that make peace and help each other become stronger Christians.*
ROMANS 14:19 NLV

*"If he walks in My statutes and My ordinances so as to deal faithfully—he is righteous and will surely live," declares the Lord GOD.*
EZEKIEL 18:9 NASB

Too many people think that being a Christian means believing but not doing. Being a Christian means living a godly life and rejecting many things that the world says are okay.

*I live with a foot in two worlds, Lord. Reach out and pull me into the kingdom, that I might step from this world into Yours. Amen.*

*Evening* —————————————————————

*This Christian life is a great mystery, far exceeding our understanding, but some things are clear enough: He appeared in a human body, was proved right by the invisible Spirit, was seen by angels. He was proclaimed among all kinds of peoples, believed in all over the world, taken up into heavenly glory.*
1 TIMOTHY 3:16 MSG

*Everyone should live the life the Lord gave to him. He should live as he was when he became a Christian. This is what I teach in all the churches.*
1 CORINTHIANS 7:17 NLV

The Christian's calling is to leave an imprint on all the lives we touch, sharing our relationship with Jesus through our words and actions. The nature of Christianity is to bring others to a saving knowledge of Christ, sowing seeds of truth wherever we can.

*Dear Lord, I want to mark trails that will lead others to the wonder of knowing You as Savior. Amen.*

DAY 316 – *Comfort*

## *Morning*

*And it shall come to pass in the day that the LORD shall give thee
rest from thy sorrow, and from thy fear, and from the hard bondage
wherein thou wast made to serve.*
ISAIAH 14:3 KJV

*For the Lord himself shall descend from heaven with a shout, with the voice of the
archangel, and with the trump of God: and the dead in Christ shall rise first:
Then we which are alive and remain shall be caught up together with them in the
clouds, to meet the Lord in the air: and so shall we ever be with the Lord.
Wherefore comfort one another with these words.*
1 THESSALONIANS 4:16–18 KJV

The Word of God can be a powerful source of comfort for us. In times of
danger and dread, the Lord will come close to us, to comfort and protect
us. Rest in the Lord, and He will save you.

*Heavenly Father, thank You for Your comforting words. Amen.*

## *Evening*

*The Spirit of the Lord GOD is upon me; because the LORD hath anointed me to preach
good tidings unto the meek; he hath sent me to bind up
the brokenhearted. . .to comfort all that mourn.*
ISAIAH 61:1–2 KJV

*Comfort ye, comfort ye my people, saith your God.*
ISAIAH 40:1 KJV

There comes a point where there are no more tears to cry. In our times of
desperation, the Lord will give us comfort.

*When there are no more tears to cry, Lord, fill me with Your peace and consolation.
Heal my wounded emotions, Father. Amen.*

# DAY 317 – *Commitment*

*It's certainly possible to say, "Other branches were pruned so that I could be grafted
in!" Well and good. But they were pruned because they were deadwood, no longer
connected by belief and commitment to the root. The only reason you're on the tree
is because your graft "took" when you believed, and because you're connected to that
belief-nurturing root. So don't get cocky and strut your branch.
Be humbly mindful of the root that keeps you lithe and green.*
ROMANS 11:19–20 MSG

*I am saying this for your own good, not to restrict you, but that you may
live in a right way in undivided devotion to the Lord.*
1 CORINTHIANS 7:35 NIV

God doesn't want worthy people nearly as much as He wants committed
people. Those individuals who stand up and say, "Here am I, Lord! Take
me," are the ones who please Him most.

*I want to give my all to You, Lord. Make me a reflection of Your divine light. Amen.*

*Remember his covenant forever—the commitment
he made to a thousand generations.*
1 CHRONICLES 16:15 NLT

*God-devotion makes a country strong; God-avoidance leaves people weak.*
PROVERBS 14:34 MSG

The Lord loves to see real commitment that changes lives. To live for the
Lord means to give oneself to Him: body, mind, and spirit. As the deer
pursues the cooling brook with all it has, so must we pursue our Lord.

*You are my goal, Lord. Keep my eyes focused on You.
Make sure that I don't turn away. Amen.*

# DAY 318 - *Compassion*

*Morning* —

> *Just as a father has compassion on his children, so the LORD has*
> *compassion on those who fear Him.*
> PSALM 103:13 NASB

> *So the LORD must wait for you to come to him so he can show you his love and*
> *compassion. For the LORD is a faithful God. Blessed are those who wait for his help.*
> ISAIAH 30:18 NLT

In a rough-and-tumble world, there's great need for compassion. Hurting people seek it and often receive the hardness of this world instead. Compassion is one of Christianity's hallmarks. When we offer it to others, we reflect God's love and draw sinners to Him.

> *I want to touch hearts for Christ. Help me, Father, radiate the gentle,*
> *tender virtue of compassion in this world. Amen.*

*Evening* —

> *For no one is abandoned by the Lord forever. Though he brings grief, he also shows*
> *compassion because of the greatness of his unfailing love.*
> LAMENTATIONS 3:31–32 NLT

> *When he saw the crowds, he had compassion on them because they were confused*
> *and helpless, like sheep without a shepherd.*
> MATTHEW 9:36 NLT

We need the Lord's eyes to see people's hearts. Then compassion will compel us to reach out. People need to know that they are loved unconditionally. They need to understand God has a purpose for their lives. They need the hope of heaven. Let's be compassionate and share the good news!

> *Dear Lord, open my eyes to see the lost sheep around me. May I be used*
> *to introduce them to You, the Good Shepherd. Amen.*

## *Morning*

*And God said, Let us make man in our image, after our likeness: and let them have dominion over the fish of the sea, and over the fowl of the air, and over the cattle, and over all the earth, and over every creeping thing that creepeth upon the earth.*
GENESIS 1:26 KJV

*The Scriptures say, "The earth and everything in it belong to the Lord."*
1 CORINTHIANS 10:26 CEV

God has given us the earth to have dominion over it. We must remember that this is the only place we have to live in and treat it accordingly.

*Lord, when I take this earth for granted, remind me of Your care for Your creation. Help me care for the world as You do. Amen.*

## *Evening*

*Good people are kind to their animals, but a mean person is cruel.*
PROVERBS 12:10 CEV

*"For the land which you go to possess is not like the land of Egypt from which you have come, where you sowed your seed and watered it by foot, as a vegetable garden; but the land which you cross over to possess is a land of hills and valleys, which drinks water from the rain of heaven, a land for which the LORD your God cares; the eyes of the LORD your God are always on it, from the beginning of the year to the very end of the year."*
DEUTERONOMY 11:10–12 NKJV

Though God does not explain how to solve all our conservation problems, He tells us about His creation of the earth and the stewardship role He expects humans to fulfill.

*Father, I want to be a faithful steward of this land. Show me ways I can conserve. Amen.*

## *Morning*

*"If I say to corruption, 'You are my father,' and to the worm, 'My mother' or 'My sister,' where then is my hope—who can see any hope for me?"*
JOB 17:14–15 NIV

*God made great and marvelous promises, so that his nature would become part of us. Then we could escape our evil desires and the corrupt influences of this world.*
2 PETER 1:4 CEV

It is frightening to listen to the decrees made by some of our world leaders. If it were true that they really had the ultimate power, there would be no reason for hope. We know better, however. The only true power in this world is the power of God, and our fate will not be decided by men and women, but by God.

*Father God, hear the prayers of Your people, and give us peace and confidence of a bright new age to come. Amen.*

## *Evening*

*One whose heart is corrupt does not prosper.*
PROVERBS 17:20 NIV

*Corruption makes fools of sensible people, and bribes can ruin you.*
ECCLESIASTES 7:7 CEV

We are created for eternity, and so we do not need to fear the decisions made by corrupt human beings in our age. Our trust is in the Lord of all creation, and in Him there is never reason to fear or doubt.

*Lord, when our world looks hopeless, help me rest in Your sovereignty and the hope of eternity with You. Amen.*

# DAY 321 – *Creation*

*"For behold, I create new heavens and a new earth; and the former shall
not be remembered or come to mind."*
ISAIAH 65:17 NKJV

*The LORD is good to everyone. He showers compassion on all his creation.*
PSALM 145:9 NLT

Human beings in all their wisdom and genius have created nothing to
compare with the least of God's creations. His power, might, and majesty
humble us and help us remember that He alone is God.

*Show forth Your might through Your creations, O Lord. Remind me of Your greatness
and power throughout the day. You are wonderful, Lord! Amen.*

*Evening* ─────────────────────────────────────

*Take a good look at God's work. Who could simplify and reduce
Creation's curves and angles to a plain straight line?*
ECCLESIASTES 7:13 MSG

*He chose to give birth to us by giving us his true word. And we,
out of all creation, became his prized possession.*
JAMES 1:18 NLT

We have the capacity to truly appreciate the beauty and splendor of God's
creation. Why, then, do so many people trash God's gift? The Lord gave us
His ability to see the beauty in things. Let us use that gift, to protect and
defend the wonders of the world in which we live.

*Do not let me stomp through life like some wild animal. Help me see all creation as
You see it. Fill me with the beauty of this world. Amen.*

# DAY 322 – *Death*

———————————————————

> When calamity comes, the wicked are brought down,
> but even in death the righteous seek refuge in God.
> PROVERBS 14:32 NIV

> For this is God, our God forever and ever; He will be our guide even to death.
> PSALM 48:14 NKJV

We often hope that we can leave a legacy, a testament to our life, after we die. There is no more fitting legacy than helping other people learn to love life and enjoy it every day.

*Father, I pray that my life is a reflection of You so that others embrace the joy I have been given. Amen.*

———————————————————

> "I tell you for certain that if you obey my words, you will never die."
> JOHN 8:51 CEV

> So when this corruptible shall have put on incorruption, and this mortal shall have put on immortality, then shall be brought to pass the saying that is written, Death is swallowed up in victory. O death, where is thy sting? O grave, where is thy victory?
> 1 CORINTHIANS 15:54–55 KJV

The longer Christ is with us, the more He readies us to leave this place and to enter into heaven. Death need hold no fear. On the other side waits God and an eternity spent in His loving care.

*Whatever Your will for my life, Lord, whether it will be long or short, help me accept it. Amen.*

# DAY 323 – *Descision Making*

*Where there is no guidance, a people falls, but in an abundance
of counselors there is safety.*
PROVERBS 11:14 ESV

*A good name is rather to be chosen than great riches,
and loving favour rather than silver and gold.*
PROVERBS 22:1 KJV

When it comes to decision making, we need to ask ourselves, *Who do I get advice from?* If our primary counselor is not God, we may be headed for trouble. But He also puts wise people in our paths. Are we making the most of their advice?

*Father, be my first source when I am faced with a decision. Lead me to others who
will guide me in Your way. Amen.*

*Evening* ────────────────────────────────

*"But if you refuse to serve the LORD, then choose today whom you will serve.
Would you prefer the gods your ancestors served beyond the Euphrates?
Or will it be the gods of the Amorites in whose land you now live?
But as for me and my family, we will serve the LORD."*
JOSHUA 24:15 NLT

*Powerful LORD God, all who stay far from you will be lost, and you will destroy
those who are unfaithful. It is good for me to be near you. I choose you as my
protector, and I will tell about your wonderful deeds.*
PSALM 73:27–28 CEV

Christ works inside of us to make us kingdom people, but we have to make choices on our own. We need to take the things Christ teaches and use them in our relationships, actions, and lives.

*Lord God, grant me the encouragement and wisdom I need
to make the right decisions. Amen.*

# DAY 324 - *Commitment*

*So let's keep focused on that goal, those of us who want everything God has for us.*
*If any of you have something else in mind, something less than total commitment,*
*God will clear your blurred vision—you'll see it yet! Now that we're*
*on the right track, let's stay on it.*
PHILIPPIANS 3:15–16 MSG

*My love (that true love growing out of sincere devotion to God)*
*be with you all in Christ Jesus. Amen (so be it).*
1 CORINTHIANS 16:24 AMP

God is not someone that we should turn to only in times of trial. He should
be a part of our whole life, both in good times and bad. We must be sure to
include God in everything we do.

*Dear God, forgive those times when I seem to forget You. Help me to include You in*
*all I do, think, and feel. Amen.*

*The people stood in affirmation; their commitment was unanimous.*
2 KINGS 23:3 MSG

*When he came and saw the grace of God, he rejoiced, and he exhorted them all to*
*remain faithful to the Lord with steadfast devotion.*
ACTS 11:23 NRSV

It's wonderful to see people so in love with life and with Christ that they
make the two things one. A long life well lived is a powerful testimony to
the goodness of God. Use your life to glorify God.

*Lord, I want my devotion to You to show through my life,*
*that others might see and believe. Amen.*

# DAY 325 – *Diligence*

*But take diligent heed to do the commandment and the law, which Moses the servant*
*of the LORD charged you, to love the LORD your God, and to walk in all his ways,*
*and to keep his commandments, and to cleave unto him, and to serve*
*him with all your heart and with all your soul.*
JOSHUA 22:5 KJV

*Keep thy heart with all diligence; for out of it are the issues of life.*
PROVERBS 4:23 KJV

When something is the desire of our heart, it should possess us totally. How
many of us pursue God with the same diligence?

*Help me pursue You in all ways at all times, O Lord.*
*I want You to be the desire of my heart. Amen.*

*Therefore, as ye abound in every thing, in faith, and utterance, and knowledge,*
*and in all diligence, and in your love to us, see that ye abound in this grace also.*
2 CORINTHIANS 8:7 KJV

*Wherefore, beloved, seeing that ye look for such things, be diligent that ye may be*
*found of him in peace, without spot, and blameless.*
2 PETER 3:14 KJV

God wants us to value the time we have on earth. We take time for granted,
acting as though our earthly life will go on forever. Time on earth is too
short to waste. Number your days, and be diligent in your faith walk.

*Don't let me waste time, but let me use every moment to the fullest. Amen.*

# DAY 326 – *Doubt*

*When doubts filled my mind, your comfort gave me renewed hope and cheer.*
PSALM 94:19 NLT

*Jesus answered and said unto them, Verily I say unto you, If ye have faith, and doubt not, ye shall not only do this which is done to the fig tree, but also if ye shall say unto this mountain, Be thou removed, and be thou cast into the sea; it shall be done. And all things, whatsoever ye shall ask in prayer, believing, ye shall receive.*
MATTHEW 21:21–22 KJV

Doubt comes to us easily. It is during those times that it is most important to hold fast to the promises of God.

*Almighty God, forgive me when I doubt Your will and guidance. Help me always have the faith I need to trust and obey. Amen.*

*But if you have doubts about whether or not you should eat something, you are sinning if you go ahead and do it. For you are not following your convictions. If you do anything you believe is not right, you are sinning.*
ROMANS 14:23 NLT

*Only simpletons believe everything they're told!
The prudent carefully consider their steps.*
PROVERBS 14:15 NLT

We can't re-create God in our own image and be happy. Wrong doctrine takes the power out of faith. Instead of falling for a bunch of maybes, be renewed in the knowledge of God by believing just what He said about His plan for salvation and walking in that truth.

*Lord, I don't want to doubt Your Word. Buoy my faith, I pray. Amen.*

# DAY 327 - *Evil*

*For you have made the Lord, my refuge, even the Most High, your dwelling place.
No evil will befall you, nor will any plague come near your tent. For He will give His
angels charge concerning you, to guard you in all your ways.*
PSALM 91:9–11 NASB

*The Lord will keep you from all evil; he will keep your life. The Lord will keep
your going out and your coming in from this time forth and forevermore.*
PSALM 121:7–8 ESV

Evil is as oppressive as a thick cloud of smoke. It envelopes people and
chokes them. One day the Lord will dispel all evil as a fan dispels smoke.
On that day, all God's people will breathe richly of the fragrance of God.

*Lord, send the breath of Your Spirit to cleanse me of all evil. Free me from the
oppression of all that I have done wrong through Your blessed forgiveness. Amen.*

*Do not be wise in your own eyes; fear the Lord and turn away from evil.*
PROVERBS 3:7 NASB

*Put everything to the test. Accept what is good and don't have
anything to do with evil.*
1 THESSALONIANS 5:21–22 CEV

Perusing the daily news, you realize "good" people don't make the
headlines very often. It is easy to become overwhelmed by the stories of
evil. But look around your own neighborhood, church, and family. Aren't
there more "good" people than bad? And in the long run, good is blessed
by God.

*Lord, give me eyes to see the good amid the evil. Amen.*

*Morning* ———————————————————————

> Now the body is not for sexual immorality but for the Lord,
> and the Lord for the body.
> 1 CORINTHIANS 6:13 NKJV

> Marriage should be honored by all, and the marriage bed kept pure, for God will
> judge the adulterer and all the sexually immoral.
> HEBREWS 13:4 NIV

Adultery undermines the ultimate plan of God that men and women will join together in order that the two shall become one in spirit, mind, and body. It trades in the promise of eternal bliss for a moment of physical pleasure.

*Lift me up, Father, and raise me high above sin and temptation. Your design is perfect; help me follow Your will in my marriage. Amen.*

*Evening* ———————————————————————

> Flee sexual immorality. Every sin that a man does is outside the body, but he who
> commits sexual immorality sins against his own body.
> 1 CORINTHIANS 6:18 NKJV

> I say then: Walk in the Spirit, and you shall not fulfill the lust of the flesh.
> GALATIANS 5:16 NKJV

No one has ever said that sexual purity is easy. That's why scripture calls us to flee from temptation. The person who entertains the idea of giving in surely and quickly falls from God's standard.

*Lord, when I struggle, point me back to You.*
*When I'm tempted, help me flee. Amen.*

*Morning* —————————————————————

*Then Jesus told him, "You believe because you have seen me.*
*Blessed are those who believe without seeing me."*
JOHN 20:29 NLT

*And Jesus said unto them, I am the bread of life: he that cometh to me shall never*
*hunger; and he that believeth on me shall never thirst.*
JOHN 6:35 KJV

We all face decisions about whether to trust God. But the struggle to avoid unbelief is worth it all when we see the benefits of trusting Jesus and experience His love.

*Lord, when my human understanding causes me to lack belief, fill me with Your*
*promises that I might believe anew. Amen.*

*Evening* —————————————————————

*He that believeth on him is not condemned: but he that believeth not is condemned*
*already, because he hath not believed in the name of the only begotten Son of God.*
JOHN 3:18 KJV

*But we ought always to give thanks to God for you, brothers beloved by the Lord,*
*because God chose you as the firstfruits to be saved, through sanctification*
*by the Spirit and belief in the truth.*
2 THESSALONIANS 2:13 ESV

It is natural and human to doubt the Lord sometimes. He understands that. Just don't give up. The Lord can break through our deepest unbelief.

*Lift me, Lord, into Your loving arms. Grace me with the sweet memory*
*of Your care, that I might never doubt You. Amen.*

## *Morning*

*"For they all put in out of their surplus, but she, out of her poverty,
put in all she owned, all she had to live on."*
MARK 12:44 NASB

*The stingy are eager to get rich and are unaware that poverty awaits them.*
PROVERBS 28:22 NIV

To come before Jesus means to come before the needy of this world. Jesus said unless you do good unto your brothers and sisters, you have not done good unto Him. Let us join with our Lord in being saviors to a world in need.

*Forgive me for wrong priorities, Lord. I worship often in word, but not in deed.
Let my actions reinforce the faith I confess with my heart. Amen.*

## *Evening*

*"One person dies in prosperity, completely comfortable and secure,
the picture of good health, vigorous and fit. Another person dies in bitter poverty,
never having tasted the good life. But both are buried in the same dust,
both eaten by the same maggots."*
JOB 21:23–26 NLT

*For you know the grace of our Lord Jesus Christ, that though He was rich, yet for
your sake He became poor, so that you through His poverty might become rich.*
2 CORINTHIANS 8:9 NASB

All too often, poor people are made out to be lazy when nothing could be further from the truth. The poor are our brothers and sisters, and they are worthy of our help, just because Christ said so. God blesses the poor and those who help them. Take hold of your blessing. Help someone in need.

*Lord, all Your children deserve dignity. Let me give to others with respect.
Humble my heart when I feel myself looking down on those around me. Amen.*

# DAY 331 – *Family*

*Morning* ———————————————————————

"A family splintered by feuding will fall apart."
LUKE 11:17 NLT

So I bow in prayer before the Father from whom every family in heaven
and on earth gets its true name.
EPHESIANS 3:14–15 NCV

In homes where Christ is King and ruler, it is easy to feel God's blessing.
There is no conflict or problem that can upset the blessing that God puts
upon a faithful household.

*Come, O Lord, to be the head of my household and the unifier in my family. Amen.*

*Evening* ———————————————————————

God decided in advance to adopt us into his own family by bringing us to himself
through Jesus Christ. This is what he wanted to do, and it gave him great pleasure.
EPHESIANS 1:5 NLT

Suppose someone doesn't know how to manage his own family.
Then how can he take care of God's church?
1 TIMOTHY 3:5 NIrV

Before we can hope to spread the love of God in our own private worlds,
we must first learn to spread it in our home, with our families. It is often
harder to keep peace with and care for those closest to us, but with God's
help it can be the most blessed peace of all.

*Heavenly Father, let my home be a haven of comfort and joy, and help me spread
that peace to those outside my home. Amen.*

*"Don't fear: I am First, I am Last, I'm Alive. I died, but I came to life,
and my life is now forever."*
REVELATION 1:17–18 MSG

*"And do not fear those who kill the body but cannot kill the soul. But rather fear Him
who is able to destroy both soul and body in hell. Are not two sparrows sold for a
copper coin? And not one of them falls to the ground apart from your Father's will.
But the very hairs of your head are all numbered. Do not fear therefore;
you are of more value than many sparrows."*
MATTHEW 10:28–31 NKJV

There are two kinds of fear: fear of (or reverence for) God and the doubtful
fear that focuses on all the things that could go wrong in our lives. Fear of
God is a good thing, because it draws us closer to Him in respect and love.
But doubtful fears show our lack of reliance on Him.

*Lord, with You I have nothing to fear. When doubtful fear creeps into my life,
remind me of Your power and faithfulness. Amen.*

*But the* LORD *said to him, "Peace be to you. Do not fear; you shall not die."*
JUDGES 6:23 ESV

*The* LORD *is on my side; I will not fear. What can man do to me?*
PSALM 118:6 ESV

Fear can be a healthy thing for us when it forces us to clean up our lives and
walk the straight path. Once on the right path, though, we can leave fear
behind, for nothing can harm us once we are in the Lord's camp.

*When I begin to fear the consequences of wrongdoing,
lead me back to You, Lord. Amen.*

# DAY 333 – *Revenge*

*The LORD is a jealous and avenging God; the LORD is avenging and wrathful;
the LORD takes vengeance on his adversaries and keeps wrath for his enemies.*
NAHUM 1:2 ESV

*Never take your own revenge, beloved, but leave room for the wrath of God, for it is
written, "VENGEANCE IS MINE, I WILL REPAY," says the Lord.*
ROMANS 12:19 NASB

A lot of people live for revenge. They hold grudges, let them burn inside,
then explode forth to do whatever damage they can. When someone
wrongs you, your duty is to forgive, not to punish.

*Heavenly Father, pride often causes me to plot in my heart against those who have
wronged me. Create in my heart a spirit of forgiveness instead. Amen.*

*Evening*

*Go ahead and be angry. You do well to be angry—but don't use your anger as fuel
for revenge. And don't stay angry. Don't go to bed angry. Don't give
the Devil that kind of foothold in your life.*
EPHESIANS 4:26-27 MSG

*"The LORD says, 'Am I not storing up these things, sealing them away in my
treasury? I will take revenge; I will pay them back. In due time their feet will slip.
Their day of disaster will arrive, and their destiny will overtake them.'"*
DEUTERONOMY 32:34-35 NLT

Nothing good can come from a spirit of hurt and revenge. It is through
forgiveness that God can enter our lives and make everything all right.

*Lord, create in my heart a spirit of forgiveness, that I may do everything
in my power to heal with Your healing love. Amen.*

## *Morning*

*If you live right, the reward is a good life.*
PROVERBS 10:16 CEV

*In the future there is laid up for me the crown of righteousness, which the Lord,
the righteous Judge, will award to me on that day; and not only to me,
but also to all who have loved His appearing.*
2 TIMOTHY 4:8 NASB

Truly faithful people don't have to go seeking acclaim. When we pursue recognition, we open ourselves to failure and disgrace. We should focus on the work that we need to do rather than the credit we will receive for doing it.

*Destroy in me, O Lord, the desire to do things that make me look good.
Rather, let me do things for Your glory. Amen.*

## *Evening*

*Would you do me a favor, friends, and give special recognition to the family
of Stephanas? You know, they were among the first converts in Greece,
and they've put themselves out, serving Christians ever since then.
I want you to honor and look up to people like that.*
1 CORINTHIANS 16:15–16 MSG

*Blessed are those who have learned to acclaim you,
who walk in the light of your presence, LORD.*
PSALM 89:15 NIV

Christ never looked for personal acclaim; all He did was for the glory of God. As committed Christians, it is important that we also learn to live our lives not for ourselves, but always for the glory of God.

*Help me be the person You want me to be, God; not selfish or vain,
but more like Christ in every way. Amen.*

# DAY 335 – *Fulfillment*

*My eyes long for your salvation and for the fulfillment of your righteous promise.*
PSALM 119:123 ESV

*Now if their transgression is riches for the world and their failure is riches for the
Gentiles, how much more will their fulfillment be!*
ROMANS 11:12 NASB

Life is a privilege that God wants us to value. When we turn from Him and
pursue our own selfish desires, we lose sight of the sacredness of His gift.
We may think that we can find fulfillment in life on our own, but it is through
God and God alone that we can come to know the wonder of life most fully.

*Help me see the beauty and wonder of this life You have given to me, O Lord. Amen.*

*"And blessed is she who believed that there would be a fulfillment
of what was spoken to her from the Lord."*
LUKE 1:45 ESV

*But now you have arrived at your destination: By faith in Christ you are in direct
relationship with God. Your baptism in Christ was not just washing you up for a fresh
start. It also involved dressing you in an adult faith wardrobe—Christ's life,
the fulfillment of God's original promise.*
GALATIANS 3:25–27 MSG

God is the author of life, and He will bless us with its richness if we will only
let Him. A full and happy life, rich in meaning and honorable in all ways, is
the prize of any believer who will keep God centered in his or her life.

*Dear God, open my eyes so that I might come to know the richness and fullness You
intend my life to have. Grant me this, I pray. Amen.*

# DAY 336 – *God's Correction*

*For they verily for a few days chastened us after their own pleasure; but he for our profit, that we might be partakers of his holiness. Now no chastening for the present seemeth to be joyous, but grievous: nevertheless afterward it yieldeth the peaceable fruit of righteousness unto them which are exercised thereby.*
HEBREWS 12:10–11 KJV

*As many as I love, I rebuke and chasten: be zealous therefore, and repent.*
REVELATION 3:19 KJV

Often we know what God says, but we do other things instead. When we find ourselves in trouble, we look to God to bail us out, then wonder why He doesn't jump to our aid. Sometimes God allows us to struggle through adversity in order to learn that He means what He says.

*Dear heavenly Father, I so often do what I know You do not want me to. Forgive my disobedience. Help me heed Your will, not my own. Amen.*

*The LORD hath chastened me sore: but he hath not given me over unto death.*
PSALM 118:18 KJV

*"Behold, blessed is the one whom God reproves; therefore despise not the discipline of the Almighty."*
JOB 5:17 ESV

Just as a parent disciplines his child, God disciplines us. Sometimes He hones our character by allowing challenges. Even hardships that are caused by other people are an opportunity for growth. He disciplines not to punish us, but because He loves us.

*Lord, thank You for loving me enough to discipline me. Help me accept those things You ask of me. Amen.*

# DAY 337 – *Healing*

And suddenly, a woman who had a flow of blood for twelve years came from behind
and touched the hem of His garment. For she said to herself, "If only I may touch His
garment, I shall be made well." But Jesus turned around, and when He saw her He
said, "Be of good cheer, daughter; your faith has made you well."
And the woman was made well from that hour.
MATTHEW 9:20–22 NKJV

And the prayer offered in faith will make the sick person well; the Lord will
raise them up. If they have sinned, they will be forgiven. Therefore confess
your sins to each other and pray for each other so that you may be healed.
The prayer of a righteous person is powerful and effective.
JAMES 5:15–16 NIV

Whether it's our bodies or our spirits, we all need God's healing touch. And
God is always willing to offer it to us. Look how often Jesus healed during
His ministry—not only hurting bodies but also souls that had been severely
damaged.

*Lord, touch my heart today, that I may be healed. Amen.*

Heal me, O LORD, and I shall be healed; save me, and I shall be saved,
for you are my praise.
JEREMIAH 17:14 ESV

O LORD my God, I cried unto thee, and thou hast healed me.
PSALM 30:2 KJV

Abuse has far-reaching consequences, but healing and redemption
are valuable for those who seek it. Only God can take the most hurtful
circumstances of our lives and weave them into His plan for us.

*Father, take my pain and redeem it. Use it for Your glory. Amen.*

DAY 338 – *Righteousness*

*Morning* ———————————————————

*Your righteousness is like the highest mountains, your justice like the great deep.*
PSALM 36:6 NIV

*Because I have sinned against him, I will bear the LORD's wrath,*
*until he pleads my case and upholds my cause. He will bring me out into the light;*
*I will see his righteousness.*
MICAH 7:9 NIV

Through the death and resurrection of Jesus, Christ's righteousness becomes the righteousness of all who believe in Him and turn their hearts over to Him. Jesus paid the penalty that would have come to us. We have no fear of condemnation. All we have is the promise of love and forgiveness.

*Though I do not deserve Your great love, Father God, I thank You that You give it so freely. Embrace me as Your child, and help me remember that I am Yours. Amen.*

*Evening* ———————————————————

*"I will fetch my knowledge from afar, and I will ascribe righteousness to my Maker."*
JOB 36:3 NASB

*"Blessed are those who hunger and thirst for righteousness, for they shall be filled."*
MATTHEW 5:6 NKJV

When we do what is truly right, we need to rejoice. God celebrates with us, and He will honor our righteousness. To do right is to affirm who God wants us to be. The peace that comes from doing right is wonderful.

*Lord, let me know the triumph that comes from standing up for my values.*
*Let me feel the power You share with those who strive for what is right. Amen.*

# DAY 339 – *Guilt*

*And I will cleanse them from all their iniquity, whereby they have sinned against me; and I will pardon all their iniquities, whereby they have sinned, and whereby they have transgressed against me.*
JEREMIAH 33:8 KJV

*But if we walk in the light, as he is in the light, we have fellowship one with another, and the blood of Jesus Christ his Son cleanseth us from all sin.*
1 JOHN 1:7 KJV

Too often we come before the Lord with the feeling that we shouldn't be there. True, we have sinned, but God does not want us to dwell on the fact that we have sinned. Instead, remember that we have been forgiven.

*Your grace has made me worthy, Lord. What I could not do on my own, You have done for me. Thank You, Father, from the depths of my soul. Amen.*

*For if ye turn again unto the LORD, your brethren and your children shall find compassion before them that lead them captive, so that they shall come again into this land: for the LORD your God is gracious and merciful, and will not turn away his face from you, if ye return unto him.*
2 CHRONICLES 30:9 KJV

*I write unto you, little children, because your sins are forgiven you for his name's sake.*
1 JOHN 2:12 KJV

The love of God is greater than any sin we might commit. God makes us able to look up, because he lifts the burden of guilt from our shoulders.

*Lord, when shame overwhelms me, remind me of Your forgiveness, which washes me clean. I don't deserve Your grace, but Your love redeems me. Amen.*

# DAY 340 – *God's Omniscience*

## *Morning*

*Be not ye therefore like unto them: for your Father knoweth what things ye have need of, before ye ask him.*
MATTHEW 6:8 KJV

*This then is the message which we have heard of him, and declare unto you, that God is light, and in him is no darkness at all.*
1 JOHN 1:5 KJV

From the very beginning of time, God has had each and every one of us in His mind. He knows us completely. There is never even one moment when we are out of God's vision.

*Heavenly Father, You are amazing! I am just one,
but I am alwaysin Your care. Amen.*

## *Evening*

*For the ways of man are before the eyes of the LORD, and he pondereth all his goings.*
PROVERBS 5:21 KJV

*He telleth the number of the stars; he calleth them all by their names.*
PSALM 147:4 KJV

God rejoices when we walk in the paths of righteousness, and He mourns for us when we fall into paths that lead from His glory. We can't fool God, because He knows us so well.

*O Lord, You know me so much better than I know myself.
Help me know myself as You know me. Amen.*

# DAY 341 – *Guidance*

*He guides me along the right paths for his name's sake.*
PSALM 23:3 NIV

*Guide me in your truth and teach me, for you are God my Savior,*
*and my hope is in you all day long.*
PSALM 25:5 NIV

God has given us a conscience, a "still, small voice," an inner wisdom that guides us and comforts us when we remain true to its instruction.

*O heavenly Father, I reach out to Your guidance and will.*
*Help me listen for Your instruction. Amen.*

*"Because of the tender mercy of our God, whereby the sunrise shall visit us from on*
*high to give light to those who sit in darkness and in the shadow of death,*
*to guide our feet into the way of peace."*
LUKE 1:78–79 ESV

*I praise you, LORD, for being my guide. Even in the darkest night,*
*your teachings fill my mind.*
PSALM 16:7 CEV

Doing what we know to be right offers not only freedom from guilt, but also joy which comes forth from our soul. Christ rejoices each time we obey the guidance of the Holy Spirit.

*Lord God, fill me with a special wisdom so that I might always*
*choose to follow the right path. Amen.*

# DAY 342 – *God's Protection*

*All of you worship the L*ORD*, so you must trust him to help and protect you.*
PSALM 115:11 CEV

*The L*ORD *shall preserve thee from all evil: he shall preserve thy soul.*
*The L*ORD *shall preserve thy going out and thy coming in from this time forth,*
*and even for evermore.*
PSALM 121:7–8 KJV

If we will set our sights on the Lord, He will make our steps sure. No snare, trap, or pitfall can stop us when our eyes are on the Lord. He will guard us each step of the way.

*I am uncertain, Lord, and often afraid. Instill Your holy confidence in me.*
*I place my trust in Your protection, that I might walk a good walk of faith*
*and never stumble. Amen.*

*The L*ORD *helps them and delivers them; he delivers them from the wicked and saves*
*them, because they take refuge in him.*
PSALM 37:40 NIV

*The name of the L*ORD *is a strong tower: the righteous runneth into it, and is safe.*
PROVERBS 18:10 KJV

Our fortress is the Lord. In times of desperate need, we should immediately turn to Him. There is no better place to rest and be safe.

*Never let me stray too far from Your loving protection, almighty God. I need You*
*more than I even realize. Open Your arms to me, Lord. Amen.*

DAY 343 – *God's Provision*

*Morning* ——————————————————————

*Or what man is there of you, whom if his son ask bread, will he give him a stone?
Or if he ask a fish, will he give him a serpent? If ye then, being evil, know how to give
good gifts unto your children, how much more shall your Father
which is in heaven give good things to them that ask him?*
MATTHEW 7:9-11 KJV

*I have provided all kinds of fruit and grain for you to eat.*
GENESIS 1:29 CEV

God has given good things to His children, and when one thing doesn't
work out, we can rest assured that something else is soon to come along. In
good and bad, the Lord is with us, helping us make the best of things.

*You give so many good things, Lord. Help me see past the things that are wrong.
Thank You for providing the support I need. Amen.*

*Evening* ——————————————————————

*Who covers the heavens with clouds, who provides rain for the earth,
who makes grass to grow on the mountains.*
PSALM 147:8 NASB

*"Then this city will bring me joy, glory, and honor before all the nations of the earth!
The people of the world will see all the good I do for my people, and they will tremble
with awe at the peace and prosperity I provide for them."*
JEREMIAH 33:9 NLT

Our God provides us with everything we need to be the best people we
can be. Call upon the Lord to load you daily with benefits. He will do even
more than you expect.

*Lord, I do not even know what I need to be better than I am today,
but in Your wisdom, You see my every need. Give me what You will,
in order that I might honor and glorify You. Amen.*

# DAY 344 - *Grace*

*Being made right with God by his grace, we could have the hope of
receiving the life that never ends.*
TITUS 3:7 NCV

*But when grace is shown to the wicked, they do not learn righteousness; even in a
land of uprightness they go on doing evil and do not regard the majesty of the LORD.*
ISAIAH 26:10 NIV

It is through God's grace that we can avoid the pain that sin brings. It is in
His will that we find the path that leads to true happiness.

*Dear Lord, let me know that I can be forgiven for the things I do wrong, and that I
can start afresh, if I will just focus my eyes and my soul on You. Amen.*

*Evening* ——————————————————————

*And God is able to make all grace abound to you, so that always having all
sufficiency in everything, you may have an abundance for every good deed.*
2 CORINTHIANS 9:8 NASB

*The grace of our Lord Jesus Christ be with you all. Amen.*
2 THESSALONIANS 3:18 KJV

Nothing beats the real thing. Once we are touched by the grace of God,
nothing else compares. What this world has to offer us is but a snapshot of
what we can really have. The real thing is best. Embrace God and all that
He is and all that He does. You'll never need anything else.

*Lord, nothing can compare with You. In my life I have experienced wonderful things,
but none so wonderful as Your grace. Thank You. Amen.*

# DAY 345 – *Gratitude*

As ye have therefore received Christ Jesus the Lord, so walk ye in him:
Rooted and built up in him, and stablished in the faith, as ye have been taught,
abounding therein with thanksgiving.
COLOSSIANS 2:6–7 KJV

And whatsoever ye do in word or deed, do all in the name of the Lord Jesus,
giving thanks to God and the Father by him.
COLOSSIANS 3:17 KJV

What do we offer to God when we are blessed with good things? Do we
even remember to say thank You? The Lord has given us so much, and we
should always and everywhere give Him thanks and praise.

*In bad times, please be my strength; in good times, celebrate with me, Lord. Thank
You for being with me, doing so much for me, and giving so much to me. Amen.*

For everything created by God is good, and nothing is to be rejected
if it is received with gratitude.
1 TIMOTHY 4:4 NASB

Let the message of Christ dwell among you richly as you teach and admonish one
another with all wisdom through PSALMS, hymns, and songs from the Spirit,
singing to God with gratitude in your hearts.
COLOSSIANS 3:16 NIV

God wants us to truly appreciate what we have before we start asking
for more. He gives good things to His children, and He is willing to give
abundantly, but He desires us to learn the real meaning of thankfulness.

*Dear God, make me appreciative of all the wonderful gifts You give.
When I take things for granted, show me the error of my ways.
Fill my mind and heart with gratitude. Amen.*

DAY 346 - *Advice*

*Morning* ———————————————————————————————

*Plans are established by seeking advice; so if you wage war, obtain guidance.*
PROVERBS 20:18 NIV

*"Now listen to me, and let me give you a word of advice, and may God
be with you. You should continue to be the people's representative before God,
bringing their disputes to him."*
EXODUS 18:19 NLT

Without the counsel of the Lord, everything is ignorance. In trying to deal with
our problems apart from God, we are creating more problems than we can
handle. The answer is not in running from the Lord, but in running to Him.

*O Lord, be close to me, building me up and keeping me ever
in Your loving care. Amen.*

*Evening* ———————————————————————————————

*"I've followed him closely, my feet in his footprints, not once swerving from his way.
I've obeyed every word he's spoken, and not just obeyed his advice—I've treasured it."*
JOB 23:11–12 MSG

*Let me give you some good advice; I'm looking you in the eye
and giving it to you straight.*
PSALM 32:8 MSG

"Let me give you some advice." Either we cringe at those words or
welcome them with open arms. The Bible has some advice on wise counsel:
take it!

*Lord, help me accept godly advice with grace. Amen.*

*Morning*

*The violence of the wicked will destroy them, because they refuse to do what is right.*
PROVERBS 21:7 NCV

*Do not be afraid of sudden terror or of the ruin of the wicked, when it comes.*
PROVERBS 3:25 ESV

Terrible things are done all around us. We must hold on to God's goodness and His strength so we can endure such inconceivable crimes. Our Lord is greater than anything on earth. His will be done!

*Lord, while the evil days keep coming, grant me strength enough*
*to endure until the end. Amen.*

*Evening*

*You will not fear the terror of the night, nor the arrow that flies by day.*
PSALM 91:5 ESV

*He will redeem them from oppression and violence, for their lives are precious to him.*
PSALM 72:14 NLT

God's great power stands against the worst that humankind can do. So far we have not done irreparable damage, and by God's grace we never will; but it is good to know that the Lord is with us, to heal all wounds and make all things new.

*The power of humankind does not even compare to Your might, Lord.*
*Save us from our own destructiveness, and renew us. Amen.*

## *Morning*

*Honor is no more associated with fools than snow with summer or rain with harvest.*
PROVERBS 26:1 NLT

*Our Father in heaven, help us to honor your name.*
MATTHEW 6:9 CEV

One of the best ways we can honor our Lord is to pay attention and be careful. Other people see the way we live our lives, and if we are sloppy and sinful, we can hardly hope to make others see the benefits of honoring God with their own lives.

*Make me a good example, Lord, of a life made new through Your love.
I desire to honor You all my days. Amen.*

## *Evening*

*To those who by persistence in doing good seek glory, honor and immortality,
he will give eternal life.*
ROMANS 2:7 NIV

*"Let your light shine in front of men. Then they will see the good things you do and
will honor your Father Who is in heaven."*
MATTHEW 5:16 NLV

It is our duty to remain faithful to Christ, and to work to bring honor upon Him by our virtue. Our lives can be crowns upon the head of Christ for all the world to see.

*Lord, I pray that my actions might be a source of honor in Your sight. Amen.*

# DAY 349 - *Hope*

*Even when there was no reason for hope, Abraham kept hoping—believing that he*
*would become the father of many nations. For God had said to him,*
*"That's how many descendants you will have!"*
ROMANS 4:18 NLT

*But I will hope continually, and will yet praise thee more and more.*
PSALM 71:14 KJV

Sometimes we need a boost. God sees that, and He is ready to lift us up—
to give us a new vantage point of hope. Reach up to the Lord, and He will
lead you to Himself, a Rock that is higher than any problem we might have.

*Pick me up, Lord, and hold me in Your loving arms. Inspire me*
*with the hope only You can bring. Amen.*

*For in hope we have been saved, but hope that is seen is not hope;*
*for who hopes for what he already sees? But if we hope for what we do not see,*
*with perseverance we wait eagerly for it.*
ROMANS 8:24–25 NASB

*Thou art my hiding place and my shield: I hope in thy word.*
PSALM 119:114 KJV

When we despair of life itself, the Lord comes to us gently and with love.
He stays beside us, bringing us hope when we need it most.

*Sometimes I feel like my life is hopeless, Lord. Lift that burden from me*
*and let me experience life the way You meant for it to be. Amen.*

## *Morning*

*Surely God will not hear vanity, neither will the Almighty regard it.*
JOB 35:13 KJV

*Pride goes before destruction, a haughty spirit before a fall.*
PROVERBS 16:18 NIV

Humility is the antithesis of pride. Jesus is the perfect example of humility—putting others above self. Although He was God, He humbled Himself and became obedient to His heavenly Father by dying on the cross.

*Dear Lord, convict me of any prideful spirit within me and teach me humility. Amen.*

## *Evening*

*"When I fed them, they were satisfied; when they were satisfied, they became proud; then they forgot me."*
HOSEA 13:6 NIV

*For we are the circumcision, who worship God in the Spirit, rejoice in Christ Jesus, and have no confidence in the flesh.*
PHILIPPIANS 3:3 NKJV

How do we retain a humble spirit when the world is constantly telling us how great it is to be self-reliant? One way is to acknowledge our spiritual poverty and neediness before our heavenly Father. Each breath we draw is a gift from God.

*Heavenly Father, help me remember who I am before You. Keep me mindful of my constant dependence on You. Amen.*

DAY 351 – *Reflecting Christ*

 *Morning* ———————————————————————

*"Anyone working and living in truth and reality welcomes God-light so the work can be seen for the God-work it is."*
JOHN 3:21 MSG

*Just as water mirrors your face, so your face mirrors your heart.*
PROVERBS 27:19 MSG

One of the greatest sins we can ever commit is to call ourselves Christians, then act in ways that are unacceptable in the sight of the Lord. We must devote ourselves to imitating Christ in all ways possible.

*I pray that I might learn to walk carefully in the steps of Jesus Christ, almighty Father. Grant that I might be an honor to Your truth in all ways. Amen.*

*Evening* ———————————————————————

*What is man and woman that you bother with them; why take a second look their way? You made them not quite as high as angels, bright with Eden's dawn light; then you put them in charge of your entire handcrafted world.*
HEBREWS 2:6–8 MSG

*"Because God made humans in his image reflecting God's very nature. You're here to bear fruit, reproduce, lavish life on the Earth, live bountifully!"*
GENESIS 9:6–7 MSG

As much as we might like to be a reflection of Jesus Christ, for each success there are a dozen failures where we stray from the path. God still believes in us and helps us to be the best people we can be.

*Grant me spiritual wings that I might soar as an angel on this earth, O Lord. Amen.*

# DAY 352 – *Infertility*

*"Worship the LORD your God, and his blessing will be on your food and water. I will take away sickness from among you, and none will miscarry or be barren in your land. I will give you a full life span."*
EXODUS 23:25–26 NIV

*Isaac prayed to the LORD on behalf of his wife, because she was barren; and the LORD answered him and Rebekah his wife conceived.*
GENESIS 25:21 NASB

Some couples who would like to have children never do. That does not mean God is punishing them. He simply has another plan for their lives.

*Father, when I see those struggling with infertility, pour out Your compassion through me. May I be an encouragement in their pain. Amen.*

*"Your relative Elizabeth is also going to have a son, even though she is old. No one thought she could ever have a baby, but in three months she will have a son. Nothing is impossible for God!"*
LUKE 1:36–37 CEV

*And we know that all things work together for good to them that love God, to them who are the called according to his purpose.*
ROMANS 8:28 KJV

Scripture promises to bless those who follow the Word of God, but it also tells the stories of a number of women who were infertile, or barren, and eventually had children. Whether a woman has children or cannot conceive, God can bless her.

*Lord, Your blessings come in many forms. Help us trust in Your will, knowing You have our best interests in mind. Amen.*

*Morning*

*"I know, my God, that you test the heart and are pleased with integrity. All these things I have given willingly and with honest intent. And now I have seen with joy how willingly your people who are here have given to you."*
1 CHRONICLES 29:17 NIV

*May integrity and honesty protect me, for I put my hope in you.*
PSALM 25:21 NLT

Just as faith is not simply an outward thing, integrity shows what a person is from the inside out. What we really believe on the inside shows in our thoughts and actions. But all our efforts at integrity cannot earn us God's favor. Sometimes He simply pours out His favor on us, despite our failings.

*Father, lead me in integrity. I want to be a witness for You from the inside out. Amen.*

*Evening*

*In everything set them an example by doing what is good. In your teaching show integrity, seriousness and soundness of speech that cannot be condemned, so that those who oppose you may be ashamed because they have nothing bad to say about us.*
TITUS 2:7–8 NIV

*By this I know that You are pleased with me, because my enemy does not shout in triumph over me. As for me, You uphold me in my integrity, and You set me in Your presence forever.*
PSALM 41:11–12 NASB

There is nothing to be gained by resting on our laurels. Hard work and integrity are important values to possess. If we can learn to be disciplined in our daily lives, we can improve our spiritual discipline as well.

*Help me do what is right, Lord. Amen.*

DAY 354 – *Joy*

## *Morning*

*"Ask, using my name, and you will receive, and you will have abundant joy."*
JOHN 16:24 NLT

*But the fruit of the Spirit is. . .joy.*
GALATIANS 5:22 NKJV

The saying goes, misery loves company. Miserable people spread their misery around. On the other hand, people who possess joy can also share it.

*My Lord, You have filled my heart with Your love. Whenever I see sadness,
let me try to meet it with a measure of Your joy. Amen.*

## *Evening*

*Let the sea roar, and all it contains; let the field exult, and all that is in it.
Then the trees of the forest will sing for joy before the LORD;
for He is coming to judge the earth. O give thanks to the LORD,
for He is good; for His lovingkindness is everlasting.*
1 CHRONICLES 16:32–34 NASB

*Be glad in the LORD, and rejoice, ye righteous: and shout for joy,
all ye that are upright in heart.*
PSALM 32:11 KJV

There are many breathtaking experiences in this life that God has given to us. They remind us just how great He is. Embrace life fully. Try new things. The Lord is offering you new excitement and joy every day of your life.

*Grant me wings to soar, Father. Set me upon high places, and show me
the wonders of Your love. Open my heart to joy. Amen.*

## *Morning*

*And God has placed in the church first of all apostles, second prophets,
third teachers, then miracles, then gifts of healing, of helping,
of guidance, and of different kinds of tongues.*
1 CORINTHIANS 12:28 NIV

*Therefore it says, "When he ascended on high he led a host of captives,
and he gave gifts to men."*
EPHESIANS 4:8 ESV

We have been given many wonderful gifts and talents. When we affirm the
talents we have been given, then God will surely bless us, and we will be a
sign to others of His goodness.

*Teach me to use the gifts I have been given, Lord. Be patient with me, and touch me
with Your touch of peace and grace. Amen.*

## *Evening*

*I wish that all of you were as I am. But each of you has your own gift from God;
one has this gift, another has that.*
1 CORINTHIANS 7:7 NIV

*"I've filled him with the Spirit of God, giving him skill and know-how and expertise in
every kind of craft to create designs and work in gold, silver, and bronze; to cut and
set gemstones; to carve wood—he's an all-around craftsman."*
EXODUS 31:3–5 MSG

God has given us hands, feet, power, grace, and a multitude of other gifts.
Embrace them, and know that the Lord is good.

*Lord, thank You for the many ways, even small ones, that I am gifted.
My desire is to use my talents for Your good. Amen.*

# DAY 356 – *Justice*

*Morning* ————————————————————

The L ORD loves righteousness and justice; the earth is full of his unfailing love.
P SALM 33:5 NIV

How blessed are those who keep justice, who practice righteousness at all times!
P SALM 106:3 NASB

So often it seems like the evil will inherit the earth, rather than the meek.
Bad people with evil intentions appear blessed in many ways that good
people are not. It is a hard lesson to learn that the rain falls on the just and
the unjust alike.

Help me be patient and turn from bitter feelings toward those who do wrong, Lord.
May I always remember that Your will is perfect. Amen.

*Evening* ————————————————————

When justice is done, it brings joy to the righteous but terror to evildoers.
P ROVERBS 21:15 NIV

Commit your way to the L ORD; trust in him and he will do this: He will make your
righteous reward shine like the dawn, your vindication like the noonday sun.
P SALM 37:5–6 NIV

Justice is God's responsibility. Ours is to do those things that we know are
pleasing to God, and to avoid doing things that He dislikes—like judging
our neighbors.

Lord God, let me love others with Your love, even when that love seems undeserved.
Help me look at my own life to see that it is pleasing in Your sight. Amen.

# DAY 357 – *Sharing the Gospel*

*But even if we, or an angel from heaven, should preach to you a gospel contrary to
what we have preached to you, he is to be accursed!*
GALATIANS 1:8 NASB

*God has seen how I never stop praying for you, while I serve him
with all my heart and tell the good news about his Son.*
ROMANS 1:9 CEV

The Lord wants us to know Him completely and share our faith with all
those we meet. Hear what the Lord has to say, and proclaim it with your
mouth and with your actions.

*Speak through us when we have the opportunity to share
Your good news, Lord. Amen.*

*"For whoever wants to save their life will lose it, but whoever loses
their life for me and for the gospel will save it."*
MARK 8:35 NIV

*The gospel is bearing fruit and growing throughout the whole world—just as it has
been doing among you since the day you heard it and truly understood God's grace.*
COLOSSIANS 1:6 NIV

It matters little whether you are big, strong, smart, or powerful. What
matters is that you have the truth of Christ to share, and there is no greater
force in all creation.

*Father, thank You for the truth of the Gospel! Give me courage
to share the life-changing news. Amen.*

# DAY 358 – *Marriage*

## *Morning*

*In God's plan women need men and men need women.*
1 CORINTHIANS 11:11 NLV

*Do not be unequally yoked together with unbelievers. For what fellowship has righteousness with lawlessness? And what communion has light with darkness?*
2 CORINTHIANS 6:14 NKJV

Marriage is a picture of the relationship between God and His people. So, not surprisingly, God bans marriage between believers and those who have no faith in Him.

*Lord, when our hearts are blind, remind us of Your loving commands.*
*They are meant for our good. Amen.*

## *Evening*

*Wives, submit yourselves unto your own husbands, as it is fit in the Lord. Husbands, love your wives, and be not bitter against them.*
COLOSSIANS 3:18–19 KJV

*Let your fountain be blessed, and rejoice in the wife of your youth.*
*As a loving hind and a graceful doe, let her breasts satisfy you at all times;*
*be exhilarated always with her love.*
PROVERBS 5:18–19 NASB

The marital relationship is a very special covenant between God and two people and must be honored by all. Partners are to remain faithful to each other for life.

*Faithfulness can be hard, Lord. Remove our tendency to wander.*
*Keep us faithful in marriage. Amen.*

# DAY 359 – *Mercy*

*Therefore God has mercy on whom he wants to have mercy,
and he hardens whom he wants to harden.*
ROMANS 9:18 NIV

*Blessed are the merciful: for they shall obtain mercy.*
MATTHEW 5:7 KJV

As we draw near to God in faith, our understanding of His mercy grows. We recognize our own deep need for Him in every corner of our lives, and we begin to respond to His love by living mercifully with others.

*Lord God, left to myself, I am engulfed by sin. But You mercifully sent Your Son
to die for my every wrong thought and deed. Thank You! Amen.*

*"For I desire mercy and not sacrifice, and the knowledge of God
more than burnt offerings."*
HOSEA 6:6 NKJV

*No, O people, the LORD has told you what is good, and this is what he requires of
you: to do what is right, to love mercy, and to walk humbly with your God.*
MICAH 6:8 NLT

We can trust in the God who is slow to anger because we have experienced His mercy. When we err or even sin intentionally, He is slow to retaliate so that we can have time to come to Him in repentance.

*Lord God, thank You for Your mercy—undeserved
by me but supplied by Your vast love. Amen.*

*Morning* ────────────────────────────────

*I will meditate on your majestic, glorious splendor and your wonderful miracles.*
PSALM 145:5 NLT

*So then, does He who provides you with the Spirit and works miracles among you,*
*do it by the works of the Law, or by hearing with faith?*
GALATIANS 3:5 NASB

A miracle is a miracle is a miracle. The how is not nearly as important as the fact that it did happen. Our God is a God of miracles and wonders. Praise Him for what He does, rather than how He does it; and you will find your faith grows by leaps and bounds.

*When Your miracles get reduced to topics of debate, I find I lose interest, Father.*
*Refresh me with the strangeness and awe of Your power, Lord. Amen.*

*Evening* ────────────────────────────────

*Come and see what our God has done, what awesome miracles*
*he performs for people!*
PSALM 66:5 NLT

*Of all the miracles God works, we cannot understand a one.*
JOB 9:10 CEV

For the disciples, life with Jesus included sudden miracles. A Christian's journey with Jesus—whether walking in His earthly footsteps or following the steps shown to us in His Word—is a walk of faith. Seeing isn't always believing, but believing is seeing.

*Stir our hearts to faith, Lord, even when our minds become*
*confused by the miraculous. Amen.*

## *Morning*

*Honor the LORD with your wealth, with the firstfruits of all your crops;
then your barns will be filled to overflowing.*
PROVERBS 3:9–10 NIV

*Command those who are rich in this present age not to be haughty, nor to trust in
uncertain riches but in the living God, who gives us richly all things to enjoy. Let
them do good, that they be rich in good works, ready to give, willing to share.*
1 TIMOTHY 6:17–18 NKJV

Not only does He give us money, He also gives the promise that He will
always provide for us. That doesn't mean we can spend uproariously, but as
we follow Him, we will not lack what we need.

*Lord, help me use Your money wisely, and to always remember
that You will provide. Amen.*

## *Evening*

*A hard worker has plenty of food, but a person who
chases fantasies ends up in poverty.*
PROVERBS 28:19 NLT

*Owe no one anything except to love one another.*
ROMANS 13:8 NKJV

The way people handle money shows God a lot about their trustworthiness.
God knows how much He can trust us with spiritual blessings when He
looks at the way we handle our cash.

*Lord Jesus, may we be wise stewards of the money You have given us. Amen.*

# DAY 362 – *Obedience*

————————————————————

*And his affection for you is even greater, as he remembers the obedience of you all,*
*how you received him with fear and trembling.*
2 CORINTHIANS 7:15 ESV

*Children, obey your parents in the Lord, for this is right.*
EPHESIANS 6:1 NIV

If we learn to be obedient to the will of God, we will find that life becomes
a little easier to live, and a lot more fulfilling. Life ceases to be such a
struggle, and it becomes a joy.

*Dear God, life can be so difficult, and I know I cannot handle everything on my*
*own. Be with me, guiding me and helping me to follow Your commandments. Amen.*

*Evening* ————————————————————

*Through him we received grace and apostleship to call all the Gentiles to the*
*obedience that comes from faith for his name's sake.*
ROMANS 1:5 NIV

*Obey them that have the rule over you, and submit yourselves: for they watch for*
*your souls, as they that must give account.*
HEBREWS 13:17 KJV

Coming to know Jesus is priceless but not free. He paid the cost of our sin,
but if we treat that lightly, we show we don't understand its worth. Nothing
on earth could buy His friendship, yet all He asks of us is simple obedience.
Our submission to His will shows we don't hold His life cheap.

*Such love as You offer us, Lord, can only be answered by our hearts.*
*We seek to show our gratitude through our obedience. Amen.*

*You have already won a big victory over those false teachers, for the Spirit
in you is far stronger than anything in the world.*
1 JOHN 4:4 MSG

*Someday a prophet may come along who is able to perform miracles or tell what
will happen in the future. Then the prophet may say, "Let's start worshiping
some new gods—some gods that we know nothing about." If the prophet
says this, don't listen! The LORD your God will be watching to find
out whether or not you love him with all your heart and soul.*
DEUTERONOMY 13:1–3 CEV

There is no substitute for the truth and saving power of Jesus Christ.
Other groups and sects may appear to be sincere and good, but they
lure us from what is right and good to things we should avoid.

*Father, protect me from the things that would lead me far from You. Amen.*

*"I know that false teachers, like vicious wolves, will come in among you
after I leave, not sparing the flock."*
ACTS 20:29 NLT

*"Many false religious teachers will come. They will fool many people
and will turn them to the wrong way."*
MATTHEW 24:11 NLV

Jesus warned that many false prophets would come preaching harmony
and love, but that they were wolves in sheep's clothing. He will expose the
darkness of lies and deceit through His holy light.

*Lord, make sure that I use the common sense You have given me. Amen.*

## *Morning*

*Through patience a ruler can be persuaded, and a gentle tongue can break a bone.*
PROVERBS 25:15 NIV

*God's Spirit makes us loving, happy, peaceful, patient.*
GALATIANS 5:22 CEV

Patience is a difficult virtue to obtain, but its rewards are greater than we can begin to comprehend. Shortcuts may look promising, but it is the person who learns the benefits of waiting who is on the road to true wisdom.

*Keep my feet on the right path, O Lord. Keep me from straying onto roads that seem to be easier to travel but lead nowhere. Amen.*

## *Evening*

*For ye have need of patience, that, after ye have done the will of God, ye might receive the promise.*
HEBREWS 10:36 KJV

*Such things were written in the Scriptures long ago to teach us. And the Scriptures give us hope and encouragement as we wait patiently for God's promises to be fulfilled. May God, who gives this patience and encouragement, help you live in complete harmony with each other, as is fitting for followers of Christ Jesus.*
ROMANS 15:4–5 NLT

Patience is not a strong virtue in the twenty-first century. Unfortunately, we worship a God of eternity who chooses to operate on His time schedule, not ours. Therefore, patience is a vital component of the happy Christian life. Ask the Lord for patience. You'll need it.

*Father, I need to learn to wait graciously and patiently. Fill my heart with peace and give me a spirit of acceptance, that I might know happiness even when things don't happen fast enough to suit me. Amen.*

# DAY 365 – *Peace*

*Finally, brothers, rejoice. Aim for restoration, comfort one another, agree with one another, live in peace; and the God of love and peace will be with you.*
2 CORINTHIANS 13:11 ESV

*And let the peace that comes from Christ rule in your hearts. For as members of one body you are called to live in peace.*
COLOSSIANS 3:15 NLT

Our mission in this world is to spread the peace of Christ wherever we go. As we spread peace, we find comfort in facing the future, and we come to know the peace that passes all understanding: God's own peace.

*Make me an instrument of Thy peace, O Lord. Where I find discord, let me bring harmony. Where there is hatred, bring love. Amen.*

*Evening* ———————————————————

*And the fruit of righteousness is sown in peace of them that make peace.*
JAMES 3:18 KJV

*Now the Lord of peace himself give you peace always by all means. The Lord be with you all.*
2 THESSALONIANS 3:16 KJV

Our Lord is a Lord of compromise, sacrifice, and caring. No Christian should be our enemy. We are all members of the same body, and Christ blesses those who strive to live in peace and harmony with one another.

*Remind me, Lord, that I am a Christian first and foremost. The causes I support are second to the fact that I follow Jesus Christ. Let Him rule in my heart, and lead me in the ways I should walk. Amen.*

# Topical Index

# Read Through the Bible in a Year

| | | | |
|---|---|---|---|
| 1-Jan | Gen. 1-2 | Matt. 1 | Ps. 1 |
| 2-Jan | Gen. 3-4 | Matt. 2 | Ps. 2 |
| 3-Jan | Gen. 5-7 | Matt. 3 | Ps. 3 |
| 4-Jan | Gen. 8-10 | Matt. 4 | Ps. 4 |
| 5-Jan | Gen. 11-13 | Matt. 5:1-20 | Ps. 5 |
| 6-Jan | Gen. 14-16 | Matt. 5:21-48 | Ps. 6 |
| 7-Jan | Gen. 17-18 | Matt. 6:1-18 | Ps. 7 |
| 8-Jan | Gen. 19-20 | Matt. 6:19-34 | Ps. 8 |
| 9-Jan | Gen. 21-23 | Matt. 7:1-11 | Ps. 9:1-8 |
| 10-Jan | Gen. 24 | Matt. 7:12-29 | Ps. 9:9-20 |
| 11-Jan | Gen. 25-26 | Matt. 8:1-17 | Ps. 10:1-11 |
| 12-Jan | Gen. 27:1-28:9 | Matt. 8:18-34 | Ps. 10:12-18 |
| 13-Jan | Gen. 28:10-29:35 | Matt. 9 | Ps. 11 |
| 14-Jan | Gen. 30:1-31:21 | Matt. 10:1-15 | Ps. 12 |
| 15-Jan | Gen. 31:22-32:21 | Matt. 10:16-36 | Ps. 13 |
| 16-Jan | Gen. 32:22-34:31 | Matt. 10:37-11:6 | Ps. 14 |
| 17-Jan | Gen. 35-36 | Matt. 11:7-24 | Ps. 15 |
| 18-Jan | Gen. 37-38 | Matt. 11:25-30 | Ps. 16 |
| 19-Jan | Gen. 39-40 | Matt. 12:1-29 | Ps. 17 |
| 20-Jan | Gen. 41 | Matt. 12:30-50 | Ps. 18:1-15 |
| 21-Jan | Gen. 42-43 | Matt. 13:1-9 | Ps. 18:16-29 |
| 22-Jan | Gen. 44-45 | Matt. 13:10-23 | Ps. 18:30-50 |
| 23-Jan | Gen. 46:1-47:26 | Matt. 13:24-43 | Ps. 19 |
| 24-Jan | Gen. 47:27-49:28 | Matt. 13:44-58 | Ps. 20 |
| 25-Jan | Gen. 49:29-Exod. 1:22 | Matt. 14 | Ps. 21 |
| 26-Jan | Exod. 2-3 | Matt. 15:1-28 | Ps. 22:1-21 |
| 27-Jan | Exod. 4:1-5:21 | Matt. 15:29-16:12 | Ps. 22:22-31 |
| 28-Jan | Exod. 5:22-7:24 | Matt. 16:13-28 | Ps. 23 |
| 29-Jan | Exod. 7:25-9:35 | Matt. 17:1-9 | Ps. 24 |
| 30-Jan | Exod. 10-11 | Matt. 17:10-27 | Ps. 25 |
| 31-Jan | Exod. 12 | Matt. 18:1-20 | Ps. 26 |
| 1-Feb | Exod. 13-14 | Matt. 18:21-35 | Ps. 27 |
| 2-Feb | Exod. 15-16 | Matt. 19:1-15 | Ps. 28 |
| 3-Feb | Exod. 17-19 | Matt. 19:16-30 | Ps. 29 |
| 4-Feb | Exod. 20-21 | Matt. 20:1-19 | Ps. 30 |
| 5-Feb | Exod. 22-23 | Matt. 20:20-34 | Ps. 31:1-8 |
| 6-Feb | Exod. 24-25 | Matt. 21:1-27 | Ps. 31:9-18 |
| 7-Feb | Exod 26-27 | Matt. 21:28-46 | Ps. 31:19-24 |
| 8-Feb | Exod. 28 | Matt. 22 | Ps. 32 |
| 9-Feb | Exod. 29 | Matt. 23:1-36 | Ps. 33:1-12 |
| 10-Feb | Exod. 30-31 | Matt. 23:37-24:28 | Ps. 33:13-22 |
| 11-Feb | Exod. 32-33 | Matt. 24:29-51 | Ps. 34:1-7 |
| 12-Feb | Exod. 34:1-35:29 | Matt. 25:1-13 | Ps. 34:8-22 |

| | | | |
|---|---|---|---|
| 13-Feb | Exod. 35:30-37:29 | Matt. 25:14-30 | Ps. 35:1-8 |
| 14-Feb | Exod. 38-39 | Matt. 25:31-46 | Ps. 35:9-17 |
| 15-Feb | Exod. 40 | Matt. 26:1-35 | Ps. 35:18-28 |
| 16-Feb | Lev. 1-3 | Matt. 26:36-68 | Ps. 36:1-6 |
| 17-Feb | Lev. 4:1-5:13 | Matt. 26:69-27:26 | Ps. 36:7-12 |
| 18-Feb | Lev. 5:14 -7:21 | Matt. 27:27-50 | Ps. 37:1-6 |
| 19-Feb | Lev. 7:22-8:36 | Matt. 27:51-66 | Ps. 37:7-26 |
| 20-Feb | Lev. 9-10 | Matt. 28 | Ps. 37:27-40 |
| 21-Feb | Lev. 11-12 | Mark 1:1-28 | Ps. 38 |
| 22-Feb | Lev. 13 | Mark 1:29-39 | Ps. 39 |
| 23-Feb | Lev. 14 | Mark 1:40-2:12 | Ps. 40:1-8 |
| 24-Feb | Lev. 15 | Mark 2:13-3:35 | Ps. 40:9-17 |
| 25-Feb | Lev. 16-17 | Mark 4:1-20 | Ps. 41:1-4 |
| 26-Feb | Lev. 18-19 | Mark 4:21-41 | Ps. 41:5-13 |
| 27-Feb | Lev. 20 | Mark 5 | Ps. 42-43 |
| 28-Feb | Lev. 21-22 | Mark 6:1-13 | Ps. 44 |
| 1-Mar | Lev. 23-24 | Mark 6:14-29 | Ps. 45:1-5 |
| 2-Mar | Lev. 25 | Mark 6:30-56 | Ps. 45:6-12 |
| 3-Mar | Lev. 26 | Mark 7 | Ps. 45:13-17 |
| 4-Mar | Lev. 27 | Mark 8 | Ps. 46 |
| 5-Mar | Num. 1-2 | Mark 9:1-13 | Ps. 47 |
| 6-Mar | Num. 3 | Mark 9:14-50 | Ps. 48:1-8 |
| 7-Mar | Num. 4 | Mark 10:1-34 | Ps. 48:9-14 |
| 8-Mar | Num. 5:1-6:21 | Mark 10:35-52 | Ps. 49:1-9 |
| 9-Mar | Num. 6:22-7:47 | Mark 11 | Ps. 49:10-20 |
| 10-Mar | Num. 7:48-8:4 | Mark 12:1-27 | Ps. 50:1-15 |
| 11-Mar | Num. 8:5-9:23 | Mark 12:28-44 | Ps. 50:16-23 |
| 12-Mar | Num. 10-11 | Mark 13:1-8 | Ps. 51:1-9 |
| 13-Mar | Num. 12-13 | Mark 13:9-37 | Ps. 51:10-19 |
| 14-Mar | Num. 14 | Mark 14:1-31 | Ps. 52 |
| 15-Mar | Num. 15 | Mark 14:32-72 | Ps. 53 |
| 16-Mar | Num. 16 | Mark 15:1-32 | Ps. 54 |
| 17-Mar | Num. 17-18 | Mark 15:33-47 | Ps. 55 |
| 18-Mar | Num. 19-20 | Mark 16 | Ps. 56:1-7 |
| 19-Mar | Num. 21:1-22:20 | Luke 1:1-25 | Ps. 56:8-13 |
| 20-Mar | Num. 22:21-23:30 | Luke 1:26-56 | Ps. 57 |
| 21-Mar | Num. 24-25 | Luke 1:57-2:20 | Ps. 58 |
| 22-Mar | Num. 26:1-27:11 | Luke 2:21-38 | Ps. 59:1-8 |
| 23-Mar | Num. 27:12-29:11 | Luke 2:39-52 | Ps. 59:9-17 |
| 24-Mar | Num. 29:12-30:16 | Luke 3 | Ps. 60:1-5 |
| 25-Mar | Num. 31 | Luke 4 | Ps. 60:6-12 |
| 26-Mar | Num. 32-33 | Luke 5:1-16 | Ps. 61 |
| 27-Mar | Num. 34-36 | Luke 5:17-32 | Ps. 62:1-6 |
| 28-Mar | Deut. 1:1-2:25 | Luke 5:33-6:11 | Ps. 62:7-12 |
| 29-Mar | Deut. 2:26-4:14 | Luke 6:12-35 | Ps. 63:1-5 |
| 30-Mar | Deut. 4:15-5:22 | Luke 6:36-49 | Ps. 63:6-11 |
| 31-Mar | Deut. 5:23-7:26 | Luke 7:1-17 | Ps. 64:1-5 |

| Date | Reading 1 | Reading 2 | Reading 3 |
|---|---|---|---|
| 1-Apr | Deut. 8-9 | Luke 7:18-35 | Ps. 64:6-10 |
| 2-Apr | Deut. 10-11 | Luke 7:36-8:3 | Ps. 65:1-8 |
| 3-Apr | Deut. 12-13 | Luke 8:4-21 | Ps. 65:9-13 |
| 4-Apr | Deut. 14:1-16:8 | Luke 8:22-39 | Ps. 66:1-7 |
| 5-Apr | Deut. 16:9-18:22 | Luke 8:40-56 | Ps. 66:8-15 |
| 6-Apr | Deut. 19:1-21:9 | Luke 9:1-22 | Ps. 66:16-20 |
| 7-Apr | Deut. 21:10-23:8 | Luke 9:23-42 | Ps. 67 |
| 8-Apr | Deut. 23:9-25:19 | Luke 9:43-62 | Ps. 68:1-6 |
| 9-Apr | Deut. 26:1-28:14 | Luke 10:1-20 | Ps. 68:7-14 |
| 10-Apr | Deut. 28:15-68 | Luke 10:21-37 | Ps. 68:15-19 |
| 11-Apr | Deut. 29-30 | Luke 10:38-11:23 | Ps. 68:20-27 |
| 12-Apr | Deut. 31:1-32:22 | Luke 11:24-36 | Ps. 68:28-35 |
| 13-Apr | Deut. 32:23-33:29 | Luke 11:37-54 | Ps. 69:1-9 |
| 14-Apr | Deut. 34-Josh. 2 | Luke 12:1-15 | Ps. 69:10-17 |
| 15-Apr | Josh. 3:1-5:12 | Luke 12:16-40 | Ps. 69:18-28 |
| 16-Apr | Josh. 5:13-7:26 | Luke 12:41-48 | Ps. 69:29-36 |
| 17-Apr | Josh. 8-9 | Luke 12:49-59 | Ps. 70 |
| 18-Apr | Josh. 10:1-11:15 | Luke 13:1-21 | Ps. 71:1-6 |
| 19-Apr | Josh. 11:16-13:33 | Luke 13:22-35 | Ps. 71:7-16 |
| 20-Apr | Josh. 14-16 | Luke 14:1-15 | Ps. 71:17-21 |
| 21-Apr | Josh. 17:1-19:16 | Luke 14:16-35 | Ps. 71:22-24 |
| 22-Apr | Josh. 19:17-21:42 | Luke 15:1-10 | Ps. 72:1-11 |
| 23-Apr | Josh. 21:43-22:34 | Luke 15:11-32 | Ps. 72:12-20 |
| 24-Apr | Josh. 23-24 | Luke 16:1-18 | Ps. 73:1-9 |
| 25-Apr | Judg. 1-2 | Luke 16:19-17:10 | Ps. 73:10-20 |
| 26-Apr | Judg. 3-4 | Luke 17:11-37 | Ps. 73:21-28 |
| 27-Apr | Judg. 5:1-6:24 | Luke 18:1-17 | Ps. 74:1-3 |
| 28-Apr | Judg. 6:25-7:25 | Luke 18:18-43 | Ps. 74:4-11 |
| 29-Apr | Judg. 8:1-9:23 | Luke 19:1-28 | Ps. 74:12-17 |
| 30-Apr | Judg. 9:24-10:18 | Luke 19:29-48 | Ps. 74:18-23 |
| 1-May | Judg. 11:1-12:7 | Luke 20:1-26 | Ps. 75:1-7 |
| 2-May | Judg. 12:8-14:20 | Luke 20:27-47 | Ps. 75:8-10 |
| 3-May | Judg. 15-16 | Luke 21:1-19 | Ps. 76:1-7 |
| 4-May | Judg. 17-18 | Luke 21:20-22:6 | Ps. 76:8-12 |
| 5-May | Judg. 19:1-20:23 | Luke 22:7-30 | Ps. 77:1-11 |
| 6-May | Judg. 20:24-21:25 | Luke 22:31-54 | Ps. 77:12-20 |
| 7-May | Ruth 1-2 | Luke 22:55-23:25 | Ps. 78:1-4 |
| 8-May | Ruth 3-4 | Luke 23:26-24:12 | Ps. 78:5-8 |
| 9-May | 1 Sam. 1:1-2:21 | Luke 24:13-53 | Ps. 78:9-16 |
| 10-May | 1 Sam. 2:22-4:22 | John 1:1-28 | Ps. 78:17-24 |
| 11-May | 1 Sam. 5-7 | John 1:29-51 | Ps. 78:25-33 |
| 12-May | 1 Sam. 8:1-9:26 | John 2 | Ps. 78:34-41 |
| 13-May | 1 Sam. 9:27-11:15 | John 3:1-22 | Ps. 78:42-55 |
| 14-May | 1 Sam. 12-13 | John 3:23-4:10 | Ps. 78:56-66 |
| 15-May | 1 Sam. 14 | John 4:11-38 | Ps. 78:67-72 |
| 16-May | 1 Sam. 15-16 | John 4:39-54 | Ps. 79:1-7 |
| 17-May | 1 Sam. 17 | John 5:1-24 | Ps. 79:8-13 |

| | | | |
|---|---|---|---|
| 18-May | 1 Sam. 18-19 | John 5:25-47 | Ps. 80:1-7 |
| 19-May | 1 Sam. 20-21 | John 6:1-21 | Ps. 80:8-19 |
| 20-May | 1 Sam. 22-23 | John 6:22-42 | Ps. 81:1-10 |
| 21-May | 1 Sam. 24:1-25:31 | John 6:43-71 | Ps. 81:11-16 |
| 22-May | 1 Sam. 25:32-27:12 | John 7:1-24 | Ps. 82 |
| 23-May | 1 Sam. 28-29 | John 7:25-8:11 | Ps. 83 |
| 24-May | 1 Sam. 30-31 | John 8:12-47 | Ps. 84:1-4 |
| 25-May | 2 Sam. 1-2 | John 8:48-9:12 | Ps. 84:5-12 |
| 26-May | 2 Sam. 3-4 | John 9:13-34 | Ps. 85:1-7 |
| 27-May | 2 Sam. 5:1-7:17 | John 9:35-10:10 | Ps. 85:8-13 |
| 28-May | 2 Sam. 7:18-10:19 | John 10:11-30 | Ps. 86:1-10 |
| 29-May | 2 Sam. 11:1-12:25 | John 10:31-11:16 | Ps. 86:11-17 |
| 30-May | 2 Sam. 12:26-13:39 | John 11:17-54 | Ps. 87 |
| 31-May | 2 Sam. 14:1-15:12 | John 11:55-12:19 | Ps. 88:1-9 |
| 1-Jun | 2 Sam. 15:13-16:23 | John 12:20-43 | Ps. 88:10-18 |
| 2-Jun | 2 Sam. 17:1-18:18 | John 12:44-13:20 | Ps. 89:1-6 |
| 3-Jun | 2 Sam. 18:19-19:39 | John 13:21-38 | Ps. 89:7-13 |
| 4-Jun | 2 Sam. 19:40-21:22 | John 14:1-17 | Ps. 89:14-18 |
| 5-Jun | 2 Sam. 22:1-23:7 | John 14:18-15:27 | Ps. 89:19-29 |
| 6-Jun | 2 Sam. 23:8-24:25 | John 16:1-22 | Ps. 89:30-37 |
| 7-Jun | 1 Kings 1 | John 16:23-17:5 | Ps. 89:38-52 |
| 8-Jun | 1 Kings 2 | John 17:6-26 | Ps. 90:1-12 |
| 9-Jun | 1 Kings 3-4 | John 18:1-27 | Ps. 90:13-17 |
| 10-Jun | 1 Kings 5-6 | John 18:28-19:5 | Ps. 91:1-10 |
| 11-Jun | 1 Kings 7 | John 19:6-25a | Ps. 91:11-16 |
| 12-Jun | 1 Kings 8:1-53 | John 19:25b-42 | Ps. 92:1-9 |
| 13-Jun | 1 Kings 8:54-10:13 | John 20:1-18 | Ps. 92:10-15 |
| 14-Jun | 1 Kings 10:14-11:43 | John 20:19-31 | Ps. 93 |
| 15-Jun | 1 Kings 12:1-13:10 | John 21 | Ps. 94:1-11 |
| 16-Jun | 1 Kings 13:11-14:31 | Acts 1:1-11 | Ps. 94:12-23 |
| 17-Jun | 1 Kings 15:1-16:20 | Acts 1:12-26 | Ps. 95 |
| 18-Jun | 1 Kings 16:21-18:19 | Acts 2:1-21 | Ps. 96:1-8 |
| 19-Jun | 1 Kings 18:20-19:21 | Acts 2:22-41 | Ps. 96:9-13 |
| 20-Jun | 1 Kings 20 | Acts 2:42-3:26 | Ps. 97:1-6 |
| 21-Jun | 1 Kings 21:1-22:28 | Acts 4:1-22 | Ps. 97:7-12 |
| 22-Jun | 1 Kings 22:29-2 Kings 1:18 | Acts 4:23-5:11 | Ps. 98 |
| 23-Jun | 2 Kings 2-3 | Acts 5:12-28 | Ps. 99 |
| 24-Jun | 2 Kings 4 | Acts 5:29-6:15 | Ps. 100 |
| 25-Jun | 2 Kings 5:1-6:23 | Acts 7:1-16 | Ps. 101 |
| 26-Jun | 2 Kings 6:24-8:15 | Acts 7:17-36 | Ps. 102:1-7 |
| 27-Jun | 2 Kings 8:16-9:37 | Acts 7:37-53 | Ps. 102:8-17 |
| 28-Jun | 2 Kings 10-11 | Acts 7:54-8:8 | Ps. 102:18-28 |
| 29-Jun | 2 Kings 12-13 | Acts 8:9-40 | Ps. 103:1-9 |
| 30-Jun | 2 Kings 14-15 | Acts 9:1-16 | Ps. 103:10-14 |
| 1-Jul | 2 Kings 16-17 | Acts 9:17-31 | Ps. 103:15-22 |
| 2-Jul | 2 Kings 18:1-19:7 | Acts 9:32-10:16 | Ps. 104:1-9 |
| 3-Jul | 2 Kings 19:8-20:21 | Acts 10:17-33 | Ps. 104:10-23 |

| | | | |
|---|---|---|---|
| 4-Jul | 2 Kings 21:1-22:20 | Acts 10:34-11:18 | Ps. 104: 24-30 |
| 5-Jul | 2 Kings 23 | Acts 11:19-12:17 | Ps. 104:31-35 |
| 6-Jul | 2 Kings 24-25 | Acts 12:18-13:13 | Ps. 105:1-7 |
| 7-Jul | 1 Chron. 1-2 | Acts 13:14-43 | Ps. 105:8-15 |
| 8-Jul | 1 Chron. 3:1-5:10 | Acts 13:44-14:10 | Ps. 105:16-28 |
| 9-Jul | 1 Chron. 5:11-6:81 | Acts 14:11-28 | Ps. 105:29-36 |
| 10-Jul | 1 Chron. 7:1-9:9 | Acts 15:1-18 | Ps. 105:37-45 |
| 11-Jul | 1 Chron. 9:10-11:9 | Acts 15:19-41 | Ps. 106:1-12 |
| 12-Jul | 1 Chron. 11:10-12:40 | Acts 16:1-15 | Ps. 106:13-27 |
| 13-Jul | 1 Chron. 13-15 | Acts 16:16-40 | Ps. 106:28-33 |
| 14-Jul | 1 Chron. 16-17 | Acts 17:1-14 | Ps. 106:34-43 |
| 15-Jul | 1 Chron. 18-20 | Acts 17:15-34 | Ps. 106:44-48 |
| 16-Jul | 1 Chron. 21-22 | Acts 18:1-23 | Ps. 107:1-9 |
| 17-Jul | 1 Chron. 23-25 | Acts 18:24-19:10 | Ps. 107:10-16 |
| 18-Jul | 1 Chron. 26-27 | Acts 19:11-22 | Ps. 107:17-32 |
| 19-Jul | 1 Chron. 28-29 | Acts 19:23-41 | Ps. 107:33-38 |
| 20-Jul | 2 Chron. 1-3 | Acts 20:1-16 | Ps. 107:39-43 |
| 21-Jul | 2 Chron. 4:1-6:11 | Acts 20:17-38 | Ps. 108 |
| 22-Jul | 2 Chron. 6:12-7:10 | Acts 21:1-14 | Ps. 109:1-20 |
| 23-Jul | 2 Chron. 7:11-9:28 | Acts 21:15-32 | Ps. 109:21-31 |
| 24-Jul | 2 Chron. 9:29-12:16 | Acts 21:33-22:16 | Ps. 110:1-3 |
| 25-Jul | 2 Chron. 13-15 | Acts 22:17-23:11 | Ps. 110:4-7 |
| 26-Jul | 2 Chron. 16-17 | Acts 23:12-24:21 | Ps. 111 |
| 27-Jul | 2 Chron. 18-19 | Acts 24:22-25:12 | Ps. 112 |
| 28-Jul | 2 Chron. 20-21 | Acts 25:13-27 | Ps. 113 |
| 29-Jul | 2 Chron. 22-23 | Acts 26 | Ps. 114 |
| 30-Jul | 2 Chron. 24:1-25:16 | Acts 27:1-20 | Ps. 115:1-10 |
| 31-Jul | 2 Chron. 25:17-27:9 | Acts 27:21-28:6 | Ps. 115:11-18 |
| 1-Aug | 2 Chron. 28:1-29:19 | Acts 28:7-31 | Ps. 116:1-5 |
| 2-Aug | 2 Chron. 29:20-30:27 | Rom. 1:1-17 | Ps. 116:6-19 |
| 3-Aug | 2 Chron. 31-32 | Rom. 1:18-32 | Ps. 117 |
| 4-Aug | 2 Chron. 33:1-34:7 | Rom. 2 | Ps. 118:1-18 |
| 5-Aug | 2 Chron. 34:8-35:19 | Rom. 3:1-26 | Ps. 118:19-23 |
| 6-Aug | 2 Chron. 35:20-36:23 | Rom. 3:27-4:25 | Ps. 118:24-29 |
| 7-Aug | Ezra 1-3 | Rom. 5 | Ps. 119:1-8 |
| 8-Aug | Ezra 4-5 | Rom. 6:1-7:6 | Ps. 119:9-16 |
| 9-Aug | Ezra 6:1-7:26 | Rom. 7:7-25 | Ps. 119:17-32 |
| 10-Aug | Ezra 7:27-9:4 | Rom. 8:1-27 | Ps. 119:33-40 |
| 11-Aug | Ezra 9:5-10:44 | Rom. 8:28-39 | Ps. 119:41-64 |
| 12-Aug | Neh. 1:1-3:16 | Rom. 9:1-18 | Ps. 119:65-72 |
| 13-Aug | Neh. 3:17-5:13 | Rom. 9:19-33 | Ps. 119:73-80 |
| 14-Aug | Neh. 5:14-7:73 | Rom. 10:1-13 | Ps. 119:81-88 |
| 15-Aug | Neh. 8:1-9:5 | Rom. 10:14-11:24 | Ps. 119:89-104 |
| 16-Aug | Neh. 9:6-10:27 | Rom. 11:25-12:8 | Ps. 119:105-120 |
| 17-Aug | Neh. 10:28-12:26 | Rom. 12:9-13:7 | Ps. 119:121-128 |
| 18-Aug | Neh. 12:27-13:31 | Rom. 13:8-14:12 | Ps. 119:129-136 |
| 19-Aug | Esther 1:1-2:18 | Rom. 14:13-15:13 | Ps. 119:137-152 |

| | | | |
|---|---|---|---|
| 20-Aug | Esther 2:19-5:14 | Rom. 15:14-21 | Ps. 119:153-168 |
| 21-Aug | Esther. 6-8 | Rom. 15:22-33 | Ps. 119:169-176 |
| 22-Aug | Esther 9-10 | Rom. 16 | Ps. 120-122 |
| 23-Aug | Job 1-3 | 1 Cor. 1:1-25 | Ps. 123 |
| 24-Aug | Job 4-6 | 1 Cor. 1:26-2:16 | Ps. 124-125 |
| 25-Aug | Job 7-9 | 1 Cor. 3 | Ps. 126-127 |
| 26-Aug | Job 10-13 | 1 Cor. 4:1-13 | Ps. 128-129 |
| 27-Aug | Job 14-16 | 1 Cor. 4:14-5:13 | Ps. 130 |
| 28-Aug | Job 17-20 | 1 Cor. 6 | Ps. 131 |
| 29-Aug | Job 21-23 | 1 Cor. 7:1-16 | Ps. 132 |
| 30-Aug | Job 24-27 | 1 Cor. 7:17-40 | Ps. 133-134 |
| 31-Aug | Job 28-30 | 1 Cor. 8 | Ps. 135 |
| 1-Sep | Job 31-33 | 1 Cor. 9:1-18 | Ps. 136:1-9 |
| 2-Sep | Job 34-36 | 1 Cor. 9:19-10:13 | Ps. 136:10-26 |
| 3-Sep | Job 37-39 | 1 Cor. 10:14-11:1 | Ps. 137 |
| 4-Sep | Job 40-42 | 1 Cor. 11:2-34 | Ps. 138 |
| 5-Sep | Eccles. 1:1-3:15 | 1 Cor. 12:1-26 | Ps. 139:1-6 |
| 6-Sep | Eccles. 3:16-6:12 | 1 Cor. 12:27-13:13 | Ps. 139:7-18 |
| 7-Sep | Eccles. 7:1-9:12 | 1 Cor. 14:1-22 | Ps. 139:19-24 |
| 8-Sep | Eccles. 9:13-12:14 | 1 Cor. 14:23-15:11 | Ps. 140:1-8 |
| 9-Sep | SS 1-4 | 1 Cor. 15:12-34 | Ps. 140:9-13 |
| 10-Sep | SS 5-8 | 1 Cor. 15:35-58 | Ps. 141 |
| 11-Sep | Isa. 1-2 | 1 Cor. 16 | Ps. 142 |
| 12-Sep | Isa. 3-5 | 2 Cor. 1:1-11 | Ps. 143:1-6 |
| 13-Sep | Isa. 6-8 | 2 Cor. 1:12-2:4 | Ps. 143:7-12 |
| 14-Sep | Isa. 9-10 | 2 Cor. 2:5-17 | Ps. 144 |
| 15-Sep | Isa. 11-13 | 2 Cor. 3 | Ps. 145 |
| 16-Sep | Isa. 14-16 | 2 Cor. 4 | Ps. 146 |
| 17-Sep | Isa. 17-19 | 2 Cor. 5 | Ps. 147:1-11 |
| 18-Sep | Isa. 20-23 | 2 Cor. 6 | Ps. 147:12-20 |
| 19-Sep | Isa. 24:1-26:19 | 2 Cor. 7 | Ps. 148 |
| 20-Sep | Isa. 26:20-28:29 | 2 Cor. 8 | Ps. 149-150 |
| 21-Sep | Isa. 29-30 | 2 Cor. 9 | Prov. 1:1-9 |
| 22-Sep | Isa. 31-33 | 2 Cor. 10 | Prov. 1:10-22 |
| 23-Sep | Isa. 34-36 | 2 Cor. 11 | Prov. 1:23-26 |
| 24-Sep | Isa. 37-38 | 2 Cor. 12:1-10 | Prov. 1:27-33 |
| 25-Sep | Isa. 39-40 | 2 Cor. 12:11-13:14 | Prov. 2:1-15 |
| 26-Sep | Isa. 41-42 | Gal. 1 | Prov. 2:16-22 |
| 27-Sep | Isa. 43:1-44:20 | Gal. 2 | Prov. 3:1-12 |
| 28-Sep | Isa. 44:21-46:13 | Gal. 3:1-18 | Prov. 3:13-26 |
| 29-Sep | Isa. 47:1-49:13 | Gal 3:19-29 | Prov. 3:27-35 |
| 30-Sep | Isa. 49:14-51:23 | Gal 4:1-11 | Prov. 4:1-19 |
| 1-Oct | Isa. 52-54 | Gal. 4:12-31 | Prov. 4:20-27 |
| 2-Oct | Isa. 55-57 | Gal. 5 | Prov. 5:1-14 |
| 3-Oct | Isa. 58-59 | Gal. 6 | Prov. 5:15-23 |
| 4-Oct | Isa. 60-62 | Eph. 1 | Prov. 6:1-5 |
| 5-Oct | Isa. 63:1-65:16 | Eph. 2 | Prov. 6:6-19 |

| | | | |
|---|---|---|---|
| 6-Oct | Isa. 65:17-66:24 | Eph. 3:1-4:16 | Prov. 6:20-26 |
| 7-Oct | Jer. 1-2 | Eph. 4:17-32 | Prov. 6:27-35 |
| 8-Oct | Jer. 3:1-4:22 | Eph. 5 | Prov. 7:1-5 |
| 9-Oct | Jer. 4:23-5:31 | Eph. 6 | Prov. 7:6-27 |
| 10-Oct | Jer. 6:1-7:26 | Phil. 1:1-26 | Prov. 8:1-11 |
| 11-Oct | Jer. 7:26-9:16 | Phil. 1:27-2:18 | Prov. 8:12-21 |
| 12-Oct | Jer. 9:17-11:17 | Phil 2:19-30 | Prov. 8:22-36 |
| 13-Oct | Jer. 11:18-13:27 | Phil. 3 | Prov. 9:1-6 |
| 14-Oct | Jer. 14-15 | Phil. 4 | Prov. 9:7-18 |
| 15-Oct | Jer. 16-17 | Col. 1:1-23 | Prov. 10:1-5 |
| 16-Oct | Jer. 18:1-20:6 | Col. 1:24-2:15 | Prov. 10:6-14 |
| 17-Oct | Jer. 20:7-22:19 | Col. 2:16-3:4 | Prov. 10:15-26 |
| 18-Oct | Jer. 22:20-23:40 | Col. 3:5-4:1 | Prov. 10:27-32 |
| 19-Oct | Jer. 24-25 | Col. 4:2-18 | Prov. 11:1-11 |
| 20-Oct | Jer. 26-27 | 1 Thes. 1:1-2:8 | Prov. 11:12-21 |
| 21-Oct | Jer. 28-29 | 1 Thes. 2:9-3:13 | Prov. 11:22-26 |
| 22-Oct | Jer. 30:1-31:22 | 1 Thes. 4:1-5:11 | Prov. 11:27-31 |
| 23-Oct | Jer. 31:23-32:35 | 1 Thes. 5:12-28 | Prov. 12:1-14 |
| 24-Oct | Jer. 32:36-34:7 | 2 Thes. 1-2 | Prov. 12:15-20 |
| 25-Oct | Jer. 34:8-36:10 | 2 Thes. 3 | Prov. 12:21-28 |
| 26-Oct | Jer. 36:11-38:13 | 1 Tim. 1:1-17 | Prov. 13:1-4 |
| 27-Oct | Jer. 38:14-40:6 | 1 Tim. 1:18-3:13 | Prov. 13:5-13 |
| 28-Oct | Jer. 40:7-42:22 | 1 Tim. 3:14-4:10 | Prov. 13:14-21 |
| 29-Oct | Jer. 43-44 | 1 Tim. 4:11-5:16 | Prov. 13:22-25 |
| 30-Oct | Jer. 45-47 | 1 Tim. 5:17-6:21 | Prov. 14:1-6 |
| 31-Oct | Jer. 48:1-49:6 | 2 Tim. 1 | Prov. 14:7-22 |
| 1-Nov | Jer. 49:7-50:16 | 2 Tim. 2 | Prov. 14:23-27 |
| 2-Nov | Jer. 50:17-51:14 | 2 Tim. 3 | Prov. 14:28-35 |
| 3-Nov | Jer. 51:15-64 | 2 Tim. 4 | Prov. 15:1-9 |
| 4-Nov | Jer. 52-Lam. 1 | Ti. 1:1-9 | Prov. 15:10-17 |
| 5-Nov | Lam. 2:1-3:38 | Ti. 1:10-2:15 | Prov. 15:18-26 |
| 6-Nov | Lam. 3:39-5:22 | Ti. 3 | Prov. 15:27-33 |
| 7-Nov | Ezek. 1:1-3:21 | Philemon 1 | Prov. 16:1-9 |
| 8-Nov | Ezek. 3:22-5:17 | Heb. 1:1-2:4 | Prov. 16:10-21 |
| 9-Nov | Ezek. 6-7 | Heb. 2:5-18 | Prov. 16:22-33 |
| 10-Nov | Ezek. 8-10 | Heb. 3:1-4:3 | Prov. 17:1-5 |
| 11-Nov | Ezek. 11-12 | Heb. 4:4-5:10 | Prov. 17:6-12 |
| 12-Nov | Ezek. 13-14 | Heb. 5:11-6:20 | Prov. 17:13-22 |
| 13-Nov | Ezek. 15:1-16:43 | Heb. 7:1-28 | Prov. 17:23-28 |
| 14-Nov | Ezek. 16:44-17:24 | Heb. 8:1-9:10 | Prov. 18:1-7 |
| 15-Nov | Ezek. 18-19 | Heb. 9:11-28 | Prov. 18:8-17 |
| 16-Nov | Ezek. 20 | Heb. 10:1-25 | Prov. 18:18-24 |
| 17-Nov | Ezek. 21-22 | Heb. 10:26-39 | Prov. 19:1-8 |
| 18-Nov | Ezek. 23 | Heb. 11:1-31 | Prov. 19:9-14 |
| 19-Nov | Ezek. 24-26 | Heb. 11:32-40 | Prov. 19:15-21 |
| 20-Nov | Ezek. 27-28 | Heb. 12:1-13 | Prov. 19:22-29 |
| 21-Nov | Ezek. 29-30 | Heb. 12:14-29 | Prov. 20:1-18 |

| | | |
|---|---|---|
| 22-Nov | Ezek. 31-32 | Heb. 13 | Prov. 20:19-24 |
| 23-Nov | Ezek. 33:1-34:10 | Jas. 1 | Prov. 20:25-30 |
| 24-Nov | Ezek. 34:11-36:15 | Jas. 2 | Prov. 21:1-8 |
| 25-Nov | Ezek. 36:16-37:28 | Jas. 3 | Prov. 21:9-18 |
| 26-Nov | Ezek. 38-39 | Jas. 4:1-5:6 | Prov. 21:19-24 |
| 27-Nov | Ezek. 40 | Jas. 5:7-20 | Prov. 21:25-31 |
| 28-Nov | Ezek. 41:1-43:12 | 1 Pet. 1:1-12 | Prov. 22:1-9 |
| 29-Nov | Ezek. 43:13-44:31 | 1 Pet. 1:13-2:3 | Prov. 22:10-23 |
| 30-Nov | Ezek. 45-46 | 1 Pet. 2:4-17 | Prov. 22:24-29 |
| 1-Dec | Ezek. 47-48 | 1 Pet. 2:18-3:7 | Prov. 23:1-9 |
| 2-Dec | Dan. 1:1-2:23 | 1 Pet. 3:8-4:19 | Prov. 23:10-16 |
| 3-Dec | Dan. 2:24-3:30 | 1 Pet. 5 | Prov. 23:17-25 |
| 4-Dec | Dan. 4 | 2 Pet. 1 | Prov. 23:26-35 |
| 5-Dec | Dan. 5 | 2 Pet. 2 | Prov. 24:1-18 |
| 6-Dec | Dan. 6:1-7:14 | 2 Pet. 3 | Prov. 24:19-27 |
| 7-Dec | Dan. 7:15-8:27 | 1 John 1:1-2:17 | Prov. 24:28-34 |
| 8-Dec | Dan. 9-10 | 1 John 2:18-29 | Prov. 25:1-12 |
| 9-Dec | Dan. 11-12 | 1 John 3:1-12 | Prov. 25:13-17 |
| 10-Dec | Hos. 1-3 | 1 John 3:13-4:16 | Prov. 25:18-28 |
| 11-Dec | Hos. 4-6 | 1 John 4:17-5:21 | Prov. 26:1-16 |
| 12-Dec | Hos. 7-10 | 2 John | Prov. 26:17-21 |
| 13-Dec | Hos. 11-14 | 3 John | Prov. 26:22-27:9 |
| 14-Dec | Joel 1:1-2:17 | Jude | Prov. 27:10-17 |
| 15-Dec | Joel 2:18-3:21 | Rev. 1:1-2:11 | Prov. 27:18-27 |
| 16-Dec | Amos 1:1-4:5 | Rev. 2:12-29 | Prov. 28:1-8 |
| 17-Dec | Amos 4:6-6:14 | Rev. 3 | Prov. 28:9-16 |
| 18-Dec | Amos 7-9 | Rev. 4:1-5:5 | Prov. 28:17-24 |
| 19-Dec | Obad-Jonah | Rev. 5:6-14 | Prov. 28:25-28 |
| 20-Dec | Mic. 1:1-4:5 | Rev. 6:1-7:8 | Prov. 29:1-8 |
| 21-Dec | Mic. 4:6-7:20 | Rev. 7:9-8:13 | Prov. 29:9-14 |
| 22-Dec | Nah. 1-3 | Rev. 9-10 | Prov. 29:15-23 |
| 23-Dec | Hab. 1-3 | Rev. 11 | Prov. 29:24-27 |
| 24-Dec | Zeph. 1-3 | Rev. 12 | Prov. 30:1-6 |
| 25-Dec | Hag. 1-2 | Rev. 13:1-14:13 | Prov. 30:7-16 |
| 26-Dec | Zech. 1-4 | Rev. 14:14-16:3 | Prov. 30:17-20 |
| 27-Dec | Zech. 5-8 | Rev. 16:4-21 | Prov. 30:21-28 |
| 28-Dec | Zech. 9-11 | Rev. 17:1-18:8 | Prov. 30:29-33 |
| 29-Dec | Zech. 12-14 | Rev. 18:9-24 | Prov. 31:1-9 |
| 30-Dec | Mal. 1-2 | Rev. 19-20 | Prov. 31:10-17 |
| 31-Dec | Mal. 3-4 | Rev. 21-22 | Prov. 31:18-31 |